STRATEGIES FOR COMMUNITY EMPOWERMENT

Direct-Action and Transformative Approaches to Social Change Practice

Mark G. Hanna

and

Buddy Robinson

EmText
Lewiston/Queenston/Lampeter

Library of Congress Cataloging-in-Publication Data

Hanna, Mark G.
   Strategies for community empowerment : direct action and
transformative approaches to social change practice / Mark G. Hanna,
Buddy Robinson.
       p.   cm.
   Includes bibliographical references (p.   ) and index.
   ISBN 0-7734-2297-8
   1. Social change--United States. 2. Social action--United States.
3. Community organization--United States. I. Robinson, Buddy.
II. Title. III. Title: Community empowerment.
HN65.H356   1994
361.2'0973--dc20   93-51033
                                                                   CIP

Editorial Inquiries and Order Fulfillment:

The Edwin Mellen Press
Box 450
Lewiston, New York
USA 14092-0450

Printed in the United States of America

This book is dedicated to our parents:

Orville Allen Hanna (in memoriam) and Virginia Hanna Rehm
&
Saul and Lillian Robinson

Contents

PREFACE

When we first thought about writing this book, it was because we wanted to share with social work students, practitioners, and educators our excitement about the diversity of community organizing and social change training opportunities which we had observed throughout the United States. Our collaboration seemed unique, as Buddy has been a practicing grassroots organizer for 20 years, while Mark has been a social work administrator and teacher. Overall, we think this marriage has strengthened the book, balancing the emphasis on theory and practice. Even though we decided to emphasize the social work perspective in much of the writing, we did not lose sight of the fact that many organizers without social work training could also benefit from our analysis and description of current organizing methods.

It also seemed to us that social workers and other professionals involved with community work had limited knowledge of the unique and interesting approaches to training and practice witnessed in nonacademic organizing training programs. We and several MSW students at CSU, Fresno, participated in hundreds of hours of training in locations across the country and we had experienced remarkable changes in our understanding of who and why people get involved with community organizing. This training experience and the people who participated, were so unlike our previous classroom education and yet so directly relevant to professional work that we thought everyone ought to know about it.

A review of the literature revealed that other books and articles had looked at some of the organizing projects undertaken by the major training centers (Bettin & Austin, 1990; Cox, Erlich, Rothman, & Tropman, 1987; Delgado, 1986; Fisher, 1984; Pruger & Specht, 1969; Rubin & Rubin, 1992), but that very few books had documented the training process itself (Reitzes & Reitzes, 1987). Even as there was a growing recognition among academics that popular education and models of adult education were relevant to university-based social work education, researchers had not yet looked closely at how grassroots community organizing training methods and concepts might be applied to the classroom. So we took the time to go to the trainings, to visit the organizing projects and to survey the training participants to find out what they liked and didn't like, what they used and didn't use. Then we sat down to write this book.

That was 4 years ago. For the next 2 years, we argued and experimented with both the grassroots training approaches and the adult education model in the university classroom. Social work students were very adept critics when it came time to evaluate the practicality of these ideas. And then we rewrote the manuscript twice to focus more on comparing the approaches to organizing and social change and on helping social work students choose a strategy and method which fits their individual requirements. We downplayed traditional political strategies because these had already been written about at great length and because frankly, we think, as do others, that traditional electoral politics has been oversold, particularly for low-income people, minorities and other oppressed groups (Watts, 1986/87). We think some of the kinks got worked out in the process. We finally settled on describing three principal strategies of social change: traditional, direct action, and transformative. We use actual case illustrations and composites of actual organizing campaigns to spice up the presentation, even though we would like to think the analysis and critique of the various methods and tactics stands on its own. We also cut back from three theory chapters to one combined theory/history/philosophy/ideology chapter, at the advice of students. The book is now pretty "user friendly," and most of the chapters have plenty of illustrations and stories to make the concepts understandable and suggested classroom exercises and study questions so students can try out the new roles and skills.

While we hope that many readers will contemplate making organizing their life's work, it is more realistic to hope that many more social work professionals will join the large number of people across the country who participate in organizing projects and campaigns on a part-time, voluntary basis, as part of an overall commitment to community service and public citizenship.

ACKNOWLEDGEMENTS

This book would not have been written but for the curiosity and support of many social work students from the Department of Social Work Education, California State University, Fresno, who participated in one or more phases of the research for the book: Kelly Woodard, MSW, Lanny Knight, MSW, and Tom Hall, who assisted with early interviewing and traveled the length of California gathering data; David Crabtree, MSW, Amy Self, MSW, Maria Espinoza-Helm, MSW, Eliezer Risco, and Richard Mendelsohn, all of whom attended trainings across the country and assisted with the initial training participant survey; and Carl Dragt, MSW, Loma Hollett, MSW, Rena Belluomini, MSW, and Jennifer Solorio, MSW, who helped conduct the followup survey of the training participants. In addition, the many students who worked to make adult education a reality in the classroom while struggling to understand and apply the concepts and skills of organizing deserve our thanks.

Others at California State University, Fresno who supported this research and writing with financial and logistical help, including a sabattical for Mark Hanna to complete the manuscript, are Dean Richard Ford, School of Health and Social Work, and Dr. Benjamin Cuellar, Chair, Department of Social Work Education. We thank Kathleen Vander Meer, Division of Graduate Studies thesis consultant, for her fine editorial assistance near the end of this project.

We are also indebted to the many fine people who consented to be interviewed for this book, and several people in particular associated with the organizing training centers who assisted with access to important resources. Among these people are June Rostan and Walter Davis with the Southern Empowerment Project; Jackie Kendall and Steve Max, Midwest Academy; Heather Booth and Bob Creamer, Citizen Action; John Baumann, S.J., of the Pacific Institute for Community Organizing (PICO); Mike Miller, Organized Training Center (OTC); Lew Finfer, Organizing and Leadership Training Center (OLTC); Lee Staples, Boston University; John McReynolds, North County Community Project (NCCP); Don Stahlhut, San Francisco Organizing Project (SFOP); Alfredo De Avîla and Sonja Peña, Center for Third World Organizing

(CTWO), and Tim Sampson, CTWO Board member and professor of social work, California State University, San Francisco; Ed Chambers, Larry McNiel, Sr. Christine Stephens, and Ernesto Cortes, Jr., Industrial Areas Foundation (IAF); Greg Galluzzo and Joe Mariano, Gamaliel Foundation; Pat Sweeney, of the Western Organization of Resource Councils (WORC); Steve Kest and Fran Streich, ACORN; Ray Rogers, Corporate Campaign, Inc.; Ed Durkin, United Brotherhood of Carpenters and Joiners of America, AFL-CIO, Special Services Department; and Joseph Uehlein, Industrial Union Department (AFL-CIO), Special Projects/Coordinated Campaigns. Several people associated with the Mexican American Cultural Center (MACC) were helpful with early research questions, including Rev. Rosendo Urrabazo, Ph.D., President; Rev. Virgil Elizondo, S.T.D.; and Leonard Anguiano. A special thank you to Ruben Zamorano-Gamez, Lillie Lopez, Beatrice Cortez, Carmen Badillo, and Helen Ayala, all of San Antonio, for their experience and insight into the COPS organization. Also thanks to Fr. Chuck Dahm and Edgard Beltran for information about base ecclesial communites in Illinois; Fr. Shigayuki Naganosi, whose personal commitment to the landless peasant movement in Brazil is an inspiration to us; Sr. Theresa Gomez of San Bernadino, CA, and her associates, who initiated several basic Christian communites and cooperatives; Ellen Pence and members of the Women's Action Group; and to Pat Speer, who provided us with material on the corporate campaign against Pittston Coal Company.

There are several other people who provided us with encouragement and key information, among them, Msgr. Jack Egan, Tom Gaudette, Don Elmer, Richard Leucke, Bruce Leier, and Dick Blin, Director of Publications for the United Paper Workers. Mark also acknowledges an intellectual and practical debt to Professor George Brager, Columbia University School of Social Work, whose organizing wisdom and administrative judgement helped make the writing of this book possible.

Finally, we most gratefully acknowledge the patience and steadfast support of our families: Jan Witte, Sean Witte, Kendra Witte-Robinson; and Rami and Tessa Hanna. The journey would not have been started nor finished without them.

INTRODUCTION

This book is addressed primarily to social work students who learn, as part of their training, about community change strategies and organized group efforts to solve problems. For them, the book provides an in-depth analysis of the strengths and limitations, similarities and differences, and underlying values and ideology of a wide array of strategies and methods. The comparative examination allows for choices about further study or actual organizing opportunities and assists with the evaluation of particular methods based on clear impressions of the constituencies, concepts, implicit theory, types of relationships, and tactics upon which a particular method is based. We stress that the spectrum of social change strategies, as well as the styles of operationalizing them, is quite broad, and that incompatibility with one should not condemn others. One's choice of operating methods, values, and goals often hinges on a mixture of personal preferences and style, and lessons drawn from personal experience. Obviously, a wider repertoire based on familiarity with divergent methods can impart great flexibility and a broadened base of professional practice.

Exposure to a full spectrum of social change methods -- not just in their superficial "how to" manifestations, but also in their underlying theory and long-range implications, may contribute to an appreciation of more possibilities, a clarity of vision and mutuality of perception among those whose business it is to organize community and promote social and economic justice.

There may also be an audience of general interest readers or practitioners who may be curious, and perhaps inspired, to learn how activists of different stripes are earnestly toiling with great creativity, dedication, and thought to try to change our society towards a more egalitarian distribution of benefits and a rebirth of participatory democracy. In many instances, they are crafting and attempting to implement workable solutions to intractable problems that the "powers that be" are unwilling to undertake.

Key Concepts: Strategy, Community, Organizing, Empowerment

Strategy

We define strategy as a general plan to accomplish a specified goal, incorporating: (a) a consistent set of assumptions about actors, environment, and dynamics of interaction; (b) application of one's resources to impact upon other entities; and (c) expectation of a desired outcome that proceeds logically from (a) and (b). For the purposes of this book, each of the three principal strategies of social change may also be considered as distinct "approaches" to effecting desired changes in one or another level of the system. Similarly, within each general strategy or approach there may be one or more "methods" described to implement the strategy. "Method" implies a systematically developed and executed set of general procedures with operating guidelines derived from actual prior experience. Method does not imply a lock-step, rigid application of rules without concern for situational and personal factors and organizing styles. Method takes the general principles of overall strategy and refines them during the processes of planning, implementation, and evaluation.

Community

Generally, when speaking of "community" we refer to a specific population defined in terms of geographic location, demographic characteristics, or group commonality, who share a degree of relationship with each other, as well as some experiences and self-interests which can be addressed on a collective basis. This rather practical approach to defining community avoids the lengthy discussion about cultural, ethnic, or racial identification as a basis for community, which is taken up in several other places in this book. The central themes underpinning the discussion of community in subsequent chapters include values, self-interests, and human needs. We cannot ignore the fact that our working definition of community also is ideologically grounded in a social justice agenda and an empowerment perspective. This means that we think social change strategies which do not link change goals to the eradication of personal and structural oppression, and which do not recognize the latent and manifest power differences between and within social groups, fail in important respects.

Organizing

Organizing is a group process by which a number of people define a common self-interest or unmet need, and strategize and implement plans of action to meet that self-interest or need. Once again, in the interests of brevity we avoid a lengthy and complicated discussion about organizing versus mobilizing. There are several chapters which take up such differences and critically assess their advantages and disadvantages. At this juncture, it is sufficient to point out that organizing for social change is not the same thing as organizationally based program coordination or professional networking, which overall fail to meet the standard of action embodied in our conception of organizing.

Empowerment

One thing that everybody agrees on when empowerment is discussed, is that **power** is the central concept in the definition. We think **em**powerment means bringing people to a sense of their own power to act to achieve their goals, usually in the face of opposition. Utilizing the ideas of Naparstik, Biegel, and Spiro (1982), empowerment requires a convergence of capacity, which implies the ability to exercise power, to access institutions, and to nurture; and equity, which involves a sense of getting back what one invests and the idea of "fair shares" of available resources (Biegel, 1982). Empowerment also implies that power in society is not equally distributed, but it doesn't mean giving people power, which is a contradiction in terms. And it doesn't mean activating some "hyper" switch in a person which transforms them into an "activist," by someone else's definition. Personal empowerment, through collaborative, cooperative, or reciprocal processes, is generally viewed as constituting a step on the way to collective empowerment of a social group or organized community with more clearly defined goals. When someone (or some social group) is defined as not having any power in a particular situation, this doesn't mean they are powerless in every situation (Zimmerman, 1992). It's like what Alinsky (1971) said about there being no such thing as organizing a community, only reorganizing a community. So it is similar with power. A person or persons may be blocked from achieving a particular goal, or there may be such a systemic/structural oppression they cannot even define their goals anymore, or their goals may have become replaced over time with those of their oppressor. But other goals may be within their reach. So everyone who is alive has exercised power at one point or another just to stay alive, and everybody (including Ross Perot) has experienced at least once not having enough power to get their own way. As social workers, we are more concerned about the powerlessness of the "have-nots" than the "haves," the oppressed than the oppressors. The strategies and methods described in this book address these primary constituencies of social work. The achievement of social justice is the driving force of our efforts, even though it will be immensely difficult to develop the necessary power to achieve full justice anytime soon.

"Social Change" Strategies Versus
Traditional politics

This book focuses on three basic strategies -- traditional politics, direct-action community organizing, and transformative social change. The first strategy, referred to as "traditional," becomes the point of departure and signifies the status quo, in effect, reflecting the authors' perspective that interest group politics and political liberalism (the fabric of status quo politics) will yield little by way of benefits to marginalized social groups in the United States. It is undeniable that increased participation by minorities and women in elected offices is a positive step toward diminished race and gender discrimination. But electoral politics does not bring large numbers of people to a sense of their own power to effect changes in their daily lives, let alone state or national political processes.

The second strategy, referred to as "direct-action community organizing," includes mass-based community organizing projects that seek to have a significant impact on multiple public policy issues, and which sometimes (but not necessarily) use confrontational techniques; and some innovative labor movement activities that go beyond traditional workplace organizing to interact with the broader community. Direct-action organizing is clearly differentiated from strategies of mass "mobilization," which can be effective vehicles for broad social change during large-scale social movements, as well as important contexts for consciousness raising and radicalization of participants. But mobilization strategies are extremely difficult to sustain and they generally are forced to ignore long-term considerations of viable grassroots, democratic organizing structures, and promotion of stable, mutual support community.

"Transformative strategy" encompasses several methods, four of which are listed below:

1. Study circles, as they have been interpreted from the Swedish tradition and applied increasingly to labor organizations and peace and justice settings throughout the United States;

2. Citizenship schools, particularly illustrated by the role of the Highlander Folk School during the civil rights era in the United States and the early Community Service Organizations (CSO's) undertaken by Fred Ross, Sr. and Cesar Chavez;

3. Feminist support/action groups, which have developed from many social problem bases in the United States, including battered women, gender equity, sexual harassment, and sexism; and

4. Base ecclesial communities or (BEC's) which are inspired by liberation theology (most recently) and by a model of the early Catholic Church in which the congregants fulfilled mutual support functions and provided sustained relational community.

Each of these methods has many common dimensions which characterize the transformative strategy, including a small-group orientation, an emphasis on self-directed (non-hierarchical) learning, an emphasis on interpersonal bonds, an analysis linking personal oppression to societal/structural oppression, and a fully collective approach to group awareness, decision making, and social action. Each offers unique frameworks suitable to varied contexts and environments, from non-English-speaking immigrant groups to senior citizen groups wishing to learn more about cultures and technology, to students and social workers wanting to interact in non-directive settings; to women developing forums for solidarity and social transformation.

The heart of transformative strategies is the "adult model" of learning which requires strict adherence to the rules of democracy (no exclusion and no imposed authority) and the minimizing of any "instrumental" relationships, where there is some hidden or explicit "quid pro quo" required in exchange for participation. In these settings, people are extended the utmost respect based upon their essential "be-ing-ness," rather than being recognized, rejected, or promoted based upon some credential or expertise. Strict equality prevails.

The direct-action and transformative strategies can be termed "social change" ventures with a goal of fundamental reform, in contrast to traditional social betterment efforts that are fully accepted within our system and deemed noncontroversial. They differ qualitatively from traditional methods (that is, the methods of traditional political, labor, and church structures), especially regarding vision, consciousness raising, and views about power and accountability. This contrast is made evident in the matrices found in Chapter 2, in which we compare the traditional, direct action, and transformative approaches.

Supposedly, "working within the system" can afford disadvantaged groups the ability to achieve for themselves a role and voice in our pluralistic system, and gradually acquire a reasonable piece of the pie. Certainly this has been the case for various immigrant communities throughout the nation's history. Rational problem solving in both the public and private sectors should be able to assure that basic needs are met for all groups, although the degree of individual achievement depends -- as always -- on self-application, ambition, and perseverance.

The problem, of course, is that it doesn't work that way for large numbers of people, many of whom have been in this country for over 200 years. Many key social issues seem to be getting worse, not better -- not just in the context of the country's declining competitive stance in world markets, but in the distribution of available resources within the country. The gaps in income and economic class are growing steadily, and racism continues unabated -- perhaps, even is rising. Unresolved domestic policy crises face joint inaction by government and corporations: health care affordability and access, a meaningful energy policy to conserve finite resources, a shortage of low income housing, and the looting of Savings & Loans banks, to name a few of the more glaring ones. As financiers export jobs overseas, the ideal of employment for anyone who wants it (and which could help break the cycle of welfare dependence) evaporates. A manufacturing system weighted towards non-productive, capital-intensive defense industry siphons away desperately needed resources while the country's infrastructure crumbles.

The American political and social system, dominated by corporate and interest group power, seems incapable of accommodating meaningful reform to provide a decent quality of life for all. Intransigent resistance to even a partial restructuring and redistribution of wealth to provide an acceptable minimum of housing, health care, jobs, and education condemns us, increasingly, to a two-tiered society. Logic dictates that if the country cannot or will not accommodate the fundamental needs of many of its citizens, despite enormous aggregate wealth, then something must be fundamentally wrong with how the system is structured.

Guide To The Book

The first chapter provides a brief historical and philosophical review of social change efforts in this country starting at the turn of the century. This is done not to make any new points about that history, but rather to provide a context for understanding and placing today's activities. It is also to express a sense of continuity of purpose: just as there have always been injustices in America, there have always been people of conscience and courage trying to correct them.

Chapter 1 also discusses important aspects of political theory which explain the relevance of examining the theory and ideology behind social change strategies, even when these may seem apparent. The fact that the underlying ideology is often unstated in community organizing makes it all the more pertinent to reveal it, because its submerged position automatically limits critical evaluation. This chapter also stresses the importance, as an analytic tool, of dialectical argument (the method of describing the interaction of opposing or contradictory forces or ideas, to gain a better understanding of reality).

In Chapter 2, the traditional, direct-action, and transformative strategies are compared along three matrices: Theory ("Why You Do It"), Concepts ("What You Do"), and Skills ("How You Do It"). Definitions of each of the components within each strategy are played out for the three matrices, to help illustrate the contrasts. Despite the many dissimilarities between the direct-action and transformative approaches, these two social change methods differ from the traditional strategy because of their shared goal of fundamental change in how society operates. How well they each move toward that goal, however, is another matter, as will be seen.

The first two chapters having furnished a context, we move with Chapters 3 through 6 into the description and analysis of the actual methods. The material on direct-action strategies is far more extensive than that for transformative ones, reflecting the relative predominance of those activities today, as well as the fact that they have developed systematic training programs which the transformative groups generally lack. Indeed, we see the direct-action organizing centers' refined and regularized training routines as an integral strategic component. The smaller amount of discussion of transformative methods, however, in no way diminishes the significance of their dialectical contrast to the direct-action modes; it remains important to consider the complementary differences of the two processes in tandem, because we believe they have something to learn from each other.

The analysis of direct-action strategies is divided into three chapters, in 3 through 5. Chapter 3 begins with the institution-based method, which typically involves church congregations in a locally based organization that might eventually link up with similar groups in the same state. This method possesses many unique strengths in its principles of organizing around values, centering on churches as a base to mobilize people and find leaders, and using concepts as an effective training tool. However, it falls short of its own rhetoric in that only a small percentage of its participants enjoy significant training, personal development, and politicization, and in the fact that the influence and direction provided by professional organizers to the community groups they work with is often much greater than is openly acknowledged. The most striking contradiction, unfortunately, is that the professed belief in the importance of relational power -- that is, the process of building the power needed to effect social change by constantly expanding the web of relationships -- is totally ignored when it comes to the question of the organizing networks relating to each other and joining forces. Their mutual custom of staying at arm's length not only results in achieving a lower potential power than otherwise possible, but also contributes to the practice of each organizing center's acquiring its knowledge in a fairly self-contained way, from direct pragmatic experience alone.

There is tension within some of the institution-based groups' concepts as well. The typical congregation-centered focus of this method, while a key source of strength, includes inherent limitations regarding which constituencies have access to the method's benefits: people not in the targeted institutions are automatically excluded. Furthermore, the very nature of the method requires an accommodation to the traditional rules by which these mainstream structures operate.

A second conceptual tension revolves around the strict differentiation between the public arena (regarding policy issue decision making) and the private arena (concerning family and close-friend intimacy). While serving a very utilitarian purpose in the organizing method, this dichotomy can tend to emphasize accountability relations within community organizations to the point of denigrating an affective, social-support aspect which constitutes part of the bonds of group solidarity. The public/private split also excludes from the agenda discussion of issues of oppression within family and intimate relationships.

Another common thread within the operation of many institution-based organizing centers is a deliberate minimizing, conceptually, of the significance of race, gender, and cultural issues. This attitude is in conflict with the actual perceptions of people of color, and women, who attend the training programs of these same centers -- as evidenced by the results of a national survey conducted with 154 training session participants (Hanna & Robinson, 1991).

A final point on the institution-based method is that because these projects tend to restrict themselves to localized issues (and tackle issues decided on a state level of power only after several local groups have proliferated in the same state in the same network), the kind of political education and awareness that these groups' members develop is also limited to smaller-scale power levels. Larger forces operating at the national or multi-national level do not receive much scrutiny, since that arena is considered "off-limits" until enough organizational power can be constructed to deal with it. A somewhat related problem concerns the institution-based networks' common goal of achieving a political system based on true participatory democracy. Realization of this goal is an enormous undertaking that begs for a united effort; yet in contradiction to this fact, these networks hold an attitude of insisting that their local groups join forces only with other institution-based organizations within their own network.

In Chapter 4, the second direct-action strategy is examined, which is individual-based methods. There is much more variety among these than in institution-based projects, since some are local, some regional, and some are linked nationally. There are also some hybrid qualities such as Citizen Action state organizations, which typically consist of an organizational coalition of interest groups, but whose primary organizational strength derives from thousands of individual member-supporters solicited through systematic canvassing.

A key strength of many of the individual-based organizations is that they focus on state and national decision makers, carefully strategizing on issues that impact in important ways on large sectors of the population. And while they may not very often have sufficient power to win on these issues, they are at least influencing the debate in a consistent manner. The potential negative is that, since these issue campaigns are usually coordinated with a top-down approach, the assessment from above of the issue's appeal runs the risk of not being in synchrony with people's perceptions of their own self-interest. The risk is in fact minimized with a canvassing system, however, since there is immediate feedback from the public.

The individual-based methods tend to be staff dependent, with two noticeable characteristics. One is that some of these generally rely on staff to play the visible leadership and public spokesperson roles. There is nothing intrinsically wrong with doing this, as long as the organization does not try to claim that it is a "grass roots" operation in the fullest sense (of both membership and leadership). The other distinction is that, in comparison to many institution-based groups, the individual-based organizations tend to have smaller showings at mass events. The poorer turnouts are a result of the staff-intensive nature of the individual-based method, since these projects cannot support enough staff to compensate for the absence of unpaid grassroots leaders' efforts.

The individual-based methods do not make nearly as extensive a use of concepts as do the institution-based groups, and this seems to contribute to less thorough development of staff and leaders -- which in turn could result in their achieving a lesser degree of effectiveness per person. In similar fashion, the individual-based organizing centers taken as a whole generally have less comprehensive training programs than do their institution-based counterparts; this also likely adds to a lower effectiveness, in aggregate.

Some of the individual-based organizations are in fact producing leaders at the local level. However, a further limitation on their effectiveness can occur to the extent that, as opposed to grass-roots leaders in institution-based projects, they may not tend to be "backbones of the community" -- that is, established leaders in mainstream community institutions. Not having those connections and networks translates to not being able to mobilize as many people. This is more likely to be a problem for projects that tend to seek out marginalized low-income people, who have a limited power potential precisely because they are not a majority. In contrast, institution-based projects with a low-income constituency may have a better chance of succeeding because they are tapping directly into more of the established leaders within such a community.

Chapter 5 concludes the discussion of direct-action methods with non-traditional labor movement community organizing. One chief method in this category is the corporate comprehensive campaign, in which a union expands its struggle with a particular employer by seeking allies in the consumer, community, and financial markets whose self-interests can be appealed to. Secondary "targets" are often dealt with to create indirect pressure on the corporation in question. A second variety is the labor-initiated issue coalition, in which consumer and other groups are united with unions around a common primary self-interest.

Labor unions bring some significant resources to these undertakings, including financial strength, sophisticated, high-tech research capabilities and highly skilled staff. However, the corporate comprehensive campaigns are somewhat limited by a narrow vision centered on the union's short-term objectives, without much extensive relationship-building with allies. There is usually not much attention spent on listening to the full range of self-interests of the allies, or even-handed quid pro quo trade-offs of support for each other's agendas. Some of the issue coalitions have a greater likelihood or potential for more solid and permanent relationship-building, but these efforts tend to depend on how long the work on the common issue lasts.

Chapter 6 presents a description and assessment of several of the transformative methods. A common trait of these approaches is a dependable effectiveness in the consciousness-raising, or politicization of their participants. On the other hand, the process tends to be fairly slow. The first method is the study circle, which originated from the European labor movement. Study circles have a solid background with connections to American labor, and a growing visibility with general citizen groups engaged in the "Public Talk Series," initiated through the Study Circle Resource Center in Connecticut.

Citizenship schools, another transformative example, already proved their effectiveness in the civil rights movement, and can continue to be a viable model for meaningful political education. We also include feminist support/action groups as a transformative approach. They served an extensive consciousness-raising function in the development of the modern women's movement. That movement has undergone many changes, and some of these groups are now struggling, on a local level, to utilize their support functions as bases from which to step into effective action. We do not pretend to fully explore the dimensions of feminist social change practice, nor do we represent ourselves as the most informed observers of the women's movement. We do think, however, that the few illustrations provided in this book may be useful, even inspirational, for social workers unfamiliar with this rapidly changing terrain.

The fourth transformative method, the base ecclesial community (BEC), starts from the assumption that much more attention on the part of social workers needs to be given to the religious context for practice. In central cities, with varied ethnic populations whose heritage and cultural identification remains strongly religious, approaches which fail to incorporate these values and even the rituals themselves miss important and powerful opportunities for sustained change efforts.

An extensive history of the BEC movement, including an elaboration of liberation theology originating from a Latin America context and several contemporary illustrations drawn from across the United States, are provided. Important criticisms of the BEC methodology are discussed, including the problems of adapting the Latin American ideology of liberation theology to the U.S. Also, it is noted that one of the original goals of the strategy of BEC's and the theology of liberation -- reform of the church itself -- gets muted into abstraction. However, liberation theology's base ecclesial community approach can serve as an effective vehicle for developing mutual support networks with the advantages of decentralized, small-group/family involvement. Its religiously centered progam emphasis also invokes strong value convergence of participants, which, when coupled with a justice interpretation (hermeneutic) of the principal scripture and an explicit acceptance of the "preferential option for the poor" (central to liberation theology), holds potential for unifying social action.

In all of the transformative methods mentioned above, the question of translating their reflection and politicization processes into effective organized action remains problematic, and awaits much more development. Up to now, the trend has been to place full priority on the integrity of the group support process, which in turn has de-emphasized the setting of an intentional focus on results-oriented action. But it is critical to bear in mind that an important flaw in traditional and direct action approaches to social change practice has been precisely the short shrift given to early stages or "pre-political" stages of community organization.

The authors have identified five interrelated stages of the evolution of political behavior:

1. The recognition of sentiment systems among group participants;
2. The establishment of dialogical inquiry (a largely self-directed stage);
3. The development of critical consciousness (based on a recognition of contradictions between daily reality and the "promise" of scripture or the secular "American dream;"
4. Political socialization (a consideration of change options); and
5. Mobilization of bias (the stage when conscious choices are made to yield personal "consent" for specific purposes, a vastly different arrangement than the current manipulative system of courting votes of uninformed citizens.

We make the point that premature mobilization of bias reduces the depth of consciousness raising which is necessary to develop sustained motivation and participation among oppressed populations. Social workers who are engaged with their communities will want to consider the implications of these stages for their practice interventions.

Chapter 7 presents some decision rules for social workers and others who are interested in pursuing social change training opportunities or careers in social change practice. Descriptions of the major training centers and organizing networks are provided, including a listing many of current cities where organizing is taking place (particularly direct action type). Contact names, addresses, and phone numbers are included.

CHAPTER 1

History and Philosophy of Social Change Strategies

The spirit of protest walks across America with a middle-class gait. The reform group is a precipitate of class, although its middle-class outlines are rarely perceived by either its members or the society at large. (Philip Abbott)

Traditional Social Change Practice

A recurring thread woven throughout our nation's life is the desire to create social change by reforming our traditional political institutions. Despite repeated frustration over the decades, the endeavors still persist today. From campaign reform to curb the influence of special interests, to reliance on management efficiency experts and measures to promote "good government," the collective efforts to make government more responsive to the needs of citizens abound.

Social workers and other human service professionals who work in public agencies or who otherwise observe governmental processes locally or nationally may not fully appreciate how deeply these roots of reform have run throughout the history of our country. Also, a brief review of the development of the American political system may shed light on a few of the characteristics of our constitutional democracy which begin to explain why social change through traditional strategies is so difficult to achieve.

Our Republican Legacy

What is referred to here as "traditional social change practice" might also be called "politics in the modern age." Politics wasn't always sullied and its practitioners vilified. At the time of the Greek city-state or polis (from which the modern "politics" is drawn), politics was a noble enterprise, consisting of "great deeds and speech" (praxis and lexus).

Democracy itself was derived from the Greek "demos" (the people), and "kratia" (to rule). Citizenship in the polis meant inclusion on an equal and free basis in the great issues of the day, with members competing fiercely to outdo each other in acts or works of persuasion. To be "public" in this context meant that whatever was brought forward could be "seen and heard" by everyone and that it was "common to all of us and distinguished from our privately owned place in it" (Arendt, 1958, p.25). One needs to add that not everyone in the Greek city-state was awarded full citizenship. Women and slaves were restricted to the private sphere of the household where the male head of the household ruled with complete authority.

But equally important to the "ruled by the people" legacy of the early Greek system of governance was the republican doctrine of other civilizations including Sparta, Rome, and Venice. In these systems a deep distrust of rule by the people or rule by leaders was resolved by "a constitution that reflects and somehow balances the interests of the one, the few and the many by providing for a mixed government of democracy, aristocracy, and monarchy so constituted that all three components will finally concur in the good of all" (Dahl, 1989, p.25).

Constitutional Compromise

If the seeds of American government and politics, and hence the "traditional approach" to social change practice, are to be found in ancient Greek and Roman experience, then the blossom of youthful American experience can be traced to the British influence. American colonists were not simply some merry band of British adventurers. They represented specific classes and a band of occupational skill. They were merchants and craftsmen as well as agrarian gentry. Ideologically, these people were a product of "Lockian liberalism" which favored enlightened self-interest, individualism, "and supported a state with parliamentary political forms and a laissez-faire stance toward economic and private matters" (Ash, 1972, p. 31).

Given the vast geographical expanse of North America and its isolation from the intellectual and political evolution of Europe, it is not hard to understand how American sociopolitical institutions became "fragmented and fossilized" (Ash, 1972, p. 31). The legendary "free enterprise" system of the merchant class of early immigrants went largely unchallenged by the kind of ideological competition which swept over Europe. Even the revolutionary fervor which brought with it independence for the colonies had little to do with questioning the dominance of economic liberalism.

This doesn't mean, however, that there was a political consensus among the colonial powers. In fact, each colony and later each region developed its own political culture (LeLoup, 1986, p. 62). Such fragmentation, as well as a deep-seated mistrust of centralized authority, largely accounts for the system of shared powers and separation of powers among the three branches of government.

Hence, America adopted a system of government which maximizes material self-interest and the autonomy of small constituencies and decentralized politics. We have a constitution which was designed to protect the right to own property. It fosters stability to institutional arrangements by requiring super-majorities to amend it. The arrangement of small legislative units in the House of Representatives promotes corruption and log-rolling to achieve even limited policy goals. The smaller a unit of government, the more likely a majority will be obtained, perhaps at the cost of a permanently oppressed minority. The virtues of this order of politics have been noted to include important basic individual freedoms, the limitation of centralized power as well as protections against the rise of mass movements, and the promotion of diversity of political forms (McConnell, 1966, p. 353).

But there is also great danger to the fragmented, decentralized (pluralist) organization of governments and society. This danger is found in the exercise of private power over the policy process. While it is true that a fear of irrational mass movements helped to nurture our system of narrowly focused interest-groups, these same interest-groups have ultimately come close to subverting any larger public interests.

James Madison recognized the dangers of faction in his famous Federalist Paper #10, and political scientists have joined the debate ever since. The two major competing political philosophies, pluralism and elitism, each describe the political system according to their perspectives. Pluralists such as Robert Dahl point out that the existing system, better than any other democratic system, insures that large numbers of private interests have access to the policy system and that there is a rough balance achieved through the pulling and hauling of competing interests. Elitists such as Grant McConnell, C.W. Mills, and E.E. Schattschneider point out that not all interests are equal, that power is not evenly distributed, and that it is the nature of small constituencies that the interests of the less powerful are effectively blocked. As Schattschneider says: "The flaw in the pluralist heaven is that the heavenly chorus sings with a strong upper-class accent. Probably about 90 percent of the people cannot get into the pressure system" (Schattschneider, 1975, pp. 34-35).

This background has been provided to orient the social work student to a number of the inherent structural characteristics of the American political system. With this background one can reasonably predict the limits of reform efforts or other variations of policy advocacy which seek social change utilizing "traditional" institutional procedures. To the extent that the mature system of special interests has been fostered by the original "founding fathers," even if inadvertently, it is quite clear that the power of money has corrupted and eviscerated many of the early virtues of the system. Still, a passing review of important examples of "traditional" reform efforts will at least permit social workers to make informed choices about their participation in such ventures.

The Rise of Social Movements

It will be useful to begin with a working definition of a social movement as a:

set of attitudes and self-conscious action on the part of a group of people directed toward change in the social structure and/or ideology of a society and carried on outside of ideologically legitimated channels or which uses these channels in innovative ways (Ash, 1972, p. 1)

Although the maneuvering of special interests to influence the policy process has more recently been characterized by quiet, "professional" influence-peddling and sophisticated campaigns, there are examples of mass movements which have sought to reform government on behalf of greater public interests than those associated with interest groups.

Despite what was said earlier about the ability of our constitutional system to suppress mass movements, there have been two noteworthy periods in our history as a nation during which times dramatic and widespread popular mobilization has occurred. Unlike the conditions which brought about the Revolutionary and Civil Wars, however, even the most radical of these subsequent movements from either of the two periods never seriously threatened the dominant political or economic institutions of the time.

In fact, the incredible speed with which industrialization took place after the Civil War reinforced industrial capitalism, which was abetted by vast subsidy of public land and corporate protection through suppression of labor unions and lack of enforcement of anti-trust and interstate commerce law, as well as the 14th Amendment which prohibited state regulation of corporations, which gained status as individuals under the constitution, with no more social responsibility than any person (Ash, 1972, p. 118).

The most radical of the labor movement players, among them the "Molly McGuires," a secret terrorist organization of Pennsylvania miners and socialist and anarchist organizations actually perpetrated little violence in comparison to the violence used against workers during strikes of the day. Some of these labor groups subscribed to Marxian and socialist ideology, or at least had an alternative philosophy to oppose capitalist production. This was not the case for the much larger American Federation of Labor (AFL) under Samuel Gompers, which actively fended off socialist entreaties and pursued an agenda of limited economic gains and improvements in working conditions.

Populist Movement

The Populist Movement of the 1880s and 1890s was at once an agrarian movement of small commercial farmers seeking more favorable railway rates and the vehicle for a political party with the central platform of currency inflation and switching from a gold to silver standard. At its best the Populist Movement maintained ideological solidarity with radical labor organizations and used a marxian analysis which explained the farming crisis in terms of capitalist distribution instead of overproduction (Ash, 1972, p. 132).

Unfortunately, as with so many American movements, the analysis was divisive because of the rural character of the movement leadership, especially "isolation, competition, suspicion of outsiders, and a primitive conspiratorial world view" (Ash, 1972, p. 133). For example, many Southern Populists supported the Ku Klux Klan movement, while William Jennings Bryan, the charismatic party leader and presidential candidate of the Populists speechified against evolution (Ash, 1972, p. 133). Accordingly, this agrarian movement, after the 1890s, fragmented and pursued the same kind of narrow legislative remedies as other emerging interest groups, legislation which was "often detrimental to the rest of the nation" (Ash, 1972, p. 134).

The Progressive Era, 1905-1916

The emergence of private power became the flash point for the greatest reform movement of the 19th century, the Progressive Movement. But just as with the Populist Movement, the Progressive Movement later became fragmented, if not counter-productive.

Inherited from the Populists was "the theory of conspiracy, a notion that runs like a scarlet thread through the claims of American reform" (McConnell, 1966, p. 32). There was also a clear sense that in the preceding century power had shifted from the public sphere to the private sphere. Also the concentration of private power went hand in hand with the concentration of private wealth and especially corporate capital.

The focal point of the movement was the corruption of the "system," and the reform agenda sought to regulate corporations, to reform political parties and state and local government by instituting direct popular reform measures like statewide referenda, initiatives, the right of recall, as well as direct primaries and multiple party-filing so people could be candidates on multiple party ballots. There were demands for the professional and scientific management of government, for improved working conditions and universal female suffrage, as well as calls for improvements in the integration of immigrants and "middle class, outposts" in urban ghettos (Ash, 1972, p. 155).

Despite the fact that the Progressive Movement was broader than the Populist Movement and had far more people mobilized, it suffered from many similar flaws. It was essentially a "middle class" movement which drew support from some working class factions, but also involved humanitarian and Protestant reform elements, an emerging class of corporate professionals interested in efficiency and civic reform of "political boss" systems, as well as corporations interested in market stability and economic integration with government (Ash, 1972, pp. 138-160).

Such a combination of interests was bound to create huge conflicts and very mixed outcomes. Nearly two dozen states finally adopted initiative, referendum, and recall provisions and direct primary became increasingly commonplace. But, in the case of California, where it was thought that the political parties were corrupt and therefore their power should be arrested, in fact it was controlled by a few powerful private interests (the railroads dominated the legislature) which continued their dominance even after the wave of reform.

As for the much sought after professionalization of government modeled on administrative boards, commissions, and greater autonomy for central bureaucracies, within a few decades such reforms contributed to a system of government captured by "experts" from the private sector. Any hope of serving the larger public interest evaporated with the absence of measures of accountability. For example, McConnell points out the Forest Service developed "virtual autonomy" with

> *its own political ties to a particular constituency. In short, simple insistence upon the virtue of administrators as wardens of the public interest led deviously but certainly to ties with special interests, opposition to which had been the point of Progressive beginnings. (McConnell, 1966, p. 50)*

Roberta Ash is even more scathing in her criticism of the outcomes of Progressivism. "The Populists -- and the Progressive trustbusters and muckrakers -- wanted to use the political system against (emphasis in the original) the economic elite; the unanticipated and unintended end result . . . . was the fusion of these two sectors of society." In their efforts to define their reform agenda in "realistic" goals, Progressives ended up being swallowed by existing elites, "one of the worst fates that can befall a movement" (Ash, 1972, p. 161).

Contemporary Reform

One notes in passing from the Populist and Progressive eras to the New Deal of the 1930s and subsequently the Great Society and War on Poverty of the 1960s, that important reform programs have been achieved, largely through elite-sponsored "traditional" political methods. Viewing these developments historically, Abbott (1987) states:

> *The settlement house movement was turned into the social work profession. Black power became institutionalized as affirmative action. Feminism frequently appears to be dissolving into an agency for individual career advancement using the Service State as its structural support . . . the inventions of reform groups have become supporting inventions of the American welfare state. The reform group takes on the role of supervising and extending programs for its clientele. Just as the union has been unable to transform the factory, the reform group has been unable to transcend the service ideology of the welfare state (p.161).*

It is true that each successive generation of reform leaders gained their experience from some preceding movement or quasi-movement, and that the reform programs have shaped the ideology of the American democracy, especially as these programs have defined the domain of social welfare for generations. Nonetheless, it must be recognized that whatever success has been achieved as a result of these reforms has also reinforced the power of the existing system of political capitalism.

This form of social change practice in which social workers assume roles as policy advocates and active members of larger system-adjusting efforts is time-honored and its virtues are self-evident. There is no need to belabor the central points of this section by reviewing in detail the more widely understood history of social welfare institutions and programs. It is the overall context of the political system within which reform takes place which is salient. As Roberta Ash states "There is a kind of mutual parasitism involved here, in which the movement professionals depend for their livelihood on the elite-sponsored movement while the state in turn gains legitimacy and mass integration from the movement" (Ash, 1972, p. 232). This is co-optation on a grand scale and such change practice is flawed when it foregoes any analysis of the unchanging quality of the political capitalism which so easily integrates or marginalizes reform movement activity.

There are also important lessons to be learned from the failure of the New Left period of the 1960s and early 1970s. The ideas of participatory democracy and liberated zones (Hayden, 1970, 1980) are important ideas which are further elaborated upon by Harry Boyte in *Free Spaces* and *Citizen Action and the New American Populism.* Unrestrained utopianism has given way to a more pragmatic vision of the American reform group and elements of sustainable community. But well-reasoned criticism is leveled at the "new populism" by Abbott (1987), who says: "they are collaborating with the agents of the welfare state," (p. 161) and continue to be dangerously prone to self-destruction through incestuous, elite core leadership which is homogenous to a fault.

Recent and current movements, such as anti-Vietnam war, women's, environmental, anti-nuclear power, and gay rights have not been co-opted by power elites, except perhaps for the commercial seizure of the women's and environmental causes (witness Virginia Slims, and the "greening" of corporate America). However, these movements have also not succeeded in precipitating any truly major, lasting reforms. Limited or temporary victories have been the rule, while many issues such as reproductive rights and environmental regulations remain hotly contested.

The military establishment skillfully adapted by switching to a volunteer army, and by carefully spreading defense industry jobs throughout the country. Feminists found themselves stymied in promoting the ERA and now contend with glass ceilings. The nuclear power industry still chugs along, despite the unresolved question of long term waste disposal. Gays achieve only a weak compromise with the military, while battling for adequate responses to AIDS. Presidents still engage in foreign military adventures, and the environment's precarious status worsens. The small but growing movement for national health insurance reform is dramatically upstaged by the medical and insurance establishments' agenda. In general, the political system has not had to integrate and tame any of these movements, precisely because none of them has posed a serious enough threat as of yet. Without a turmoil equivalent to that of the Great Depression, or an intensity and power comparable to the civil rights movement, there is no need for the system to craft a response on the order of the New Deal or the War on Poverty.

Direct-Action Social Change Practice

For the purposes of this discussion, direct action for social change is distinguished from traditional parliamentary and electoral reform methods on the one side and revolutionary armed struggle which seeks to replace an existing structure of system, on the other side. One can readily find examples of the convergence or blending of direct action with traditional approaches, such as gay rights activists who protest nonviolently to pressure the drug companies to lower the costs of essential drugs used to combat the AIDS virus, while the same gay community develops a political action committee (PAC) to funnel campaign contributions to politicians supporting their agenda. In the same way, direct action and revolutionary approaches converge, as during the 1960s, when the Black Panthers operated cooperative urban food programs while sporadically engaging in armed struggle with police.

For our purposes, direct action occupies the middle ground in terms of tactics. Much of the tactical experience of direct action has been derived from the early labor movement in the United States, such as strikes, boycotts, rallies and marches, and sit-ins or sit-downs like the ones undertaken by the automobile unions in the 1930s and later used during the civil rights movement. Many variations on non-cooperation and civil disobedience (the intentional breaking of unjust laws) also evolved from the earlier abolitionist period prior to the Civil War, finding their way into the Gandhian movement for India's independence, civil rights, free speech, and anti Vietnam war movements.

Essentially, direct action for social change is characterized by active resistance or protest to existing or proposed laws or policies or living conditions (Carter, 1973, p. 24). People may join together, as temporary mobilizations during a crisis or large-scale movement (such as during the civil rights and anti-Vietnam war movements). Or smaller numbers of people may participate in long-term multi-issue organizations to work on immediate social or economic problems at the level of neighborhoods, municipalities, or occasionally, statewide or nationally. Many examples of this latter type of social change practice are discussed in Chapters 3 through 5 of this book.

The larger social movement type of change effort is usually directed at perceived flaws in the formal political system, such as an erosion of civil liberties, including personal freedom of expression and the freedom to protest publicly, or when political freedoms are perceived as ineffective, as when addressing structural problems (Carter, 1973, pp. 120-128).

The smaller, more local, direct-action organizations generally have less power and therefore, more limited goals of neighborhood improvement. There are some very resourceful direct action organizations which have moved from smaller to larger issues, from material goals to political goals. It should be borne in mind that direct action has been used by "left" and "right" wing groups. Ideology is no barrier to the skillful use of any of the methods of social change practice. This book has chosen to focus on the dominant liberal values of social work.

What Is Justice

The shared value of direct action, whether through movements or local organizations, is a desire for justice. Justice has something to do with "giving proper consideration to the claims of everyone concerned," as in "equal justice under the law," or it is a standard of fairness. But a definition is complicated by interpretation. For our purposes, we look to two political philosophies, liberalism and socialism, for contrasting views of justice. Found within the contrasting philosophies are the now familiar arguments of the pluralists and elitists.

Liberalism and Liberal Justice

The preeminent liberal political scientist, Robert A. Dahl, discusses and defends liberalism and liberal justice in his book *Democracy and Its Critics*. Dahl describes at some length the uneasy constitutional mix already reviewed earlier, while indicating particular structural flaws of the current liberal system: the insufficient conceptual understanding of interests; the difficulty of conflicts generated by such a diversity of interests; and the difficulty of preserving "civic virtue . . . in dedication to the public good," within "heterogeneous societies," and the problem of adapting "republican theory . . . on the scale of the nation-state" (Dahl, 1989).

When it comes to achieving justice within such a context, Dahl turns to philosopher John Rawls, whom he quotes: "pretty clearly, perfect procedural justice is rare, if not impossible, in cases of much practical interest . . . The best attainable scheme is one of imperfect procedural justice" (Dahl, 1989). While there are problems with this "imperfect procedural justice," Dahl persuasively states:

> *Viewed in this way, the democratic process endows citizens with an extensive array of rights, liberties, and resources sufficient to permit them to participate fully, as equal citizens, in the making of all the collective decisions by which they are found . . . the democratic process is not only essential to one of the most important of all political goods, the right of the people to govern themselves -- but is itself a rich bundle of substantive goods (Dahl, 1989).*

Obviously, social change practitioners with a shred of practical instinct recognize that the game of politics is based on compromise. If some interests aren't represented this time, then maybe they will be better organized next time. Imperfect justice is better than no justice.

Liberalism embraces the protection of individual liberties without apology. To the extent that power is associated with justice, distributive justice will always be unevenly achieved. When conditions get bad enough or when one or another social group is massively oppressed (in spite of the "bundle" of political rights accorded every citizen) liberal theory assumes the built-in system of checks and balances will eventually redress such grievances. Unfortunately, there is some strong indication that the "magical market," rather than creating stability and a high standard of living, actually is prone to extreme cyclic fluctuations which predictably disadvantage specific social groups.

In the late 1980s and into the 1990s, for example, we have witnessed corporate capitalism become more fully integrated as a global economy. Unemployment among American workers has increased dramatically as multi-national companies and American-owned businesses have moved manufacturing and product assembly plants to lower wage markets in third world countries. Realignment among prime military contractors, as a result of reduced federal military expenditures, has witnessed large-scale economic downturns in several western states. Inequitable tax codes and other forms of "fiscal welfare" for large corporations and high-income citizens has exacerbated the perceived economic injustice experienced by persons of low and moderate income and certain racial and ethnic minority groups.

Americans nonetheless remain doggedly optimistic that the politics of voting and a change in the stripe of the ruling party will create conditions for reform. Alternatives to the basic structure of our political and economic institutions are not realistic nor are they ever seriously considered.

Socialism and "Social" Justice

The clearest statement of the difference between liberal justice and socialist justice is noted by Kymlicka:

> *Justice exists, therefore, in the liberal capitalist system as a 'juridical' concept, a 'remedial virtue' required by the conflicting interests of individuals or as a result of material scarcity. But . . . both Marxists and communitarians believe in the supersession of justice, as an aspect of the development of a higher form of community. (Kymlicka, 1989, p. 113)*

The welfare state is perhaps a good example of an institutional arrangement of a liberal society which is intended to promote this kind of remedial justice. Unfortunately, when the market economy is in recession, as it frequently is, then the pressures to dismantle social welfare programs increase.

Socialism is not a monolithic philosophy. The state socialism of the former Soviet Union differs dramatically from the democratic socialism of France, Spain, or Sweden. "Pure" socialism is just as much a theoretical notion as is the pure "free market" of liberalism. It is essential to understand that socialism was conceived of as an oppositional political philosophy, precisely in relationship to the philosophy of liberalism and its economic superstructure, corporate capitalism. One Marxian critique of capitalism suggests this form of productive system ignores the importance of our "social nature" by turning people into objects from whom surplus value or profit is extracted. Capitalism also promotes many types of "social alienation" and divides people into a side known only as "worker" versus the whole realm of subjective experience which is only displayed away from the workplace. This split occurs along the same lines which saw Arendt describe the privatization of the slaves and women and "necessity," while freedom was reserved for the public sphere (Kymlicka, 1989, pp. 114-115).

These are structurally generated conflicts of social relations which inhere with capitalist division of labor and which "implies the contradiction between the interests of the separate individual or the individual family and communal interest of all individuals" (Kymlicka, 1989, p. 116). In one important sense, socialism was invented to complete liberalism, or at least "the economic side of the democratic ideal" (Kymlicka, 1989). Socialism rejected liberalism for its laissez-faire economics in favor of centralized planning and leadership from above, believing that an economy which operates rationally also protects "the greatest good of the greatest number." In this sense of the "social," some socialists have asserted that the inequalities of a society based upon individualism and private property could not be rectified unless it was replaced by a society in which the means of production (not all private property) were owned by society (Williams, 1976, p. 239).

There are thoughtful people who use a socialist analysis of political economy and who generally point to the tremendous concentration of economic wealth and political power when they call for fundamental change. Although we recognize the risk of reviewing Marxian concepts in this post-Soviet communist period, we think social workers are well served with a brief revisitation.

Historical Materialism

Marx's theory that alienation is related to substantive everyday conditions of life, especially the realm of economic activity, was in sharp contrast to the liberal conception of idealism, which posits that individual consciousness, made up of ideas and beliefs, determines people's attitudes and their social relations. A materialist interpretation of history was necessary to counterbalance the idealist interpretation of liberalism, which "finds in history a directing logic," while historical materialism seeks to discover the "real" causes of the historical process. "It identifies as the ultimate cause (of history) human nature as determined by certain drives. But it sees human nature . . . as a historical reality . . . bound to a given social and economic context" (Tillich, 1977, p. 114). In simpler terms, whereas idealists tend to be carried away by the mythology of say, the "American Dream," and believe that only their own hard work is required to achieve this abundant life, materialists would say there may be something bigger operating here which blocks the achievement of individual aspirations -- namely, the organization of the productive system and distribution system. One might arrive at this conclusion after engaging in dialectical analysis.

Dialectical Analysis

This is an important process of studying any social situation as it is presented in history, from the point of view of real working people. The dialectic predates Marxism. It is a broad, adaptable tool which can easily be used within a variety of social, political, or economic contexts. This type of analysis is not like a dry intellectual exercise; it is, rather, interactive, consisting of three parts: thesis (the central idea, supported by its assumptions and arguments); antithesis (the position opposite to the thesis); and synthesis, generally some middle ground or idea containing parts of the thesis and antithesis. The dialectic also implies active discovery, as critical consciousness of the causes of social alienation are uncovered in the daily life of action and reflection on action. One goes deeper and deeper into an understanding of the reality as it exists and changes. Analysis of cultural, social, economic, and political institutions as well as power relations all reveal new dimensions of reality.[1]

Contradictions in Social Relations

Dialectical analysis examines two main types of contradictions in social relations: contradictions in the distribution of goods and services under capitalism and contradictions of production. Marx believed that the distribution system under capitalism was unfair to laborers, who work for a wage, while owners and managers receive excessive returns for a monetary investment (surplus value from total investment, including labor, equals profit). In addition, modern capitalism has created a division of labor in the productive process which alienates workers from participating in making a complete product, creating alienation from production, from the product, from others, and from self (Longres, 1986, p.21).

Social workers certainly experience these contradictions. For example, many social service agencies purport to serve clients with fairness and respect, while at the same time enforcing eligibility rules which make it economically unfeasible for clients to exit from welfare, or impossible for truly needy families to receive adequate benefits or services. In the same way, many social service agencies espouse a progressive, equitable positon for their workers, while resiting unionization or even reasonable grievance procedures. While the dialectic may not serve the purpose of resolving these contradictions immediately, the process does keep the tension of these contradictions, a constant awareness of them, at a high level and drives people to figure out solutions.

It should be apparent that socialism runs the same risk as does liberalism under the circumstances of power, which is to achieve "just power," which itself requires the power groups which lead be held accountable and subject to democratic controls. Tillich calls this the "tension between the powers of origin that support the structure of society" (the "American Dream" or nationalistic feelings, for instance), "and the democratic corrective that subjects it to the demand of justice" (Tillich, 1977, p. 142).

Much of the criticism of Marxian analysis by social workers as well as critics of liberation theology stems from the false notion that Marx was exclusively concerned about the economic sphere -- "Materialism is economism." Tillich pointed out that the young Marx always understood that "economics" and "spirit" were inseparable (Tillich, 1977, p. 114). Later distortions of Marx's and Engels' work led to an overemphasis on the materialist side. Says Tillich, "It is therefore no accident that political romanticism today wages its struggle against the proletarian movement as a struggle against Marxism" (Tillich, 1977, p. 113).

Social workers, even if they do not propose to replace the existing social institutions, would be well-advised to have an analysis of reality connected to their choice of direct action strategy. The danger in not having such an analysis is the forfeit of vision. Practicing veto politics to stop a state-sponsored initiative to reduce AFDC grants may be a "hot" issue which translates into direct action and mass mobilization. But history teaches that such mobilization can't be sustained after the crisis point. A thoroughgoing analysis provides for action planning with a vision of an alternative. It produces insight into the function of repressive or oppressive proposals and argues for methodical organization to resist. Chapters 4 through 6, focusing on direct action methodologies, generally support action from a local base, rather than a national base. The participation of social workers in such action can become an important extension of traditional political social work. There are so many contradictions in the average productive work of social workers that it is essential that professional practice expand the lexicon of systems theory to embrace alternative tools of analysis such as the dialectic and an understanding of political economy. It seems unwise to let ideological changes in global politics obscure the advantages of using analytical tools well suited for today's struggles.

Whether one calls it a political economy perspective (Hasenfeld, 1983) or a neo-Marxian perspective, the basic tools of power analysis still require careful examination of political, economic, and structural dimensions of reality.

Transformative Social Change Practice

It is hard to argue with traditional and direct-action practitioners when they criticize social change practice which focuses on adult education and consciousness raising as being "weak" or a diversion from "action." One response, however, is that action without reflection, without analysis, runs the risk of moving people before they are ready or worse, of manipulating people to act on somebody else's agenda. Therefore, not all forms of social change practice will begin at the same place and it may take longer for some forms of practice to achieve concrete goals, if they are ever achieved. This is the case for transformative social change practice.

Three Types of Functional Community

Think about this distinction. There are three types of functional community: rational (political) community, which deals with all the public dimensions of life; productive community, concerned with economic transactions as well as issues of well-being (the alienation described by Marxism); and affective community which more or less deals with relationships of intimacy, friendship, and subjective fulfillment (Wolf, 1968, pp. 189-192).[2]

If social change practitioners operate almost exclusively in the productive and political communities (as traditional and direct-action organizers do), it leaves affective community entirely to the family and increasingly fragmented and isolated family members. There are some important problems with this tendency to ignore or isolate the family from the other two aspects of community. A little historical background makes the point.

The Family and Community

Profound changes in family structure occurred with the rise of a money-based economy and the shift from the dominance of a household economy (a post-feudalism device of the productive-property owning bourgeoisie) based on "the unity of personal and productive life in the form of self-contained cooperative economic units," to the capitalistic economy in which private property separated into "capital" and "labor power" (Zaretsky, 1976, p. 29). Between the "disintegration of feudalism in the fourteenth century and the rise of capitalism in the sixteenth," important changes took place in the family. Zaretsky notes two divisions of social organization which had far reaching, largely negative consequences for women, whom until the rise of capitalism had achieved relatively equal social status within a cooperative household economy. The first division was "between the socialized labor of the capitalist enterprise and the private labor of women in the home," which led to the diminished importance of women in the productive process and the increase in the male-domination of the household. The second division was "between our personal lives and our place within the social division of labor," which in combination with the first division led to the separation of "'work' and life'" much as had existed in the Greek city-state and the split between "necessity" and "freedom." The consequence for women is summarized by Zaretsky:

> *While housewives and mothers continued their traditional tasks of production -- housework, child rearing, etc. -- their labor was devolved through its isolation from the socialized production of surplus value. In addition, housewives and mothers were given new responsibility for maintaining the emotional and psychological realm of personal relations. For women within the family, work and life were not separated but were collapsed into one another. (Zaretsky, 1976, pp. 14-16)*

This trend was gradual throughout the seventeenth and eighteenth centuries in England, the leading nation in the early industrial revolution, and the sociological locus of Marxism. There was notable resistance to the trend of proletarianization as industrial capitalism visibly assaulted the "romantic individualism" of the prior period. By the early nineteenth century, the family was no longer seen as a place of social productivity, but as a haven from the inhuman and cruel factory, "and a new form of personal identity developed among men and women, who no longer defined themselves through their jobs" (Zaretsky, 1976, p. 49).

Feminism and the Family

The oppression of women in the idealized nuclear family, regarded as a regrettable oversight by socialists, has been well documented in a survey of feminist writers completed by Zaretsky. Noting that radical feminists have disagreed with the socialist position which asserts that family relations (and all social relations) would be transformed automatically with the equal treatment of women in the work force and the expansion of participation by women in social production, Zaretsky asserts: "Instead of viewing the contemporary family as specific to developed capitalism, radical feminism takes it to be a universal form of oppression" (Zaretsky, 1976). He quotes Firestone, a prominent feminist, asserting "Beneath economics . . . reality is psychosexual" (Zaretsky, 1976, p. 63).

The feminist challenge to socialism and to liberalism (the liberal position having been successively elaborated by Locke, Mill, and Rawls), is the rejection not simply of economics as the sole unit of analysis (under socialism) but the rejection of liberal theory which is "based on the natural equality of individuals" . . but which "have in fact taken the male-headed family as the essential unit of political analysis; women's interests are defined by and submerged in, the family, which is taken to be their natural position" (Kymlicka, 1989, p. 92).

Thus, Zaretsky notes the development of two discreet tracks following feminist and socialist critique. On the one hand, early 20th century feminists emphasized the need to maintain the subjective dimension of personal life, in the developing "tradition(s) of personal liberation, expressed through cultural radicalism -- currents that accepted personal life as a question outside politics" (Zaretsky, 1976, p. 88). A more contemporary survey of feminist thinking would suggest an increasing awareness of the organizational requirements for "socializing" the dimension of the personal and forcing it into the political. Pro-choice, domestic violence, child care, and child support represent four areas in which significant politicization has developed, often in the context of intense resistance and social conflict. The difficulties encountered by women engaged in these struggles reflect to a lesser degree the theoretical confusion which derives from converting the personal into the political; to a greater degree they reflect the hegemony of the dominant ideologies expressed through corporate and religious institutions and the practical, long-term difficulties of appropriating the language and symbols of modern culture, which currently support discriminatory policies and institutions. The construction of a new social reality based upon a re-presentation of these symbols in light of women's issues may alter the strategic cleavage in lines of conflict and add valuable constituencies to the women's movement. Additional strategies which resist corporate capitalism and the inexorable pull of "alienated individualism," may promote a stronger feminist politics.

On the other hand, socialism, throughout the early 20th century, reflected "the tradition" (s) of social transformation, which viewed family life (and the condition of women in the family) as a diversion from the essential locus of the means of social production and found in psychoanalysis "a theory of 'individual solutions'-- a guide to getting by in capitalist society" (Zaretsky, 1976, p. 100).

A feminist perspective also contributes an essential intellectual critique of patriarchy, dualism, and hierarchy as the dominant social, cultural, political, economic, and theological organizing principles. It also emphasizes the importance of personal experience over narrow, sexist views of scientific predominance. While feminism in the United States has generally failed to seriously address the liberation movements of racial and ethnic minority women, particularly African American and Latina women, these movements have benefited from feminism's renewed emphasis on communal processes. There is also no disputing that the assertion of judicial protections and civil rights for women, particularly recent Supreme Court decisions supporting women's rights to sue for workplace harassment, would not have occurred without the unrelenting pressure of the broader women's movement in the United States.

Latina feminist theologians do fault Anglo women feminists in the United States for having failed to understand how important popular religious practices are to the daily struggles of Latina women. An emerging Hispanic women's liberation theology is described as insisting on a socio-political-economic analysis which rejects the elitism of feminism and individualism which seduces so many Hispanics to become absorbed by the dominant culture. This form of liberation theology for Hispanic women strengthens families and feminism, by demanding cultural integrity to resist assimilation and support self-identity, by affirming the struggle against all types of oppression by men, against political-economic discrimination, and through a commitment to change unjust structures (Isasi-Diaz & Tarango, 1988).

Feminist theology, in general, "needs to be seen as a network of solidarity that exists among many feminist communites engaged in the critique of patriarchalism in distinct cultural and religious contexts" (Ruether, 1985). With over 3000 years of religious patriarchy to contend with, an "exodus from patriarchy" will require a prolonged struggle for "autonomous spaces" from which to develop new institutions. As Rosemary Ruether stated, "Feminist theology, along with other forms of liberation theology -- black theology, Asian theology, Latin American theology -- are engaged in redefining the agenda and constituency of theology itself . . . . We must do this because patriarchy is not benign and ultimately does not wish us well." (Ruether, 1985, p. 61).

What this brief rendering demonstrates is that the feminist movement contributes in our society to a meaningful critique of the realm of the personal sphere, while an awakened socialism, moving from a recognition of labor as consisting of "production" and "reproduction" does provide an important theoretical understanding of the social relations of the household as reproducing the dominant mode of production, e.g., individualistic, competitive, male-dominated, social relations. The expectation of socialism that such unequal relations would desist upon full inclusion of women into the workplace has failed to be achieved. Instead, we have gender inequality in the workplace and in the household. The "demand" of justice has not been satisfied.

This background should contribute to an appreciation of the importance of raising the critical consciousness of people who contemplate participation in social action. But there are a least two other important elements of the analysis. The role and function of education in the process of social transformation, and the importance of cultural and religious factors in the evolution of political behavior.

Education for Social Change

It has been said that the creation of mass society led to the substitution of "behavior" for "action" (Arendt, 1958). Mass public education in the United States, in the view of another observer, "has been assigned the function of teaching people to 'get along' with one another" (Zaretsky, 1976, p. 54). Unfortunately, public education hasn't been doing a very good job of educating the young nor of teaching them to 'get along' with each other. Paulo Friere, who wrote *Pedagogy of the Oppressed* in 1970, offers insight into the role of "liberating education" in the overall transformation of a society. Even though the book was written from the perspective of Brazilian dispossessed peasants, it offers ideas of great power and use in American society.

One of the great lines from Friere's book is: "Education suffers from narration sickness" (Friere, 1970, p. 57). Friere reveals the inherent passivity and oppressive quality to what he calls the "banking" method of education. The teacher is the source of all knowledge and the student, the ignorant receptacle. This is contrasted with "problem-posing" education, which transforms the student into a co-investigator who actively participates in "demythologizing" reality. Whereas the banking method is fatalistic, problem-posing education creates a sense that reality (as it exists in oppressive, objective conditions) is "susceptible to transformation" (Friere, 1970, p. 73).

This form of education is liberating when it is developed by the oppressed in the context of their own experience. Much as the Marxist analysis uses the dialectical method to understand the bases of domination, marginalized groups, including ethnic and racial minorities, women, gays, and lesbians, welfare recipients, or even mental health clientele might use this model of education in two stages: to systematically "unveil the world of oppression" through dialogue, and second, "through the expulsion of the myths created and developed in the old order" (Friere, 1970, p. 40).

Friere's is a humanist approach to freeing people from oppression which recognizes that without a profound perceptual transformation of the oppressed, a mere change in role or status would result in more oppression. The initial praxis (action) of the oppressed is "imitative," as oppressed people have been submerged completely in the culture of domination and so, upon being "freed" tend to behave as the oppressor behaved toward them.

Later in this book, the authors argue that sometimes community organizing work -- by social workers and others -- contains the character of the oppressor acting upon "false generosity," not really trusting that people (they are "clients," or "welfare mothers" or "single parents") can find their own solutions to problems. But, as Friere says: "It is only the oppressed who, by freeing themselves, can free their oppressors. The latter, as an oppressive class, can free neither others nor themselves" (Friere, 1970, p. 42).

Transformative social change practice, therefore, must engage the oppressed as the leaders of their own liberation process. The development of critical consciousness, through problem-posing "educational projects, which should be carried out with the oppressed in the process of organizing them," is the heart of this transformative method (Friere, 1970, p.40).

The authors' criticisms of traditional and direct action approaches to social change is that such methods do not systematically consider the pervasive character of a culture of domination, nor sufficiently emphasize critical consciousness in the action/goal-oriented methods. It isn't that action isn't important to transformative practice, but that unless participants themselves are liberated from the mind-set of oppression, the result of any action may end up reproducing the identical behavior and institutions which were the goal of reform. The only difference would be that a new set of players would fill the institutional positions.

Cultural & Religious Dimensions of Social Change Practice

We wish to make very clear that the various transformative methods which are considered in this book are quite adaptable to a widely diverse ethnic, racial, and cultural society. The essential methodologies, for the most part, are equally practical for use by secular or religiously oriented grassroots organizations. At the same time, we emphasize the central importance of recognizing the religious dimension of social change practice with racial and ethnic minority populations. One simply cannot over look the fact the the church is still the central institution for African American and Latino populations. The Black church has been especially important as one of the "main sources of power in the Black community and still provides the primary spawning ground for the majority of Black leaders . . . . and does not show any signs of significant decline" (Washington & Beasley, 1988). According to Poole (1988), however, the Black church(es) have been hampered to some degree, because of "its persistent dedication to the goal of integration . . . and its adoption of the agenda of the white church (p.140). In Poole's view, Black churches need once again to utilize their historically prominent role of promoting education among Black masses, as well as to "appropriate the themes of political, economic, and social liberation generated by the movements of Martin Luther King, Jr., Malcolm X, Black Power, and Black Theology. Further, these must be translated into effective social strategies" (Poole, 1988, p. 140).

For Mexican Americans, at this juncture in the evolution of the demographics of the United States, recognition of the importance of religious values and institutions may be even more important than for African Americans. Because Mexican American populations are overwhelmingly religious and Catholic, it is impossible and perhaps elitist to neglect consideration of the one transformative methodology which has been known to successfully engage certain sectors of Latino and Mexican American groups: the basic ecclesial community or BEC approach.

Just as study circles, citizenship schools and feminist support groups contribute to the development of "affective community," the BEC approach provides a similar bridge from traditional religious values and traditional culture to a new civic culture in the United States. In fact, the BEC approach may share as much in common with the secular-oriented ideas of Friere as with the liberation theologians of Latin America. The difference is the practical necessity of engaging people in social change practice along one of the most important dimensions of their daily experience, which is religious.[3] The political importance of the Latino and Mexican American people to the future of the United States (and especially the Western and Southwestern regions) cannot be overstated.

The Demographic Imperative

Approximately 68% of the Hispanic population in the United States is accounted for by Mexican Americans, according to recent statistics, and Hispanics in the U.S. increased in population 53% in the last decade to 22.4 million people. About half this population increase is due to immigration. By the year 2020, it is projected that the Hispanic population will rise to 15.2% of the United States population, exceeding the percentage of African Americans (14.2%). By the year 2050, the percentage of non Hispanic whites will decline to 52.7%, while that of African Americans will rise to 16.2% and Hispanics to 21.1% (Current Population Reports, November, 1992).

With this veritable explosion of the Hispanic populations, and particularly Mexican-Americans, there will be powerful forces unleashed to accommodate the populations. The relative advantage which African Americans have struggled to achieve politically and economically, is already perceived in some Hispanic metropolitan areas as exclusionary to their interests. Most notably, the spring 1991 rioting in Hispanic sections of Washington, D.C. may be evidence of the repetition of historical efforts to achieve access and equality of opportunity and political participation.

While such "new immigration" problems are hardly new in the U.S., the declining economic position of Hispanics vis a vis other minority groups and Anglo-Americans in 9 of 13 U.S. cities studied (accounting for two-thirds of U.S., Hispanics) is alarming. In 2 Texas cities, Dallas and Houston, the percent of the Hispanic population living in poverty rose from 20 to 30% and 19 to 30%, respectively (Fresno Bee, 1990).

In other reports on the rate of high school completion among Hispanics, it is noted the graduation rates are actually falling in comparison to gains made by other minority groups.[4] According to Solomon D. Trujillo, Vice president and general manager of U.S. West Communications and board member of the Aspen Institute, such statistics combine to spell disaster for U.S. businesses: "The nation's competitive position cannot be maintained if a sharp division continues between stable leadership isolated in the suburbs and poor workers and an underclass isolated in deteriorating inner cities" (Fresno Bee, 1990).

Political representation is another area in which Latinos experience wide gaps between their relative population size and proportionate representation to elected local, state and national offices. In Los Angeles, where an aging white, numerical minority population has resisted the inexorable demographics, it took until 1991 to elect the first Latino County Supervisor, after an absence of Latinos in that body since the 1870's (Fresno Bee, 1990). Even while minorities grew from 33 to 43 % of the California population between 1980 and 1990, nearly 9 of 10 elected officials at all levels are white (Fresno Bee, 1991).

The authors are encouraged the most by the numerical imperative constituted by the rapidly increasing Latino (and particularly Mexican-American) population and by increasing numbers of reports of the U.S. social policy shift toward poor children and health care. We think that Texas and California in particular, so crucial to the electoral process in deciding presidential elections, may also prove to be the leverage points for social change in the 1990s.

It is not insignificant that the Archbishop of Los Angeles, Roger Mahony, a man who supported the early organizing effort of the United Farm Workers, has been elevated to cardinal in the archdiocese where Hispanics make up 3 million of the 4.5 million parishioners. In a recent news story, the Cardinal committed the Church to outreach with Hispanics "to encourage the participation of Hispanics in the political life of Southern California" and emphasizing a program of recruitment of more Hispanic priests and requiring all seminarians to be bilingual, establishing outreach centers to provide services to immigrants and the homeless, opening parochial schools at night to offer classes in English, citizenship and adult literacy, and subsidizing parochial education" (Fresno Bee, 1991).

The Development of Mexican American Consciousness: One Example

A transformation in consciousness took place for Rosendo Urrabazo when he attended the Mexican-American Cultural Center program in San Antonio (and later became its director):

Let me tell you what happened to me. Because I came here to study. For me, a Mexican-American coming here, the beautiful experience of discovery of who you are. Because when I was in school nobody told me about the history of the Mexican-Americans. Nobody told me anything about, that we had a theology, that we had a way of looking at God. Or, that the popular practices that we have at home were of consequence.

We just always said, "well that's only superstition." And so we come here, and Virgil gives these lectures on the development of the Mexican-American consciousness. And he traces the development of the consciousness of the Mexican-American and how the consciousness of the Native American mixed in with the consciousness of the Spanish European, how that emerged into the consciousness of the the Mexicano. That consciousness of the Mexicano merges with the consciousness of the North American into what he calls the Mestizo, the mixture. And that emergence forms into this new person that we call the Mexican-American, the person born out of conflict, torn between his mother and his father (in an archetypal union kind of way).

But really it has become the person born along the border, the person who lives in two worlds. Not necessarily bi-cultural, but a new culture. Not necessarily bi-lingual, a new language has happened along the borders. So a new language emerges, a new culture emerges. And Virgil Elizondo calls it the Mestizo.

So the development of the Mexican-American consciousness,

> *to me, was the first time I heard a Mexican-American telling me*
> *that I was normal . . . when I heard the lectures about the*
> *Mexican American, the history, the heroes, the different leaders*
> *in the community, that was very affirming to me and made me*
> *want to do more* (Urrabazo, 1990).

Liberation Theology and the Emancipation of Latinos in the United States

It should be apparent that absent a clearer appreciation for Mexican and Latino culture, including the claims which Mexican Americans have on equal political rights and the centrality of the religious experience to the vast majority of this ethnic group, any practitioner group (and especially social change practitioners) will be severely disadvantaged in efforts to work with them or on their behalf. Social change practitioners will be well advised to learn substantively about the central values and rituals which shape the context of social and political struggles in which Latin people engage. While "Latino (a)" is the most encompassing term to describe people of myriad national origin, and one preferred by various politically inclined subgroups, "Hispanic" remains the most commonly heard term describing several national cultures where Spanish is the preponderant language. The term "Chicano" was in frequent use among politically active Mexican Americans until the latter term became substituted and descriptive of all people of Mexican origin with legal status in the United States. The frequent confusion in terms of description, paralleled the similar evolution of descriptors for African Americans, and is not without importance as indication of altered identity and consciousness of oppression.

Liberation theology has played an essential role in the maturation of a radical reform movement within the Catholic church, and therefore in the lives of a majority of Latinos. Its emergence during the last two decades is best explained as the result of the convergence of Latin American sociohistorical development in the mid-twentieth century with the deepening commitment of the Catholic church to social justice in the world.

Two central components of traditional Christian theology, have in the view of John A. Coleman, a sociologist, led to "this emergence of political theology. The first is the privatization of religion. The second is the breakdown for both Protestants and Catholics, of earlier models of church-world engagement and the fragmentation of concerted church action in the political order" (Coleman, 1982, p. 59). Vatican II did indeed specify an emphasis on seeking to create solidarity which promotes action on behalf of global peace and justice. Latin American theologians were particularly prompt in interpreting the Vatican II documents to the circumstances of their landless peasant populations.

"Political theology calls the church to unmask and denounce the ways it gets used to bless unjust social orders" (Coleman, 1982, p. 62). What began at Vatican II, rapidly spread to all of Latin American, principally through two major church convocations at Medellin, Columbia (1968) and Puebla, Mexico (1979). The Medellin conference was responsible for contributing important writing on the theme of liberation, including papers on "Justice," "Peace," and "Poverty," which reinforced the role of "institutional violence" and "structures of sin" in lives of oppressed people (Coleman, 1982, p. 19). These proclamations also recognized the independent, legitimate role which "popular" religion plays in the lives of the mass culture and "affirms the active and creative role of the lower classes in the building up of a new society" (Coleman, 1982, p. 22). The significance of the Medellin conference cannot be understated. In the view of some theologians, it is the most important shift in emphasis to occur in the church in Latin America in centuries. For Leonardo Boff, a prominent (though censored) liberation theologian, Medellin "confirmed the church's three great 'options' or choices: for the poor, for their integral liberation, and for the base church communities" (Boff, 1988, p.13).

The Puebla, Mexico (1979) conference went even further in the recognition of popular religion as being the religion of the poor. "This people's religion is lived out in a preferential way by the poor and simple" (Boff, 1988, p. 24).

The phrase "preferential option for the poor" grew out of the Medellin conference and became one of the central tenets of liberation theology.

> *The Latin American bishops called upon the church to live in solidarity with the poor in three ways: by denouncing poverty and the sins that beget it; by preaching and living 'spiritual poverty' and openness to God; and by a lifestyle marked by detachment from material goods. (Neilson, 1989, p. 5)*

A great profusion of writings about all aspects of liberation theology has followed the initial 1968 article written by Gustavo Gutierrez titled "A Theology of Liberation." While the intellectual feast has surely turned many aspects of Catholicism upside down, the real "praxis" of the theology can be seen in the acts of bravery undertaken by "thousands of lay pastoral leaders, Protestant and Catholic, who have given their lives in the struggle for peace and justice" (Ellis & Maduro, 1989, p. xvii). Most Westerners also know of the shocking murders of two Catholic bishops and over one hundred clergy during the last 15 years. "Liberation theologies . . . are raising uncomfortable questions, questions that some find intolerable. This is the violence of economic, political and social oppression (to which) must be added the violence of systemic oppression" (Ellis & Maduro, 1989, p. 112). Liberation theology has continued to draw the ire of the Vatican, the repressive regimes of host countries as well as conservative religious and political circles within the United States (Ellis & Maduro, 1989, p.269).

As "political theology" became liberation theology, the category of social sin became defined as "the structural concealment of past personal choices for injustice into systematic institutions of economic oppression and political deprivation" (Coleman, 1982, p. 68). Given the peculiar (subservient) relationship of Latin America to dominant economic, political, and military influence, it is not surprising that Latin Americans utilize methodologies "for specific sociopolitical and economic analysis of their situation of internal poverty and external dependence" (Coleman, 1982, p. 68). Thus, liberation theology, and the entire praxis of liberation in Latin American base ecclesial communities (BEC's) fundamentally rejects the "western models of development and historic capitalism as we know it" (Coleman,1982, p. 63).[5]

The religious dimension of culture, particularly for Latinos and more so for Latina women, is absolutely central to their definitions of themselves. Isasi-Diaz and Tarango (1988) put it this way:

> *To a large extent the soul, the vivifying element, of Hispanic women's culture is the religious dimension. It is around and in relation to the religious dimension that the motivations of this culture are established. All the elements of Hispanic women's culture are united, 'the cultural values are ordered and the aspirations and ideals of the culture are centered' around religious understanding and beliefs. (p. 71)*

It is of paramount importance for the social change practitioner who works with Latino/Latina culture to grasp the reality of religious existence. Hispanic women's Liberation Theology and Hispanic women's culture goes much deeper than adherence to traditional, "official" church teachings. It encompasses profoundly symbolic and actual meanings of existence which come from the Spanish, Amerindian, and African elements and influences on this vast social group (most especially Cubans, Mexican Americans and Puerto Ricans living in the United States).

Summary

This chapter has provided an historical and philosophical context within which to view the development of traditional, direct-action, and transformative social change strategies. The virtues of a system of government based on liberal democracy are recognized, as is the predominance of traditional political social change practice. A general indictment of global capitalism, along with a review of selected concepts of Marxian analysis, are offerred by way of counterpoint. The negative effects of liberalism and the capture of government by private interests has contributed to reform movements and to the enormous growth of direct-action and transformative social change efforts.

Greater clarity and more thorough analysis of the "ideological lock" which supports oppressive structures may help people resist the pressures of cooptation or conversion to a system based on competitive individualism and false idealism. There is an insidious temptation to lower one's vision or goals, or alter one's analysis, in order to accomplish what one feels is realistic. This is the classic tension between vision and reality. If one cannot stand the tension, one can easily succumb to the comfort of pursuing a what is easily achievable, rather than what is desireable.

Classroom Study Questions

1.   Describe or discuss some of the "contradictions in social relations" which face social workers in daily life and organizational practice. How do these contradictions extend to client populations? How can social change practice alter these situations?

2.   Describe or discuss how women social workers are disadvantaged in day to day work environments. Use the dialectic to discover the true sources of the process of gender discrimination in work environments. How does the

systemic nature of the oppression of women contribute to increasing a culture of scapegoating and victimization?

3.   Read Endnote #1 dealing with ideology. Describe or discuss how social workers can promote the "free space" and relational organization conducive to worker and client empowerment.

4.   Discuss in class, your experiences with how racial, cultural, or religious factors effect the development of rational, productive, affective, or cultural community.

Endnotes

1.   One might speak of an "American Ideology" with which most of us are heavily imbued: "The idea that knowledge is inherently neutral, that there is a unitary scientific method, or that science provides the preeminent explanatory model . . . At the heart of the American ideology is an 'uncritical criticism' . . . a commitment to the Western project with second thoughts threatening, but never quite becoming, first thoughts" (Wilson, cited in Parenger, 1990, p. 63).

It is a simple yet subtle process which creates this phenomenon, one which relies heavily upon the "everyday" reality of moment to moment sensation and experience. But this is not a "natural" process insofar as the mechanisms for its maintenance are pervasive and "subconscious" or "unconscious." All the elements which constitute the idealized (ideological) creation are merely '"accepted as inventory, as components of a known world"'(Kosik, cited in Parenger, 1990, p. 122).

The powers of advertising, mass media, and mass communications, television with a vengeance, combine to instill the paralysis of passivity -- a kind of uncritical, conventional moralism without the slightest relationship to real conditions or interests, even one's own. Parenger cites Raymond Geuss on the totality of the ideological "lock": "one can't be freed from their coercive social institutions as long as they retain the ideological world-picture which legitimizes them nor can they get rid of their ideological world picture as long as their basicly coercive social institutions render it immnue to free discussion and criticism'" (Parenger, 1990, p. 125).

It is essential that social change practitioners have a detailed understanding of the processes of idealization and ideological construction and deconstruction. These are essentially political processes, despite the clear psychological mediation. We draw on the work of several social scientists to develop this line of reasoning. Since the supportive research upon which this book is based is of an essentially pedagogical nature, it will not be surprising that we view the task of achieving critical consciousness among practitioners and students-teachers to be paramount. Education, in its dimensions as a liberating praxis, is a key element in resisting the "ideological hegemony" of the varied institutional structures. Beginning the process is in one sense direct and self-initiated. Parenger quotes Karl Popper: "it is only our critical attitude which produces the antithesis . . . The only force which promotes the dialectic development is our reluctance to accept, and to put up with, the contradiction between the thesis and the antithesis" (in Parenger, 1990, p. 116).

This is a process called "deconstruction" which "involves prizing apart the meaning and assumptions fused together in the ways we understand ourselves in order to see them as historically specific products rather than timeless and uncontrovertible given facts" (Henriques, in Parenger, 1990, p. 74). It is useful to understand that social change implies altering the configuration of forces of society of the "social," which is by definition "political." Thus, our long-range vision, a "realistic utopia" (Friedman, 1987)) is necessarily and consciously the motive force and ethical fountainhead for a concrete, transformative praxis.

But it is the everyday (conditioned) experience where one must begin this work. Berger and Luckmann state in their seminal work, *The Social Construction of Reality*, that "subjective reality is thus always dependent upon specific plausibility structures . . . The plausibility structure is also the social base for the particular suspension of doubt without which the definition of reality in question cannot be maintained in consciousness" (Berger & Luckmann, 1966, p. 143).

Ideology does not therefore appear out of thin air, nor is it maintained or destroyed with the wave of a hand or the periodic victory of narrowly based, economic-political benefit organizations which perpetrate short-range "parachutist" or "reform" strategies without recognition of hegemonic (dominant and pervasive) ideological forces.

Transformation under such conditions which exist requires what Berger terms "alternations" or "switching worlds" and these "processes resemble primary resocialization because they radically reassign reality . . . the 'recipe' includes both social and conceptual conditions . . . the social serving as matrix for conceptual." Berger continues: "The most important social condition is the availability of an effective plausibility structure . . . laboratory of transformation . . . mediated to the individual by means of significant others with whom he must establish strongly affective identification . . . replicates childhood experiences of emotional dependency on significant others . . . properly segregated from the outside world" (Berger, 1966, p. 143). What occurs, according to Berger, is that there develops "counter-identity" or "counter-reality," which are "possible only when individuals congregate in socially durable groups . . . which serve as plausibility structures for counter definitions of reality" (Berger, 1966, p. 153).

It is plain to see that most "everyday" associational activities do not approach the intensity which is implied in such a process. One must consider strategies of selective reinforcement, "selective de-linking" (Friedmann, 1987) or "de-routinize" (ing) (Parenger, 1990). But despite the apparent complexity of a voluntary process which meets "unmet needs," and which makes visible (and plausible) a "true consciousness," one may be surprised to discover the rather impressive number of organizations serving these functions within the "free-space" of associational activities or even within the context of existing, dominant social structures like the Catholic church (particularly of Latin America but increasingly among Hispanic American clergy and theologians). Subsequent chapters will describe in detail the array of such entities.

To summarize this section on ideology, it might be said that the "red herring" which casts to the defensive any progressive social change practitioners into the exclusive domain of "ideologue" needs to be recast in light of the above review. The role of social change practitioners can no longer be restricted solely to the manipulation of mechanical technique or routinized skill. Such a practitioner becomes an intellectual in the "Berger" tradition of "an expert whose expertise is not wanted by the society at large . . . this person appears as the counter-expert in the business of defining reality" (Berger, 1966, p. 116). Such a person may be the "organic" intellectual of Gramsci, who emerges from among the oppressed and works along side this "bloc" as an equal, or the "liberated-oppressor" of Elizondo who is in no position to evangelize the poor but who may be well-suited to prod the rich.

Such a practitioner may also be prepared for the role of "critical social scientist" described by Parenger (citing Fay) as one "who seeks to disclose how the historical process was such that the social order which he is examining was incapable of satisfying some of the wants and needs which it engendered, and in so doing he will have accounted for the structures, conflict and accompanying social discontent which he perceives" (Parenger, 1990, p. 60).

It is in this latter sense of the "critical social scientist" to which the authors subscribe. It is not the inflexible, doctrinaire view of a fanatical ideologue that we have in mind in bringing ideology back to respectability. The concept of ideology is essential precisely as a form of methodological critique for "prizing apart" of assumptions about dominant (hegemonic) world views. Berger said it best: "Social change must always be understood as standing in a dialectical relationship to the 'history of ideas'. Both idealectic and materialistic understandings of the relationship overlook this dialectic and this distorts history . . ." What is essential is to see "all symbolic universe and all legitimations are human products" (Berger & Luckmann, 1966, p. 118).

2.   To these three types of functional community we add a fourth: cultural community, by which we refer to the legitimacy of respecting and defending cultural membership as a primary political liberty, at the same level of importance as the "liberties of equal citizenship" (Kymlicka, 1989, p. 162). Rather than viewing "cultural community" in the narrow sense of the "character of a historical community and the norms currently characterizing it," we share Kymlicka's view of culture "in terms of the existence of a viable community of individuals with a shared heritage (language, history, etc.)" (Kymlicka, 1989, pp. 167-68). Under the

second interpretation, the rights of minorities within the larger, traditionally defined "political" community (of America, for instance), are recognized from the basis of their <u>cultural</u> membership. In this context the United States would be compelled to extend minority rights "beyond non-discrimination and affirmative action" (Kymlicka, 1989, p. 146).

3. The oppression of the Mexican people, through conquest, annexation of territory, and the imposition of religious hegemony by European Catholicism, all but eliminated essential cultural and religious practices, particularly for the Mexicans living in the territory annexed by the United States. In three spans of history, covering 150 years between 1848 and 1985, Mexicans have battled to reform a church which systematically banned their indiginous clergy, degraded their status in a two-tiered system, one for whites, the other for Mexicans, and only begrudgingly accepted the role of "mother church," defending the rights of poor Mexicans. According to Cadena, the period from 1848-1940 was one marked by deep racism and ethnic oppression. From 1940-1960, there was a period of "Pastoral Paternalism," during which Mexicans received the same kind of segregated treatment as blacks did in the South (Cadena, 1987, pp. 68-72).

During the third period from 1960-1970, Cadena describes the rise of the Chicano Movement and contrasts it with the Civil Rights Movement of blacks. Whereas the Civil Rights Movement among blacks was conducted and led by their own Black Church Leaders, the Chicano Movement reflected deep resentment and confrontation with the Catholic Church. Great demands were made on the Church to fulfill not only its religious commitment, by opening up its clerical and structural elements, but more broadly to change its aggressive, culturally oppressive policies of religious and cultural assimilation (Cadena, 1987, pp. 68-72).

Cesar Chavez, the young charismatic leader of the United Farm Workers, is quoted by Cadena, summarizing the hope of large numbers of the Chicano Movement:

> We don't ask for more cathedrals, we don't ask for bigger churches or fine gifts. We ask for the churchs' presence with us, beside us, as Christ among us. We ask the Church to sacrifice with the people for social change, for justice, and for the love of brother. We don't ask for words; we ask for deeds. We don't ask for paternalism; we ask for servant-hood.
> (Cadena, 1987, pp. 77)

As a result of these pressures from within and outside the Church, a sea of change began to occur in the fourth period, from 1970-1985. For Cadena, one event stands out as the signal. This was the appointment on May 5, 1970 of Fr. Patricia Flores as auxiliary Bishop of El Paso, Texas, "the first Chicano bishop in Church history, ending 142 years of episcopal discrimination" (Cadena, 1987, pp. 68-72).

Representation of Chicanos in the priesthood and development of church offices from Latino ministry soon followed. Cadena states:

The process soon led to call for the development of 'new ways of doing theology' that reflected Chicano/Latino cultural values and their social position in society. The importance of the laity, the role of everyman, links to political empowerment, reinterpretations of the gospel, the influence of liberation theology..., set a new agenda for . . . the Chicano people. (Cadena, 1987)

Subsequent events throughout the 1970s and 1980s, including the growth of the base ecclesiastical communities and the popularization of liberation theology in the United States and the success of the three National Hispanic Pastoral Encuentros, were not universally embraced as positive changes. To be sure, there have been critics, but in Cadena's view, "it was these expressions that brought many Chicanos back to the church" (Cadena, 1987).

One of the many important developments to emerge from this period of Chicano activism were the opening of many offices for Hispanic Affairs at the regional and dioceses levels and the opening of the Mexican American Cultural Center in the summer of 1970 in San Antonio, Texas. Established with the support of the newly appointed Bishop Flores, its first director was Father Vigilio Elizondo. Fr. Elizondo had recently completed studies at the University of Manila, East Asian Pastoral Institute (Anguiano, 1990).

In an interview with Leonard Anguiano, a MACC staff teacher and administrator since 1972, it was learned that MACC had been influenced in its early days by three pastoral institutes in different parts of the world. The East Asian Pastoral Institute in Manila was influential because of its view on culture. As Anguiano stated it, "it's a good influence in saying, well, religion is part of the culture and it's not the other way around." From the institute in Quito, Ecuador came the influence of those ideas "of dehumanization and margination, of a dominant culture penetrating the subordinate culture to the point where the oppressor always lives inside the oppressed." And from Spain came the ideas of "the renewal of the sacraments. The sacraments can be life giving, can be used to inspire people and to give people hope" (Anguiano, 1990).

One of the functions of these three institutes was to interpret the documents of the second Vatican council (1961-64), which is precisely the mission entrusted to the Mexican American Cultural Center (MACC): to interpret these documents for the Mexican American people in the United States (Anguiano, 1990).

Somewhat prior to the establishment of MACC, Fr. Virgil Elizondo had already begun to bring to the United States several professors from the Philippines. With the new forum provided by MACC, Elizondo could now bring many more Spanish speaking theologians to dialogue directly with Hispanic clergy and lay audiences.

It soon become apparent to a much wider audience, what had been understood by Elizondo and a small cadre of Hispanic theologians for several years -- namely, that due to the turbulence of civil rights protests and later anti-Vietnam sentiments, the Catholic church in the United States did not promulgate the implementation of important precepts coming from Vatican II. Latin American and Filipino theologians therefore had a head start in examining the Pastoral Letters which dealt with poverty, justice and racism issues. Surely history was recording the incredible events of the 1964 civil rights and 1965 voting rights act with clear implications for Mexican Americans, but these events were not central to the secular Chicano Movement nor did they radicalize Mexican American youth to the extent that Anglo and African American youth were radicalized.

The radical theology of Gustavo Gutierez may have been basis of Latin American "liberation theology," but the frequent visits by Gutierez, and other theologians such as Enrique Dussell of Argentina and Juan Luis Segundo of Uruguay had important and widespread impact on the theology and praxis of people attending workshops and courses at the Mexican American Cultural Center (MACC). As Rosendo Urrabazo said: "There was a resonance with what was going on here in San Antonio and the Southwest. Not only among Hispanic but among Blacks, Asians, and Native Americans" (Urrabazo, 1990).

European theology was simply not speaking to the experience of Mexican Americans, particularly the priests. The convergence of the Chicano Movement, the United Farmworkers struggles, and broadening awareness of liberation theology as it could be applied to Mexican Americans, began to touch growing numbers of the Mexican-American clergy. Rosendo Urrabazo estimated that most of the Mexican American priests in the United States, perhaps 250 in number, have participated in some form of the training at MACC. Estimates of the total number of clergy, religious and lay people attending MACC by 1983 has been put at over 9,000 (Cadena, 1987).

Cadena extends our understanding of liberation theology from the Latin American Church to the United States. He emphasizes particularly that Hispanic clergy and theologians (of whom there are very few) have been surprisingly well socialized into liberation theology and widely influenced (in their views of required changes within the church) by the Mexican America Cultural Center (MACC). Although MACC has moved away somewhat from the early emphasis on liberation theology to what is referred to as a "theology of democracy" (MACC retains close affiliations with the Texas projects of the Industrial Areas Foundation), the early influences of MACC are worth noting. Among the most important influences to come from MACC is the deepened exposure to the work of Gustavo Gutierrez. It has already been stated that Gutierrez originally proposed his theology of liberation as a departure from traditional of theology. "To Gutierrez, the primary task of theology becomes to free the oppressed from their inhuman living conditions, not to convince the non-believers" (Cadena, 1987, p. 24). Cadena further paraphrases Gutierrez in describing the two acts of theology. "The first act of theology is to begin with analyzing one's historical situation . . . , and the second act of theology becomes critical reflection on praxis" (Cadena, 1987, pp. 24-25). Finally, Cadena reviews the attributes of the "overt" liberation of Gutierrez: "1. Liberation means freedom from oppressive economic, social and political conditions. 2. Liberation means that human beings take control over their own historical destiny. 3. Liberation includes emancipation from sin and the acceptance of a new life in Christ" (Cadena, 1987, p. 25).

Thus one begins to see that indeed the historical events and a broad ideological constituency (not just culturally predisposed Marxists but also the widening circle of denominational theologians and ethnically identified clergy and social scientists) are seriously struggling from within and outside the church to press for reform and reconstitution of dominant structures. While it is clear that the dominance (hegemony) which the church obtains with the "ensemble of relations" which make up the social consciousness of the faithful, remains very strong, it is also clear that a "prophetic" voice, the voice of the past in history is not to be easily silenced. The Basic Ecclesial Community (BEC) methodology is but the most recent signification of this fact. Bishops throughout the United States and across denominations are steadily increasing the visibility and adaptability of the "preferential option for the poor" as well as the theology and methodologies of liberation.

4. Liberation theology has continuously been laden with the charge that it draws upon Marxism in deriving its critical analysis of social structures. From a number of perspectives this view seems overstated. First, it is true that Latin American liberation theology casts a very dark and critical analysis of capitalism. Latin American capitalism rapaciously exploits the mass of semi-indentured peasants in agricultural and extractive industries who live at a base subsistence level. The concentration of land and wealth is obscene and all threats to the status quo, particularly movements among landless peasants in coalescence with the church will obviously be met with the most powerful symbols used to maintain the established order, e.g., the threat of communism. But what should be apparent from the outset, is that the mass of peasants are not against the ownership of private property. It is precisely the opportunity to own their own land, whether as individual families or in small cooperative arrangements, which propels the peasant movement. Arthur F. McGovern a Jesuit priest who has carefully examined the relationship between dependency theory, Marxist analysis, and liberation theology, has this to say about the relationship:

> Liberation theology operates at two very different, though interrelated levels. In practice, most of the social analysis used by base communities and Christian programs of popular education focuses on very specific problems: agricultural development, violations of human rights, health care, land reform, and so on. In most instances this type of analysis relies very little (and often not at all) on Marxist analysis or dependency theory. Liberation theologians have, however, addressed issues about the root causes of problems in Latin America, and at this level dependency theory and Marxist analysis do come into play. (McGovern, 1989, p. 273)

The basic framework of dependency theory when applied to the contemporary situation, refers to the concentrated use of capital by transnational banking and industrial interests (located among the northern tier of developed countries, the U.S., Western Europe, Japan) to initiate and shape the economic structures of southern tier countries (of Central and South America) in such a way that the south becomes wholly dependent on increasing infusions of northern capital to produce growth in the export productivity of their economies. It is a very one-sided arrangement which has increased the cumulative foreign debt of these countries to the breaking point, while systematically forcing repayment terms which has caused drastic austerity programs to be imposed upon the populations of dependent countries. But McGovern points out that while there are parallels between dependency theory and the Marxist use of scientific methods of analysis found in historical materialism, there are important differences (McGovern, 1989, p. 278).

Specifically, the leading proponent of liberation theology, Gustavo Gutierrez, states McGovern, "does not call for class struggle or view it as the driving force in history . . . Gutierrez felt that Marxist analysis could be separated from Marxism's altruistic worldview . . . Gutierrez referred also to Althusser's distinction between Marxism as a science and as a ideology" (McGovern, 1989, p. 280). McGovern does find the use of certain key Marxian concepts and principles prevalent among liberation theologians, such a "praxis" (a "transforming of the world" and "unjust structures"), "ideology" (and the method of studying the use of ideologies by dominant sociopolitical groups), "organic intellectual" and "hegemony" (from Italian Marxist Antonio Gramsci), "exploitation" and "surplus value." McGovern closes his essay by stating of the criticisms, "I have yet to find any specifically Marxist studies of Latin America that serve as guides to liberation theology analysis" (McGovern, 1989, p. 282).

5.   A frequent criticism of the base community methodology as a method promoting social change is that religious institutions themselves mirror and reinforce the very hierarchy and patriarchy which stands in the way of change. A second criticism, having to do with the BEC approach not addressing the central question of power in its formulation and operation, will be taken up at the end of the chapter.

It is true that very few social scientists have concluded or even implied that organized religion (or popular religion) does anything other than contribute to a docile, mass society who find in religion desperate escape or convenient justification for maintaining the status quo. Much of this criticism was formulated based upon theoretical treatises which predate the development of liberation theology. Liberation theologians, not social scientists, have for the most part been at the forefront of recent efforts to demonstrate the viability of religious movements and religious ideology for social change which advances the interests of marginalized social groups. These theologians include Leonardo and Clodovis

Boff (Latino), James Cone (African American), and Rosemary Ruether (American feminist).

Of course, as theologians, the central mission involves the reform of the church in light of the principles of liberation theology, articulated by Philip Berryman and quoted in the doctoral dissertation of Gilbert Cadena: "1. An interpretation of Christian faith out of the suffering struggle, and hope of the poor; 2. A critique of society and the ideologies sustaining it; 3. A critique of the activity of the church and of Christians from the angle of the poor" (Cadena,1987).

Among these theologians, there is frequent (and increasing) reference to the writings of the Italian Marxist Antonio Gramsci (who spent many years of his life in fascist prisons under the reign of Mussolini), as an authoritative and a brilliant source of theoretical insight linking scientific Marxism to the revolutionary potential of religious peasants and workers. According to Carl Boggs, a prominent socialist intellectual, Gramsci had "a vision of cultural transformation," based upon "a system of moral principles." Boggs states, "Gramsci's fixation on human 'will' and political action as the essence of historical change goes further in its celebration of subjectivity than any previous Marxist notion, even including Labriola's "praxis philosophy" (Boggs, 1984, p. 43). Boggs quotes Gramsci in an attack on narrow "scientism and utopianism":

> *They (the reformers) do not understand history as free development of freely born and integrated energies, as something unlike natural evolution, in the same way that man and human associations are different from molecules and aggregates of molecules. They have not learned that freedom is the force immanent in history which blows up all pre-established schemes. The Philistine of socialism have reduced the finely-woven cloth of socialist doctrine to a rag, have dirtied it and then ridiculed those who they think do not respect it. (Boggs, 1984, pp. 42-43)*

Gramsci also considered culture in a much more inclusive framework than simply those things we normally associate with elite "culture." "It (in Gramsci's view) incorporated the entire realm of social consciousness, popular ideas, attitudes, habits, myths, folklore, etc." Gramsci was particularly adamant that these forms of culture did not contribute to civilita, . . . based upon an encyclopedic knowledge whereby man is viewed as a mere 'container' in which to pour and conserve empirical data of brute disconnected facts which he will have to subsequently pigeon-hole in his brain" (Boggs, 1984, p. 44).

One can see clearly the influence which such views have had on subsequent writings of educators such as Friere, whose "pedagogy for the oppressed" similarly emphasizes the destructiveness of the "banking method" of education. Liberation theologians also have been interested in how historical events in Latin America seem to have reflected Gramsci's ideas. Clearly the Latin American Catholic church (60-90% of Latin America is Catholic) has been pushed into its position of preferential option as much as it has led. The peasant movements (in addition to the military police states, which have diminished the formal, institutional presence of the church) have required that the church make some movement away from it's traditional status quo legitimizing role.

Boggs quotes Gramsci, writing nearly 70 years ago:

Catholics carry out a social action which is ever deeper and more widespread. They organize the proletarian masses, found cooperatives, trusts, banks and newspapers. They plunge into practical life and they necessarily intertwine their activity with that of the secular state, thus making the fortune of their particular interests dependent on its fortune(Boggs, 1984, p. 51).

In this context, noted Gramsci, "the state absorbs the religious myth and seeks to make it into an instrument of government, well suited to drive back the assaults of the few absolutely secular forces organized by socialism" (Boggs, 1984, p. 51). It is increasingly clear, particularly among observers of Latin American conflicts, that both peasants and the rising intra-church disputes among theologians and clergy (wide clerical support at the base to visible, yet limited support at the top) are contributing to deep rifts in the church. Gilbert Cadena reviews those tendencies of the dominated social groups to seek autonomy while the dominating group seeks to maintain hegemony in its areas of influence (social and political consciousness). Cadena states:

Pierre Bourdea and Max Weber have stated that every church is in permanent danger of the rise of prophets, who are involved in a strategy of taking religious power and capable of mobilizing large sectors of the church. A prophet can be a person or a social group and in this case I argue "liberationists" represent a prophetic social group. Their success depends on both extra- and intra-religious factors. When there is a crisis in society and social movements rise up, the probability of prophetic movements increase (Cadena, 1987, p. 19).

CHAPTER 2

Matrices of Change: A Comparison of Traditional, Direct-Action, and Transformative Strategies

Chapter 2 is designed to accomplish two objectives: first, to give readers a basic "roadmap" of the terrain of social change practice, enabling them to grasp a gestalt or complete (general) picture; and second, to provide readers with enough "roadsigns" along the way to recognize: (a) the primary highways (the three strategies or social change approaches -- traditional, direct-action, and transformative); (b) the secondary roads (consisting of the theory, concepts, and skills) adhering to each strategy; (c) the tertiary streets (consisting of the 8 specific points of theory, 10 concepts, and 12 skills). Just as with roadsigns and streetsigns, the matrix cells provide only enough information to secure a "fix" or location of one item in relation to another. The comprehensive understanding of any particular idea and the consequences of choosing each will require a careful reading of the other chapters.

Using these matrices will bring greater clarity to key elements of social change practice for people entering the arena. Beginning level practitioners would do well to spend time familiarizing themselves with the three basic components of theory, concepts, and skills, as well as try to understand the meaning of the categories within each of the three. Once this is accomplished, a comparison of the three different social change methods can be made. There is some complexity to this process but in the end one should be able to answer several questions about each method:

1. What are the central values and overall change goals implied by each method?

2. What personal and situational factors might influence your choice of method?

3. What short-term and long-term consequences might there be for your community, neighborhood, organization, self, in choosing one or another method?

These are very involved questions. Other questions and exercises at the end of each chapter will assist the reader with practice and synthesis of the material. The remainder of this narrative will provide definitions and commentary about the various categories presented in each matrix.

Matrix I -- Theory

Theory is a set of ideas formulated by reasoning from known facts to explain something. Theory has most often indicated the tentative, speculative nature of ideas, and unfortunately has been placed in historical opposition to practice. But the Greek term **praxis**, meaning action, reestablishes the close link of theory and practice, as praxis embodies the qualities of systematic observation and description with the power to critique the practical and conventional. The misuse of theory can lead to its application as fanciful abstraction (and idealism) or to "impractical or fanatical" ideology (Williams, 1976).

Ideology in this politicized sense means a set of ideas or a particular definition of reality which arises from or is attached to a definite set of material or powerful interests (Boff, 1987). For example the two dominant political parties in the United States, Republican and Democratic, each represent vested interests and each portrays reality based upon those interests. Democrats attempt to sell their reality as the party of the working class, and of low, and middle-income wage earners. Republicans have always tried to appeal to values of individualism and freedom of business from government intervention. As with all ideological systems, the basic values and principles cannot be demonstrated or refuted, and all such systems can absorb new data without undermining their basic structures (Boff, 1987, p. 210) (see endnote 1 at end of Chapter 1 for extensive treatment of ideology).

As a result of these powerful ideologies, social change practitioners are hard-pressed to resist buying into the system, let alone having success in changing the system. Beginning the process requires understanding of the **dialectic**, which is a process of investigating truth through systematic reasoning. Dialectical analysis contains three parts: thesis, antithesis, and synthesis. Thesis in one sense in just a statement or theory put forward and supported by arguments, for instance, "Apple pie is best when cooked by one's mother." When a thesis involves a position of power and politics, it refers to reality as it appears (or is represented); for instance, "Apple pie is best when made in America by real American mothers," (almost always idealized people who exist only in the imaginations of advertising executives). Antithesis, or opposite of thesis, is the idea which smashes the initial premise that, in this case, apple pie is best when cooked by mother. Maybe whoever is conveying the antithesis goes so far as to say apple pie isn't even any good, and supports the position by citing environmental studies about the use of alar on apple trees. The purpose of the antithesis is to raise up an alternate possibility, however unlikely. But it needs to strike a familiar chord with the audience to be believed and to set up possible rejection or modification of the thesis. Finally, a position of synthesis can emerge from a contrasting of the different possibilities or the natural tension between these opposite poles.

We define **power** as the ability to act to obtain one's desired goals, often, but not always, in the absence of voluntary consent. Bachrach and Baratz (1970) argue that power is a relational concept rather than a quantity to be possessed. In their view, power is exercised by (A) only in relation to another individual or group (B) to obtain the compliance of (B). Compliance is given by (B), who chooses to comply out of fear of threatened sanctions or loss of something valued more highly (position, money, etc.). Power is distinguished from force because when force is exercised (the bullet is fired) (B) no longer has a choice of whether to comply or not. Power is distinguished from influence because power requires use of potential sanctions, but the line separating the two is fuzzy. Authority also differs from power. Rather than complying from fear of sanction, one regards "a quality of communication" as authoritative and one "defers" because the request seems supportable by rational argument.

Many community organizers would critique Bachrach and Baratz on at least two points: (a) compliance is prompted sometimes not out of fear, but rather by the promise of a desired benefit or reward; and (b) deference to authority sometimes hinges on "rational arguments" which are deliberately false.

Theories of power also differ on the question of the conditions under which power can demonstrably be shown to operate. If (A) dominates (B) in a visible conflict where there is a winner and loser, no one disputes that the result is an instance of power being exercised (unless force is involved). If (A) never publicly takes an opposing position to (B), but nonetheless blocks (B), by dominating the structure of debate, from discussing the issue of potential conflict, then (A) can be said to have exercised power. Thirdly, if (A) has been able to completely submerge the awareness on the part of (B) to the existence of its own interests, (A) can still be said to have exercised power.

In the instance of visible conflict, examination of who wins the decisions will usually reveal who exercised power. When conflicts are not permitted to reach a decision point, such as when ruling elites don't allow an issue to be placed on an agenda for formal consideration, looking at these "non-decisions" can reveal the instance of power. But when larger socioeconomic and political forces have shaped and constrained the range of choices, creating cultural blinders (mom's apple pie is the only choice; or, "people can have any color Ford they want . . . as long as it's black"), potential differences may be ideologically impossible to articulate. The dialectic will permit a critical assessment of whether power was exercised under such circumstances.

For our purposes, an **interest** is a benefit or advantage about which an individual or group is concerned. Traditional strategy suggests we know and vote our own best interests in a freely chosen, competitive, and diverse environment. Direct-action strategy requires an assessment of dominant interests and the respective interests of all parties involved, in light of what change is possible. Transformative strategy implies that long-term mass re-education is required before true self-interest can even be identified. It is quite possible that under many conditions people may not know their true self-interests.

Consent is an often trivialized component of power. It means giving one's permission or allowing something to be done. The ideas of power, authority, persuasion and force all hinge on whether consent is freely given, and how accurately the person is informed. This is called "informed consent." Central to the task of a democratic system is bringing people to an understanding of their own freedom to choose, what social workers sometimes call empowerment. Unfortunately, this freedom to choose is constrained by the mechanisms examined earlier: decisions, non-decisions, and latent (submerged) conflicts of interest.

Oppositional Community is considered an element of the theoretical framework of social change practice. The forms of opposition to status quo policies or conditons will vary based upon central values and status of the operative group or organization. Traditional party distinctions and interest group affiliations are contrasted with local level public actions, relational accountability within direct action groups, and closely knit cooperative, inter-family, and support groups with transformative communites. If oppositional community is to flourish in the United States, then it must embrace direct action and transformative social change strategies which reach marginalized and poor citizens, empowering them to take control of the processes of community formation and self-produced modes of living.

Reading more extensively and directly from the works of the major **proponents** of each of the strategies will take the reader to a deeper level of understanding of each. The authors listed in this cell of the matrix are illustrative, not exhaustive.

Comparison Matrix I: Theory - "Why You Do What You Do"

Dimension	Traditional	Direct Action	Transformative
Praxis	A constitutional, parliamentary context; and a "Republic of Unequals;" a utilitarian view of politics and the control over electoral processes by advertising, media, money, polling, manipulation.	At least two dimensions: a general method of protest and policy initiatives involving public action of small or large groups; and a program to develop the base of a grassroots power organization.	Small group and collectivist processes of self-directed inquiry, development of critical consciousness, and gradual political socialization.
Ideology	The "western project" of individualism and liberal capitalism; the Protestant Ethic, the "American Dream;" the goal of equal protection.	Populism; direct electoral democracy; reformist goals within the existing political structure. Judeo-Christian values of compassion & justice.	Mixed Socialism/Social Democracy; utopian goals; a new political and economic order.
Dialectic	The mythology of the magical market and an inherent belief in the scientific method to explain reality. Individual freedom versus the oppression of totalitarianism.	The world as it is and the world as it should be....Christian prophecy and labor solidarity; the revival of political community and the expansion of economic rewards.	Questions the "American Ideology" of unlimited growth, the expansion of markets; examines the contradictions in everyday life; asks where messages come from to support "acceptable" behavior; asks what structures support these messages and how dominant structures deflect or deny the existence of alternatives.
Power	The pluralist perspective of competing, balanced interests; a "one-dimensional view" of power which examines only winners and losers in the decision-making arena.	A perspective of small elites at the top and the many at the bottom; a "two-dimensional view" of power which considers decisions and non-decisions as powerful interests limit the agenda through "mobilization of bias." Relational nature of power.	A liberationist perspective or "three-dimensional view" of power which includes decisions, non-decisions, and the possibility of a "false consensus" of values due to structurally blocked knowledge.

Theory Matrix (continued)

Dimension	Traditional	Direct Action	Transformative
Interests	Interests are ascribed based upon levels of political participation on limited policy preferences; the "Liberal" view of interests.	Interests are not always given equal weight by the political system, thus one must look to hidden agendas, or preferences substituted for your own; the "Reformist" view of interests. Appreciation of complexity and fluidity of interests.	Interests may not be "real" if wants are manufactured through a system which shapes mass preference, as in mass advertising, and which works contrary to genuine interests; the "Radical" view of interests.*
Consent	Presumes primarily the use of authority to influence voluntary consent; also democratic processes to win majority support; reluctantly admits some use of manipulation when it comes to domestic policy conflict; coercion and force are restricted to suppressing "unAmerican" values.	Recognizes the use of influence (authority and manipulation) and power (coercion and force) under some circumstances, to achieve objectives; violence is rejected as a means of achieving objectives; the ideal is people getting clear about their own self-interests and giving voluntary consent on a fully informed basis.	Focuses on unperceived (latent) conflicts of interest, using ideological critique (dialectic and deconstruction) to reveal "real" interests if circumstances permit such an analysis. Imitative praxis which "reproduces" the system of domination, or a "praxis of consumerism" may be observable substitute for wants not yet understood.
Oppositional Community	Formal political party affiliations and interest group formation.	Formation of grassroots direct action organizations; resistance is based upon private values (sometimes openly articulated on a collective basis) and public actions.	Formation of support and solidarity groups; self-help economic and social cooperatives; self-directed "circles of resistance," such as study circles, citizenship schools, and base ecclesial communities.
Proponents	J. Madison; R. Dahl; D. Bell; T. Parsons	Alinsky; C.W.Mills; G. McConnell; Bachrach and Baratz.	A.Gramsci, E. Zaretsky, G. Gutierrez, P. Freire, A. Isasi-Diaz, J. Friedmann, P. Tillich, S.Lukes

*See Stephen Lukes' book, *Power: A Radical View* (Hong Kong, Macmillan, 1978), for an excellent discussion of the dimensions of power.

Matrix II -- Concepts

Concepts are ideas. In the case of social change practice, the relevant ideas are really characteristics of practice. They are not as general nor as explanatory as theory, nor are they as specific and operational as skills. Thus, the ten concepts in Matrix II are something akin to the ingredients in gasoline: each is more or less necessary, and in certain proportions to the others. Some variation is allowed to account for different types of engines (styles and types of organizations), but overall, experience has demonstrated that successful organizing and social change practice must engage these concepts. These concepts answer the question, "What Do You Do?" We organize!

Vision is the bridge between "Why Do You Do," the theory which informs practice and the choice of strategy, and "What Do You Do," the choice of appropriate ingredients. Without vision, preferably consensually formed, practitioners and their organizational vehicles tend to substitute rules and form, routinizing habituated practices which preserve the status quo. Dynamism and creativity are stifled or actively removed. Vision is synonymous with far-sightedness and always implies change. Obviously, organizational vision is linked to primary values. The choice of strategy should not precede the formation of vision.

Power has already been defined as the ability to act to achieve one's desired goals, often, but not always, in the absence of voluntary consent. However, power is not just an ability; to be real, it must be exercised at least occasionally. Power can be attributed, based upon its prior use, and its use can be overt and covert. But the key to the use of power is not so much skill as it is intention. Intention or purpose, is again a question of values, and the choice of strategies needs to be carefully weighed in light of the anticipated consequences of the use of a selected strategy.

Tension and Conflict are qualities in a situation used intentionally to heighten visibility, drama, and antagonism between the sides. Both qualities are strategic and tactical considerations. Planning an issue campaign or an action requires specification of a strategy, such as "coordinated corporate campaign," or an "electoral" approach, as well as the subsequent mixing and matching of appropriate tactical uses of tension, drama, and conflict all along the course of the campaign. The strategic choice is a question of vision, intention, and resources, while the tactical choices tend to be most prominently influenced by timing and anticipated reactions of opponents and the various attentive audiences. There are times when it is best to escalate, and times when it is politic to de-escalate. Understanding of the concept is essential, but there is no substitute for experience.

Politicization/Consciousness-Raising refers to a process which is at its core educational, but which takes place best in the context of action. Participants become aware, sometimes for the first time, of the issues and stakes involved in a campaign. More importantly, they begin to formulate a rationale or intellectual understanding of why conditions exist, the means by which conditions may be changed, and their personal role in the change process. This is a fundamentally strategic process, and the issue which unequivocally separates the direct action from the transformative approaches. There are "degrees" of variation; rarely is the choice mutually exclusive. But whether politicization/consciousness-raising comes before or after public action, is the clearest choice for a practitioner or organization to decide. Radicalization does occur in the process of action; this is not disputed. But consciousness raising must also be an intentional process.

Leadership implies both questions of governance and organizational direction. Charismatic leaders and varieties of nondirective leaders each have advantages and disadvantages within the boundaries of strategic choices. Who will lead is not nearly so important when an organization has decided upon how it will be led: through hierarchy or through consensual processes, and the myriad of choices between.

Relationships are the bedrock of organizational life. This is particularly so for grassroots social change organizations which have not been highly bureaucratized. But beyond this general proposition, practitioners make very crucial choices about the degree of formalization which will be encouraged or sanctioned. If the principal organizational goal is power for public action, accountability among internal membership may be diminished when widespread affective bonds have been encouraged to develop. A certain aloofness or "professional" distance among members has been found desirable within many of the direct action projects. On the other hand, among base ecclesial community members (frequently called solidarity groups), such artificial distance would be counterproductive.

Accountability means to be obliged to answer for one's actions. Whereas traditional accontability tends to be defined in a linear, hierarchical sense, with only those beneath accounting to those above, direct action and transformative social change practice describe a reciprocal responsibility, top to bottom and bottom to top or circular, without reference to status differences. Differences are also made between internal measures of accountability within the organization and external accountability with reference to the larger community and body politic.

Self-Interest, we have said, is the benefit or advantage which accrues to the individual or defined community. It is closely linked to all strategies of social change and human intercourse. For instance, when you choose between job offers you weigh factors such as salary, benefits, potential for advancement, proximity to family and friends, recreational opportunities, degree of congestion, and educational quality for your children. Your choice reveals which factors are the most important to you -- your self-interest. If you have a spouse with different priorities, then you may have to negotiate the decision to reach a compromise between both of your sets of self-interests. The primacy of everyone's personal motivation is similar in organizing: The process in similar in organizing: one participates out of self-interest . . . not simply for altruistic motives like "to achieve justice," but because justice for one is justice for all, which includes "me". Developing issues and committed constituencies to pursue issues, especially when pay for work done is minimal or non-existent, must tap important values but also tap concrete self-interests. Priorities and time commitments change over time. Effective organizers will therefore move people to reexamine self-interest continuously.

Communication refers to written and oral means of expression. Communication varies greatly across strategies, with important consequences. Practitioners need to carefully consider these consequences in selecting a strategy which will maximize the values cherished by the organization and its membership. Communication which maximizes efficiency may be very different from that which maximizes equality and interpersonal growth. Pay attention to the distinctions and avoid surprises.

The role of the organizer remains one of the crucial bridges among the interstices of theory, concepts, and skills. Organizers interpret organizational reality and inevitably face the dilemma of leaders: to allow members to discover through personal experience or to by-pass discovery to facilitate efficiency or goal achievement. All organizers and change agents get trapped by expedience occasionally. But direct action and transformative organizers should at least know the difference between praxis that uplifts and praxis that manipulates.

Comparison Matrix II: Concepts -- "What Do You Do?"

Dimension	Traditional	Direct Action	Transformative
Vision	Maintain the status quo within the organization and gradually enhance its power. Seek incremental improvements and some distribution of rewards within the organization, often arranged to largely benefit the group's elite while neutralizing dissent among followers.	Organization of the world around humane collective and progressive values, instead of greed and domination. Mass democratic participation in decisionmaking, and strong accountability between leaders and followers. Direct addressing of self-interests, instead of hidden agendas, manipulation and protection of personal privilege.	Personal empowerment and collective decision-making, centered on humane and moral values that should supercede and overcome oppression -- to be accomplished through the force of moral example and perhaps some form of action.
Power	Maintain the power of the existing structures; preserve the status quo. Some limited competition between rivals.	Gain organizational power to negotiate directly with primary power holders, while individuals gain power personally at the same time; or just create organizational (often coalitional) power without empowering individuals.	Personal transformation and empowerment that later should cause external changes. The group may or may not try to create and exercise organizational power.
Tension & Conflict	Minimize, neutralize, de-legitimize or paper over any public manifestations of conflict. Limited tension between power rivals as they compete for position.	Conscious of a need for it, for social change to happen. Deliberately create it. Tap into anger stemming from the frustration of humane values.	Deal with and resolve it at a personal level. Group focuses on mutual support. Group might or might not initiate tension with external structures.

52

Concept Matrix (continued)

Dimension	Traditional	Direct Action	Transformative
Politicization/ Consciousness Raising	Socialize people into accepting existing structures and the rules to play by. Encourage incremental improvements only.	Instruct people to the "real world" of power and self-interest. Legitimize the seeking of individual and group power, and the challenging and holding accountable of decision-makers. Encourage people to create a vision, out of their values, of the world as it should be -- and to organize to make it happen, a little bit at a time: starting with what is winnable, and progressing to higher levels as organizational power grows.	Understand individual oppression in terms of societal oppressive structures. Gain understanding of how different kinds of oppression are connected. Create a vision of alternate way that society should work. Focus on politicizing the consciousness of the oppressed, with the hope of eventually changing the consciousness of the oppressor.
Leadership	Hierarchical structure, top-down control. Leaders are not very accountable to their followers. Formalized system to groom and elevate replacement leaders.	Develop community leaders into significant actors in the public policy arena. Develop new leaders from people who haven't taken that role already. Leader-follower split, but with much more accountability than in traditional structures.	Leadership is limited to the role of facilitator of the process. Collective consensus decision-making is the rule.
Relationships	Public-arena relationships are limited only to the few people in leadership roles. Other people are supposed to stay restricted to the private arena. Public actors sometimes mix in or fake private-arena contact in order to manipulate and control.	Initiate public-arena relationships with emphasis on accountability, and as a means to accurately discover self-interests, including personal ones. Promote public-arena life for many people (although in fact, it is developed for only a small number). De-emphasize affective relationships, for fear they will lessen accountability.	Mutually supportive, affective relationships, stemming from sharing of the "personal is political". Might or might not develop many external relationships in the public arena.

Concept Matrix (continued)

Dimension	Traditional	Direct Action	Transformative
Accountability	Accountability is primarily between leaders, and very little between leaders and followers.	Strong emphasis on accountability within the organization (to ensure that people follow through on task commitments), and with interactions to hold public officials accountable. Leaders accountable to each other and their followers.	Mutual accountability is focused on being true to the group process, rather than on results or performance
Self-Interest	Narrowly defined in organizational terms, for self-preservation of existing structures, with the assumption that this is for the good of all.	High degree of awareness of self-interest. Sharply defined, at both individual and group levels. Focus on it in order to organize people around it. Don't assume what it is, but find out by creating relationships with people.	Not defined specifically. Common self-interest of people in the group is to understand their oppression, and to try to figure out what to do about it.
Communication	Frequent two-way communication between a small number of leaders. Occasional top-down communication from leaders to followers in routinized, superficial way.	Many one-on-ones for purpose of discovering self-interest and to build relationships in the public arena. Extensive internal communication, to keep leaders in dialogue with and accountable to their followers OR for Citizen Action types: Frequent top-down communication from leaders to keep followers informed, and limited response feedback mechanisms (canvass, surveys).	In-depth, frequent two-way communication in small-group setting. If several small groups are linked together, then regular meetings of group representatives provide intergroup communication.

Concept Matrix (continued)

Dimension	Traditional	Direct Action	Transformative
Role of Organizer	Create interest-group alliance focused on one issue area. Broker agreements with power structure figures. Occasionally, arrange professionalized lobbying and/or financial contributions.	Find and develop leaders. Instruct people on concepts including power, self-interest, and public/private. Agitate and train people to act on their values in the public arena. Define and strategize on multiple issues to build organizational power.	Facilitate full participation in group process of reflection, personal sharing and analysis. Guide the elevation of group awareness. Once people have reflected, then possibly agitate them to act.

Matrix III -- Skills

Social workers and social change practitioners understand skill as an ability to do something well. It is known that skill develops over time and with repetition. Classroom training serves well the limited purposes of exposure to theory, paradigms, models, and the variety of conceptual knowledge. But integration of knowledge and the development of ability requires practice. Practice which occurs without the advantage of mentoring, supervision and ongoing reflection is poor practice. Skill demands attentiveness of the student, but equally presupposes the watchful eye of an experienced teacher. The best teachers are life-long students. They have risen beyond the limitations of needing to impress students with fatuous exhibitions and have no need to precipitously correct, as mistakes are excellent vehicles to self-correction.

Skill is "How Do You Do What You Do?" Skilled practitioners will not be equally skilled in all aspects of practice. The most thorough training and practice regime can't possibly prepare one for every contingency. It is a truism that all practice situations are different. Some as different as night from day; others only dawn from dusk. Practitioners, particularly neophytes, need to worry less about what they don't know and stick with what needs to be done. Do the needful, avoid the needless.

Planning and executing actions, and **planning and running issue campaigns**, consisting of numerous actions as well as more general strategic, planning and administrative tasks, are complex bundles of skills. The contrasts among the three strategies reveals traditional preferences for a narrow range of experts with centralized resources and communication networks, mobilizing defensively or offensively to protect existing arrangements. Direct actionists prefer public actions as the vehicle for agitating and polarizing targets and constituencies, as well as to develop their organization. Transformative organizing is less likely to engage in regular public action to win real gains, but when they do so, it may be as much for witnessing their values/faith as for the exertion of power.

Organizational Development (OD), **Conducting Meetings**, and **One-On-One Listening and Relationship Building** are groups of skills familiar to most professionals in the human services. But there is a perspective among grassroots organizers, particularly among practitioners of the institution-based approach, which makes organizational development a virtual imperative. Up to a point, traditional and direct action use of OD is similar. But the use of the one-on-one process and the no-nonsense approach to conducting meetings makes the direct actionists uniquely efficient at combining face to face interviews and collective leadership (developed and exercised in the context of actions and meetings). The transformative approach prizes the processes themselves over goal-directedness.

Analyzing and Cutting Issues, **Power Analysis**, **Tactical Research**, and **Strategic Planning** all combine political and technical dimensions. The most skilled technician, without political intuition and a certain artistry, will never succeed in direct action organizing in the way that they might in traditional organizing, which relies on narrowly developed, specialized expertise. Direct actionists are generalists, and they are committed to sharing their experience and knowledge of resources precisely to expand the skill base of members. On the other hand, there is much utility to the skillful use of experts, particularly as grassroots organizing campaigns develop more sophistication, along the lines of technical data bases, such as those found in traditional political research and coordinated corporate campaigns.

The Choice of Tactics will normally take place within the context of a planned action or at varied points of a campaign. Tactics are any specific procedures (means) employed to maneuver for advantage, and the range is so broad as to seem limitless. Often the advantage which direct actionists have in this arena is precisely that they are not bound to standard rules of civility and narrow conformity of tactics as the traditionalists tend to be. But over time, all strategies tend to rely upon a standard range of tactics, whether attack television commercials (for traditional electoral work), theatrical, public embarrassment, on the part of direct actionists, or witness/solidarity and civil disobedience for transformationalists. Tactics are often predictable, but the trick is to link tactics together so that they build upon each other (see Chapter 5 on the corporate campaign) and draw a reaction from an opponent which creates strategic advantage. Absent sound strategy and clarity of vision and intention, tactics are mere gimmicks.

Comparison Matrix III: Skills -- "How You Do It"

Dimension	Traditional	Direct Action	Transformative
Planning and Executing Actions	Few or no actions, since most goals are achieved by brokering arrangements with top leaders and power structure figures.	Group interacts with targeted power figures to elicit desired response, combining appeals to self-interest with pressure tactics ("ability to help and ability to hurt").	Group interacts with targeted power figures to possibly elicit a desired response, or at least to publicize the group's viewpoint -- such as a moral protest.
Agitation	Very little agitation around values. Leaders sometimes agitate each other around personal self-advancement.	Mobilize individuals to action by challenging them on the discrepancy between their values and their behavior.	Occasionally agitate people to act on their values.
Planning and Running Issue Campaigns	Mobilize organizational resources, and appeal to allies, to win the group's priority issues. In so doing, enhance the status of the existing leaders and enlarge the group's resources (money and/or people).	Use issues to build the organization by: positively affecting the constituents' self-interest, revealing a conflicting interest of the power structure, training leaders, attracting new members, and involving large numbers of people.	Work on issues to express the group's values and opinions, and expose the conflicting values of the power structure.
Organizational Development	Understand and implement a logical progression of steps to construct and increase organizational structure, size, and depth.	Understand and implement a logical progression of steps to construct and increase organizational structure, size, and depth.	Foster the proliferation of small cells, and then link them up with a representative system.

Skills Matrix (continued)

Dimension	Traditional	Direct Action	Transformative
Evaluation	Reflection, evaluation and lesson-drawing from activities is done primarily by a small number of leaders.	Group reflection on each activity to draw lessons, improve skills, and gain clarity on self-interests and power relations.	Extensive small-group reflection on personal situations and their connections to societal oppressive structures.
Analyzing and Cutting Issues	Identify issues that directly affect the constituents' self-interest, within the topic that the group is organized around. Identify allies with a related secondary self-interest. Analyze opponents' self-interest to find vulnerable points.	Identify and define issues so they are actionable, winnable, focus on specific decision-making individuals, and polarize the self-interest of constituents versus the power structure (thereby revealing an underlying conflict in values).	Analyze issues in the context of larger patterns of oppression, and connections to similar issues affecting other constituencies.
Conducting Meetings	Hierarchical process to implement ongoing activities, and for leaders to assign tasks to followers. Key decisionmaking is often done ahead of time and privately by a few top leaders.	Conduct meetings to confirm action plans and secure mutually accountable task commitments from participants. Decision-making by a collective of leaders who genuinely represent their followers' views.	Non-directive, non-hierarchical process to promote full expression of each person's feelings and thoughts. Group analysis of external structures is moderated by a facilitator.
One-On-One Listening and Relationshp Building	Very few one-on-ones. When done, usually it's by leaders to evaluate a potential leader, learn self-interests of leader with whom deal must be struck, or learn about a challenger, (or figure out how to co-opt person.)	Extensive one-on-ones to discover many peoples' interests and issues, identify leadership potential, and build relationships to involve and mobilize people.	Limited one-on-ones done in an informal, unstructured way for participants to get to know each other personally. (Much personal sharing is done instead, in small-group settings.)

	Skill Matrix (continued)		
Dimension	**Traditional**	**Direct Action**	**Transformative**
Power Analysis	Understand organizational and individual self-interests or power structure figures, but usually do not publicize the relationships and degrees of control.	Analyze self-interests, decision-making influence and control to understand and uncover power relations, and identify targets for actions.	Analyze institutional structures as systems of oppression. Usually do not thoroughly analyze unique self-interests of specific power structure figures. May use dialectic or political economy analysis to trace power interests.
Tactical Research	Gain useful information for issue campaigns by researching decision-making processes, alternative resolutions for issues, organizational and individual self-interests of the players, and power structure interrelationships.	Gain useful information for issue campaigns by researching decision-making processes, alternative resolutions for issues, organizational and individual self-interests of the players, and power structure interrelationships.	Limited amount of research, since more reliance is placed on abstracted institutional analysis.
Strategic Planning	Gain clarity on long-range vision, goals, timetables, possibilities, and workplans, needed resources, participants.	Gain clarity on long-range vision, goals, timetables, possibilities, and workplans, needed resources, participants.	Limited amount of planning, geared to expanding the number of cells and facilitators, and creating link-up structures for the cells.
Choice of Tactics	Utilize traditional, accepted tactics: going through channels, power brokering. Non-traditional tactics used rarely in extreme situations.	Identify tactics that are in the experience of the constituents, and if possible outside the experience of the target. Create "rules" to play by new tactics, rather than submitting to "acceptable behavior." Often involve many people.	Sometimes use traditional tactics, but often use or create ones that are outside the "acceptable" norms.

Summary

The purpose of this chapter has been to describe specific similarities and differences between traditional, direct action, and transformative strategies. We are positiing that both direct action and transformative strategies possess some potential to achieve meaningful social change, while traditional strategies, even when pursued by well-meaning reformers, have much less inherent ability to effectively challenge existing structural inequalities and injustices.

In the following chapters, direct action and transformative strategies are examined in close detail. The matrices in this chapter can provide a framework to reflect upon how well direct action and transformative strategies might possibly effect social change. Think about their potential to do so, both in contrast to traditional methods, and also in comparison to each other.

Classroom Study Questions and Exercises

1. You are a social worker interested in getting homeless people involved in self advocacy at a local level. Write a two page memorandum explaining to your supervisor which social change approach makes the most sense to utilize, and why you chose it in preference to the other approaches.

2. Write an essay briefly comparing the advantages and disadvantages of the three social change strategies.

3. Reflecting on your personal experience with organizations, discuss the advantages and disadvantages of a hierarchical decision making model. In your view, are there any viable alternatives to this model within the direct action or transformative strategies?

Preface for Chapters 3, 4, & 5:
Direct-Action Strategies

Direct-action strategies have played the predominant role in the work of hundreds of groups seeking fundamental reform in this country over the past quarter-century. Rather than rely on the agency of a few powerful or professionalized leaders, lobbyists, lawyers, or public officials, direct-action methods embrace a more populist-minded focus on involvement of large numbers of people in concerted activity aimed at specific changes. The modern direct action mode of community organization has solid links to mass-based social change efforts in the first half of the century, as well as earlier in the nation's history. The CIO organizing drives of the 1930s are a landmark example, and it is not coincidental that Saul Alinksy (viewed by many as the father of modern direct action community organizing) was inspired by them in a significant way.

Traditional interest group tactics of ballot box pressure, lawsuits, petition drives and professional lobbying are not shunned by direct-action organizations. However, they often go beyond these by orchestrating mass demonstrations, disruption of governmental or corporate events, boycotts, public ridicule, and in-person confrontation of targeted decision makers. The readiness to play outside the accepted rules of the arena -- to make up one's own rules -- reflects the oppositional nature of direct-action organizations. Traditional authority figures and structures are to be challenged precisely because they are viewed as less than fully legitimate. Direct action organizing proponents cleave to a populist vision, usually quite generalized and nonspecific, of a more just, compassionate, and inclusive world marked by strong leader-follower accountability, highly participatory democratic process, and collective decision making.

In contrast to the transformative social change methods discussed later in this book, the direct-action approach emphasizes action rather than consciousness raising and reflection. Evaluation and analysis are still quite important, but these are embodied in pragmatic, empirical digestion of ongoing activities. Politicization, to the degree that it happens, is expected to be initiated and "taught" by the experiences themselves, aided with some guided assessment.

A second distinction from transformative strategies is that the direct-action groups are not particularly concerned with providing social support for their members. Relationships are based on a common commitment to take action on, and responsibility for, achieving the desired reforms. People who have not yet determined in their minds that they want to be part of the action will not find much willingness for hand-holding or patient development of political attitudes.

Three Varieties of Direct-Action Organizing

In this book, we examine three varieties or subsets of direct-action community organizing: institution-based, individual-based, and nontraditional labor organizing. The institution-based approach typically involves the linking of from 10 to 50 church congregations into an "organization of organizations" that tackles local issues (such as housing or public education) within a city. In areas where a network has constructed several such projects, the groups will start working together on issues decided at the state level. Extensive one-on-one listening is employed to knit together relationships and discover issues perceived by many people to be in their self-interest. Leaders within the congregations are challenged and developed to formulate a common values base, take on roles in the public arena, work as a collective team, and function in an accountable manner to their memberships.

The individual-based strategy incorporates several variations, but all are essentially characterized by their appeals, on the basis of issues, to large numbers of unconnected people. Issues are identified on the calculation that many people feel them to be important, and then efforts are made to mobilize as many individuals as possible around them. The scale of activity is most often organized on a geographic basis. In some cases it is purely local, comprising a city or part of one; in other instances it is statewide or a regional multi-state grouping, as with the Southern Empowerment Project or the Western Organization of Resource Councils. And in a few instances, the scale is national: the Citizen Action network is constituted of statewide organizations, while National People's Action and Association of Community Organizations for Reform Now each link together a mixture of mostly local organizations.

All of the groups mentioned above have a multi-issue framework, revolving around consideration for low- and middle-income economic justice and some other concerns such as environmentalism or long-range, community-wide economic development. In addition to these organizations and networks, a multiplicity of individual-based direct-action groups exist that are geared to a specific issue or constituent category (women, minorities, environment, anti-nuclear, foreign policy) and often branded as "single-issue" organizations. The distinctions with traditional pluralist interest groups sometimes blur, especially when the latter engage in occasional mass demonstration tactics. What sets the direct-action social change groups apart are their defining characteristics, observed over time, of consistent resistance to the power structures, articulation of a vision of structural change, and desire to politicize their audiences.

The third category of direct-action efforts under discussion are non-traditional strategies utilized by segments of the American labor movement. These include comprehensive corporate campaigns, and labor-community coalitions constructed around joint issue concerns. In contrast to traditional workplace organizing, legislative lobbying and electoral politics, the nontraditional, relatively recent union activities represent a move to expand beyond labor's direct base (which has been steadily shrinking) to connect with a larger audience. They also employ bolder and more imaginative tactics than what is usually seen from labor quarters. In some respects, these approaches harken back to the days of the 30s when many unions were in fact relating to wide segments of the community on a full menu of issues and thriving in a highly activist mode.

Connecting the Matrices: Theory, Concepts, and Skills

In Chapter 2, three matrices compared traditional, direct action, and transformative strategies in regard to (a) theory, (b) concepts, and (c) skills. The points made about the direct action strategy for each category in the matrices do not apply equally to our three subsets of direct action (institution-based, individual-based, and nontraditional labor). To differentiate between them, a few comments are in order.

The reader should note that these listings of strengths and weaknesses in concepts and skills are deliberately oversimplified here, for the purpose of providing a quick road map to identify in which subset(s) of direct action one can find the fullest development of any particular concept or skill. These are also general evaluations taking each subset as a whole, although there are differences in emphasis and strength of assorted skills and concepts within each organizing/training center and individual project. To a certain extent this simply reflects the unique priorities and strengths of the organizers directing the various efforts.

Theory

Most aspects of direct action theory are consistent throughout the three subsets. They share in common a praxis of resistance within the framework of existing structures; a view of power that perceives elite decision makers who must be pressured to respond in the desired fashion; a reformist belief that the interests of the majority have been submerged to the advantage of powerful elites; and a plan to create an oppositional community of citizen organizations that can acquire enough clout to enable their articulated self-interests to prevail.

In the institution-based groups, the depiction of competing interests is taken a step further and described as a "values war" between the greedy, cynical, profit-driven denizens of the upper reaches of power, versus the masses who seek fairness, compassion, and a sense of community in pursuit of the common good. These groups have a strong sense of a dialectic between the preservation of Judaeo-Christian ethics and their refutation (evident in the behavior of many who wield primary power).

The institution-based networks, and many of the individual-based groups as well, openly profess an ideology of American democratic ideals. They discuss these in populist, direct-democracy terms, and speak of reviving a lost participation found in the country's early history.

Concepts

The three direct action subsets have different emphases among the concepts listed in the second matrix. It is fair to say that the institution-based method has the most complete grounding in concepts overall, but its strengths lie in power, tension, and conflict, leadership, accountability, self-interest, communication through the one-on-one process, and the role of the organizer in developing leadership. Two concepts that are somewhat fuzzy or problematic are a less than fully articulated vision and the separation between public and private relationships. A weaker point is politicization and consciousness raising, because the institution-based approach encourages people to create their own visions but does not provide many tools to analyze deeper aspects of society's structure.

The individual-based methods are quite strong conceptually on power, self-interest, and communication -- particularly with the sophisticated Citizen Action canvass operations. They are less solid, as a group, in the areas of an articulated vision, leadership and accountability. Two other areas, tension and conflict and the role of the organizer , tend to be fairly strong in locally-based groups where organizers are actively developing grassroots leaders; but weak in some of the statewide organizations that have evolved into a more staff-driven public interest group model. The individual-based groups share a general weakness regarding politicization and relationships.

As for the nontraditional labor methods, their strong suit includes the concepts of power, tension and conflict, communication -- including use of mass media, and the role of the organizer, primarily as a strategist. Concepts that are underdeveloped include long-range vision, accountability, and self-interest -- in that too often only the union's self-interest is fully examined and not that of its allies. The weaker points are politicization, leadership, and relationships.

Skills

Similarly, different blends of skill concentrations characterize the three subsets. In the institution-based method one finds heavy emphasis on actions, agitation, evaluation, and most important, one-on-ones. Still significant, but perhaps less acutely stressed are issue campaigns, organizational development, analyzing and cutting issues, conducting meetings, power analysis, strategic planning, and choice of tactics. An area that is given less overt attention, but is addressed in the context of cutting issues, is tactical research.

In the individual-based organizations, what is evident overall (taking into account the diverse groups in this category) is the prioritization of planning and running issue campaigns, analyzing and cutting issues, power analysis, and tactical research. Medium or mixed weight is placed on planning and executing actions, organizational development, evaluation, conducting meetings, strategic planning, and choice of tactics. The weak points tend to be agitation and one-on-one listening and relationship building.

The nontraditional labor efforts have their own unique mixture of skills, reflecting their labor movement background. High on the list are action, issue campaigns, analyzing issues, power analysis, tactical research and choice of tactics. A medium priority is afforded organizational development and strategic planning. This subset contains the largest number of skill weaknesses, consisting of agitation, evaluation, conducting meetings, and one-on-ones. In the three chapters that follow (3, 4, and 5), the institution-based, individual-based, and nontraditional labor methods are respectively examined in greater detail.

Note
1.   Saul Alinsky, in *Rules for Radicals* (1971), explained the competition between interests as the "have-nots" versus the "haves" versus the "have-a-little-want-mores." He described the basic process of pressuring decision makers to respond by stressing that "the action is in the reaction" (of the power figure).

CHAPTER 3

Institution-Based
Direct-Action Organizing

Scenario: The air is thick with tension. Some 2,200 members of a community organization called Active Churches Together Improving Our Neighborhoods, or ACTION, have crowded into St. James Church this evening to get commitments from the mayor and the president of ABC Industries. Both gentlemen are quite nervous. The ABC company owns a chemical storage and transfer station near the racially-mixed neighborhoods where many of the families of ACTION's 20 member groups live. (ACTION's membership consists of five Catholic parishes; three Baptist and three Lutheran congregations; two each of Presbyterian, African- Methodist-Episcopal (AME), and Presbyterian congregations; a Jewish synagogue; a tenants' union and a neighborhood club. These groups include white, African American, and Mexican American families with low and moderate incomes.) Their concern about the chemical station arose because of several incidents of hazardous waste leaks, with school children occasionally getting sick. This time around, leaders of ACTION anticipate that their organized power, culminating from many months of hard work, will be sufficient to prevail.

What is going on here? The scenario at St. James (a fictional composite based on actual organizations) is an example of institution-based direct action community organizing at work. Often referred to as church-based and sometimes as values-based organizing, this method has become the most widely employed, and generally the most successful, form of community organizing in America today -- especially in terms of physical presence on the local scene, and the development of indigenous leaders. It proliferates from the activity of four significant organizing and training centers: Industrial Areas Foundation (IAF), Pacific Institute for Community Organizations (PICO), Gamaliel Foundation, and Direct Action and Research Training Center (DART). Some smaller organizing networks and centers also promote the institution-based method.[1]

Institution-based community organizing originated in the experience of the IAF, which was founded by Saul Alinsky in 1940. Alinsky had, from the start, seen the utility of basing organizing efforts in church congregations. However, in the mid 1970s after his death, the IAF's staff searched for new ways to organize. They wished to create more permanent structures that would transcend the limitations and short lives of the groups they had built thus far.[2] They wrestled with the problem of how to construct a permanent power base and transcend the transitory nature of individual issues which makes it difficult to hold people together over many years.[3]

Their search led to the innovation of the values-based concept, which postulates that people and institutions can be organized around a common set of values that they hold dear, and from which they can craft a collective vision of a better life. Issues are then secondary, because they are analyzed and addressed from the perspective of these values. The critical element of the strategy is to gather people to commit to each other around common values and visions **prior** to beginning any issue campaigns. This requires teaching them that they must construct enough power to actualize their values before they can begin exercising it. Creating an adequate threshold of power is thus the initial "issue" to organize around (Drake, 1988). Churches are the natural building blocks for a values-centered approach, since they are the most prominent available repositories of explicit community values (as well as a significant gathering point for large numbers of people). Institution-based organizing therefore primarily, but not exclusively, revolves around churches. The church-based, values-based method was first tested with the Communities Organized for Public Service (COPS) organization, founded in San Antonio in 1974. All IAF projects ever since have followed this method, which in turn inspired other community organizers to follow the IAF's lead.[4]

What's So Good About Churches?

Equally important to churches' conscious attention to values is their concentration of human resources. Every congregation has several communication systems, including attendance at services, bulletins, committees, phone calling trees, and informal networks. The degree of bonding varies greatly from congregation to congregation, as does the quality of leadership -- especially the pastor, but also, the lay leaders. In general, though, many churches tend to attract people with strong leadership potential and a desire to act on their values. Large memberships, extensive communication, and effective leaders are ingredients for a potent recipe for organizational results. Compared to other forms of community organizing, the church-based method (when done well) consistently yields much higher turnouts at mass gatherings: assemblies of 1,000 to 2,000 are not uncommon, and even 5,000 to 10,000 have been achieved on a few occasions. It is these large numbers which translate into organized power at the most fundamental level.[5]

Churches' concentrations of financial and physical resources are also significant. Any community organizing effort enjoys greater longevity, stability, and independence of action to the degree that it can attain financial self-sufficiency and minimize a reliance on external funding -- "other people's money." It is very feasible for churches, depending on their size, to generate a substantial contribution -- $1,000 to $5,000 -- to an organizing budget on an annual basis. Just as vital, particularly in the early stages of a project, is that local churches can serve as conduits to larger sums through their regional and national denominational affiliations. The churches' physical buildings are also quite useful for meetings and fundraising events. Some churches also own their own buses, which can come in handy.

In contrast to the type of organizing that creates a multi-issue consumer or economic justice organization around various constituencies but not centered on churches, there are yet more advantages. The focus on identifying values that are held in common enables diverse groups to unite on a shared purpose, while still harboring differences on other beliefs and identities that are outside the organizational agenda. Thus it is not surprising that church-based projects often succeed in linking unrelated denominations, constructing an ecumenicism elusive to other interfaith ventures. The values focus, very significantly, provides a natural context to craft a collective vision of how the community should function. This helps spur the organization to generate innovative, pro-active solutions and not be mired in the discouraging rut of waging only defensive fights. And in declining inner city neighborhoods as well as emerging immigrant areas, churches are often the only institutions around that harbor community values at all.

Scenario: Back at St. James Church, the ACTION group is describing the issue at hand with the mayor and Mr. Green, the ABC Industries chief. The primary spokespersons, Father Paul (the pastor at St. James) and Mrs. Jackson (a lay leader from another ACTION church, Calvary Baptist), state that they want ABC to relocate its transfer station to other property owned by the company ten miles away. They are telling the mayor that they want stiffer city regulations for the handling of hazardous materials, and beefed-up inspection and enforcement. Their comments offer a challenge to Mr. Green and his company as being interested in maximizing profit for the sake of greed, while not caring about the health and safety of their community, families and children. They assert that city govenment has been protecting big industries and wealthy citizens, while giving up on low income neighborhoods as a lost cause. Several quotes from the Bible are entwined in their speeches, to which the crowd chants a loud "Amen" in unison each time.

How did the ACTION organization come into existence? Its conception, gestation, and birth has followed a fairly standardized format typical to institution-based organizing. Here's what it looks like.[6]

The Organizing Drive

The drive to begin a new project begins with a locally based nucleus of pastors and/or lay leaders, usually initiated by one or two people who have heard of successful groups elsewhere. An organizing center may be approached by local people who learned about it, or in some cases the center may originate the activity through individual contacts that had come about earlier. In either case, the inauguration of a new project (which might entail the re-vitalization of an existing group) will need to mesh with the organizing network's overall plans with respect to geography, constituency, and availability of staff.

A local sponsoring committee is then formed, expanding from the first few initiators. Its primary function is to raise funds to subsidize the drive, in a range of about $50,000 to $300,000 for a 1 to 3 year budget. It negotiates a consulting contract with the organizing/training center, which might hold some small workshops for the benefit of the sponsoring committee, and may also assist with contacts or grant-writing to denominational funding sources at the regional or national level, such as the Catholic Campaign for Human Development.[7]

The drive begins in earnest when a professional organizer, selected or provided by the organizing center, comes on the job. He or she performs hundreds of one-on-one interviews with pastors, active church members, community leaders, agency heads, and "gatekeepers," and any relevant contacts that could shed light on the culture, networks, themes, concerns, and dreams in the community. In so doing, the organizer is able to begin identifying potential leaders for the project, and assess the prospects of each church's involvement or abstention. The organizer also gains useful initial information on the local power structure and possible issues that the group might work on; this knowledge, however, is held in reserve for use much later on.[8]

It is then time to start assembling the pieces. A temporary organizing committee is formed -- essentially selected by the organizer and the project's initiators -- from among the best contacts developed so far. Clerics and lay leaders from interested congregations are brought together for discussions and workshops on basic concepts, including power, self-interest, the public and private arenas, and the need to build a powerful organization to enable the group to implement its values in the world. Many of the exchanges on these topics challenge people to re-think assumptions they have operated on for many years. A key point that is stressed is that power will only come from organizing a large number of people, which in turn will only happen as a result of hundreds and hundreds of individual one-on-one meetings. In this early phase, the leaders of the various congregations gain a new realization of how much they have in common with their counterparts in other churches and religions.

The next stage entails a one-on-one outreach process within the participating congregations. Each church selects its own team to perform the outreach, which at this point usually does not require a firm decision to join the new organization. Churches can be invited into the process chiefly on the prospect of enhancing their own congregational unity. Prior to the outreach, however, workshops are conducted for the congregational teams on why and how to do effective one-on-ones. It is aptly described as a listening procedure, and emphasizes the need to discover what each person's unique self-interest encompasses -- including issue priorities and personal motivations. It also serves the crucial aim of initiating a multitude of personal relationships for the purpose of potential public action in the future. The preparation for the process includes an advance commitment from each church regarding how many people its team will interview; this helps establish a pattern of mutual accountability between the congregations.

The outreach process typically results in many members of the same church getting to know one another better than they ever did before, and a growing clarity about which concerns and visions (both internal and external to the church) reflect a consensus within each congregation. Overall, the extensive, open-ended listening reliably uncovers which issues are uppermost in the minds of a large number of people (often well over 1,000) -- and is far more meaningful than any opinion poll.

Meanwhile, a smaller number of the most committed congregational leaders on the organizing committee monitor the project's development, plan meetings and training sessions, and formulate an organizational structure -- including a dues schedule for the member churches. The staff organizer guides the activity of the organizing committee, but gradually prompts individuals in it to take larger roles. The organizer thereby exercises a profound, but barely visible, influence in selecting the nature of the project's leadership. Paradoxically, the organizer is also answerable to the sponsoring and organizing committees -- while being primarily accountable to the organizing network center.

Within each congregation, key participants are encouraged to promote internal discussion about a firm commitment to formally join the organizing project and agree to pay dues. If all goes well, the excitement, good feeling and air of hope generated by building a stronger sense of community -- often typified by people remarking that they now know for "the first time" people that they have been acquainted with for years -- is in itself enough to convince a congregation to pledge itself to the new organization, before the first issues have even been chosen. A critical factor is what proportion of the congregation's members and leaders become fully involved in these activities. Insufficient "depth," with only a small core enthused by it (especially if the pastor and/or key lay leaders are not in that core) will not result in a congregation -- literally buying into the project.

When a desired number of congregations (roughly about 10, but in some cases less or more) have gone through the steps outlined above, the organization is ready to be officially founded. Two to three years, and sometimes more, will have been expended up to this point.

The founding meeting, typically attended by 500 to 1,500 people, is usually integrated with an issue selection process. These are limited to a manageable number of about two to four. The choosing of issues stems from the concerns voiced in the one-on-one listening, and is based on democratic voting or balloting at the meeting. At the founding meeting, congregations (and other groups, if participating) formally announce their joining of the organization and their dues commitments. The temporary organizing committee is dissolved, and a new structure with elected leaders erected in its place.

Scenario: The creation of ACTION has involved the conducting of 2,800 one-on-one visits of members of ACTION's member groups. Within the 18 churches and the two non-church organizations, teams of 8 to 12 leaders have personally interviewed about 15 people per leader of their own members. To do this, the leaders have attended several training workshops to learn and practice the skill and art of one-on-one visits -- the "secret weapon," as the IAF calls it, of institution-based organizing.

The initial stage of training, however, does not start with skill techniques. Instead, it emphasizes concepts that provide the underlying rationale. Two key ones are power and self-interest.[9]

Power

Power is the most central concept in direct action organizing. However, it can be problematic for church-goers who identify with an ethos of "the meek shall inherit the earth." The common attitude towards power is negative, invoking images of abusive authority figures, corrupt officials, or ruthless dictators. To want power, people have to realize that there is no other way to enact their values in the world around them. In the training sessions, power is defined simply as the ability to accomplish what you wish. According to this approach, power can and must be employed for virtuous ends, as opposed to greedy and inconsiderate purposes.

The institution-based groups say something else about power which is fairly unique: How much power you have -- your ability to get what you want -- depends on how many, and which, people you are in relationship with, and the nature of those relationships. The best kind of power is mutual and relational, in which both sides understand what the other wants, and make a deal based on that. Unfortunately, the way we usually see power exercised is linear and unilateral: one side doing what it wants to the other side by force or fear. An understanding of relational power, in contrast, leads logically to a desire to link forces, and find allies in unexpected quarters. It implies that confrontational tactics are not always inevitable once there is sufficient power to deal with the target. If a group must be confrontative, that is because it has not yet achieved a relationship of adequate power. As soon as the group's power is acknowledged, it can move to the bargaining table to negotiate its demands.

Power is evidenced in our society by two forms: organized money, and organized people. Citizen groups have the potential to gather large amounts of organized people (and modest amounts of money) to counterbalance the sources of power built on organized money. The analysis of power structures has always been an essential part of community organizing, and the institution-based method relies on it as well. At the top sit the primary institutions of the corporate and financial worlds, real estate interests, and organized crime. The secondary layer beneath these consists of politicians, bureaucrats, the news media, many unions, the advertising industry, and various professionals (lawyers, academics, consultants). The secondary institutions do the bidding of the primary power-holders who control the concentrations of money and property, and whom they shield from the general population below. The public's own institutions, including churches and typical community groups and agencies, are at the bottom with little power.[10] They make the frequent mistake of interacting with the middle layer (such as petitioning legislators to fix problems) instead of trying to deal directly with the corporations at the primary level which are wielding the real power. Church-based community organizations, however, have the potential to become effective mediating institutions to directly deal with primary power institutions. In building this type of citizen power, a simultaneous process takes place: the creation of power on the individual level -- personal empowerment of the active members and leaders of the group. The two processes are not only inseparable but mutually necessary.

Self-Interest: What's in It for Me?

Once you have decided to build power -- by organizing large numbers of people -- you have to grapple with the notion of self-interest. The only reliable way to organize many people, according to direct action community organizers, is by appealing to people's self-interests. Just as with the idea of power, the concept of self-interest has been developed chiefly by the IAF, elaborating from Alinsky's first references. The organizing viewpoint on self-interest is foreign to the thinking by which we are socialized. Most people equate the term with the repugnant traits of selfishness and self-centeredness. Selfishness and its opposite, self-sacrifice, describe poles of behavior.[11]

Self-interest, on the other hand, does not define a type of behavior; rather, it is simply, all that is important to a person -- what motivates his or her actions. The latin root -- inter esse -- is translated as the self among others, which underlines the fact that self-interests do not just exist within an isolated person, but only make sense in relation to other people. The paradox of selfish and selfless impulses, which are both within all of us (generating an inner dialectical tension), stems from our need to relate to others. Often, people are not fully aware of their own self-interests, which frequently leads to being manipulated to serve someone else's.

Certain universals are contained in each person's self-interests, including physical survival, personal values, connection to spirituality, a need for recognition, and a desire for significance after our death. Some elements pertain to common life stages, such as the concerns of a parent, a homeowner, or a retiree. Still other components are unique to the individual, defined by the shaping of one's childhood and parents, lessons absorbed from life experiences, and how one has coped with watershed personal events. An important rule is that a person's self-interests are never static, and change over time. The point is that you can never assume anything about anyone's self-interest. It can only be discovered through forming a direct relationship with the other person. And, since people can only be organized around their self-interests, the creation of relationships in order to discover self-interest is absolutely essential. This brings us to the one-on-one visit.

One-on-Ones

The IAF has led the way in evolving the critical skill of one-on-ones. Ultimately, the ability to create relational power rests entirely on the success of the one-on-one meetings in learning people's core motivational drives and forming relationships. This is much more than a superficial survey of demographics, position, property, family and career interest. The indispensable tool for discovering a person's self-interest is one's ears, to listen with. Judicious use of probing questions steers the conversation. The most important word to employ is why: Why did he do what he did? Why does she feel this way? Why is the person concerned about this issue? The answers to these questions will reveal the person's value system. One-on-one outreach has a judgmental element in which one seeks people with a strong and similar values base. As Mary Gonzalez, a chief trainer with the Gamaliel Foundation, says, "You're on a talent search -- for people like yourself."

The goal is to learn the person's self-interests in order to be able to relate to him or her in the public arena around values and issues of substance. The interviewer must be perfectly clear on this, or else the visit will fail as an exercise in voyeurism, superficial chit-chat, or a sales pitch. The mutual, even intimate nature of the one-on-one elicits honesty about a person's motivations and quickly creates a bond. The interviewer's prompting causes the person to reflect on and express -- often better than they have done before -- what he or she actually believes in and wants. Helping the person to gain clarity on this is a goal, for obvious reasons: you can't organize someone around their self-interest if the person isn't sure what their self-interest is.

Key traits that ensure successful one-on-ones are genuine curiosity and compassion about other people, and the personal courage to take the emotional risk of drawing out the other person's pain and dreams. The interviewer should reveal some key components of his or her own self-interest, to elicit comparable disclosures. Some questions can be agitational, but the tension must be resolved at the end, to foster a continued relationship. The initial one-on-one encounter should last only 30 to 45 minutes, and not seek any strong commitment. This sets the relationship in motion and obtains a fundamental reading of the person. The interviewer should write notes, from memory, shortly after leaving. Notes must not be taken during the meeting, since that would destroy the mutual, relational nature of the visit. Later, the notes are digested, to analyze the person's self-interest. In a subsequent encounter, the person can be propositioned with a good chance of success.

Scenario: Within each of the congregations of the ACTION organization, the one-on-one team meets regularly to improve their skills, and compare notes on what they have learned: in particular, issues that were frequently mentioned, and individuals who displayed the potential to become active leaders. Over several months, as the one-on-ones continue, the team members trade tips for success, and hold each other accountable to meeting their goals for total numbers of visits to do. They also begin to discern the predominant issues on their members' minds.

From this process, the leaders of ACTION learn that the ABC chemical station is the object of widespread complaint. But, so also is substandard housing, gangs, and the quality of the public schools. At an "Issues Assembly" 4 months earlier, 1,800 ACTION members had voted to work on these concerns, with the ABC station as top priority. Immediately after the Issues Assembly, the second phase of issue-narrowing was launched: research by task forces. Again, one-on-ones were undertaken, but this time with people in the power establishment with a role in or knowledge about the concerns that ACTION had decided to investigate.

Cutting the Issue

The third phase of ACTION's issue selection has been less visible. A small number of task force leaders, together with the paid staff organizer have evaluated the details uncovered in the task forces' investigations. Their goal has been to frame the issues, or "cut" them, in ways that would maximize the organization-building benefits: increase the organization's power by advancing its leaders' abilities, recruiting new leaders, gaining recognition and respect for the group, enhancing the ability to raise money, attracting more churches, and forming relationships with more power figures. This phase also teaches people lessons on how power works, both generally and specifically in the community.

Problems Versus Issues

Yet another concept is at work here: the distinction between problems and issues -- pioneered, of course, by Alinsky. Problems are common gripes which are discussed in general terms, characterized by overall agreement that they need to be addressed, but never are. Issues, however, are specific, selected aspects of a problem defined in manageable parts of solutions that can be acted upon successfully. For example, "speeding cars" is a problem, while getting Mr. Jones, head of the traffic department, to allocate $10,000 in his budget for installing a stoplight at Elm and Main is an issue. As Alinksy stressed, issues must be polarized and personalized in order to focus people on winning a goal. Tension and a division of opinion are deliberately created. Once a compromise has been struck (which the solution usually consists of), then the issue must be de-polarized, and a victory can be claimed.

A critical question is how winnable the issue is. Especially in the early years of an organization, victories are needed to provide a sense of progress, and avoid destructive demoralization. This stance necessarily defers consideration of structural political or economic issues of any weight to some undefined time in the future, when it is hoped the group will have gradually built up enough power to even the odds. "Winnability" relates to how tenaciously the power structure will try to preserve the status quo, the magnitude of the pressure the organization can realistically bring to bear; and what tactical advantages are at hand. These are all judgment calls, and the staff organizers typically direct the assessment, thereby exerting enormous influence on the way that organizations approach issues, even though grass-roots members generate the general categories. Choosing among these topics and converting generalized problems into specific, actionable issues with a probability of victory is chiefly the staff organizer's responsibility, as he or she guides the leaders who make the actual decisions. The ability to "cut the issues" successfully usually depends on the talent of the organizer.

Once the issue of ABC's chemical station was selected, however, why did Father Paul and Mrs. Jackson frame it in the terms they used? Their focus on the safety of children and the integrity of the community, in conflict with the uncaring greed of the company and the disinterest of city hall, depicts a war of values. The formation of church-based groups includes discussions about the forces assailing church congregations, families and communities. Powerful institutions, driven by the imperative of profit and dominance, are rooted in the value of personal greed - while family and community-sustaining concerns take a back seat. High-paid CEOs, in their role as corporate captains, play the part of narrowly-focused, economically-rational pursuers of the bottom line. This conflicts with the values emphasized in religious faith of compassion for the needy, social justice that opposes greed and arrogance, and the nurturing of children and families. Instead of just sermonizing about these values on Sunday, however, churches in groups like ACTION decide to put their faith into motion, and heed God's mandate to transform the world. They have resolved to make their churches live up to their own missions, and become vastly more relevant by doing so.[12]

Scenario: Now things are heating up at St. James. With the issue having been fully described, Father Paul turns to the ABC president. "Mr. Green," he says, "your company has a suitable site ten miles from here, where you could relocate this storage station. We also know that you have a proposal for municipal industrial revenue bonds, to expand another division of your company, coming before the city council next week. We are here to tell you that ACTION is prepared to block your bond issue if you don't relocate the chemical station. If you do, we will endorse the bond issue." The entire crowd claps loudly; the noise is deafening. Mr. Green, who had an idea of what to expect, gives his answer. "We are prepared to make plans to relocate the station. It will be moved within 6 months. I have authorized our Vice-President for Chemicals Division to negotiate the details with you. We look forward to your support at the council." A loud cheer erupts. Mr. Green shakes hands with the ACTION leaders on the stage.

Mrs. Jackson then faces the mayor. "Mayor Roberts, we want a commitment from you to propose a ban on extended storage of hazardous wastes in mixed-use zones, and a ban on overnight storage of toxic industrial wastes within one mile of any school. We also want city inspections twice a year of all locations handling these materials, and a doubling of the penalties for violations. If you pledge to push for these, we pledge to work with you, and support your plan at the council." Again, everyone claps on cue. Mayor Roberts responds, "I'm in full agreement with your goals, but we have to consider the burden on industry. We're all friends here -- I'm sure we can figure something out to everyone's satisfaction." Mrs. Jackson wheels around to the crowd and says, "I didn't hear him give a definite yes. Do you think he gave a good enough answer?" "Nooo!" the crowd shouts back. "Mayor Roberts," she then says, "re-election is only 8 months away. We're pleased to hear you say you agree with our goals, but we need a straight answer from you. We are making you a very specific request. Are you or aren't you willing to push for our reforms?" An uncomfortable Mayor Roberts finally replies, "Yes, all right, I'll propose your reforms. We can meet next week to hammer out the language." "Thank you, Mayor," Mrs. Jackson says, and the crowd breaks into applause.

The exchanges with Mr. Green and Mayor Roberts represent the application of additional concepts and skills, besides power and self-interest. The concepts of public and private arenas, anger and tension, and leadership are being employed in ACTION's event, as well as the skill of planning and executing actions.

Public and Private Arenas

The distinction between public and private arenas is an important concept in institution-based direct action organizing. It, too, was evolved by the IAF and then borrowed by other networks engaged in similar methods. The private category includes family and very close friends, while the public sphere contains all other people one interacts with, such as employers and co-workers, service personnel and professionals, politicians and bureaucrats. The behaviors and assumptions governing the two categories of relationships are contrasted: private relationships operate with the rules of love, permanence, and unconditional acceptance, while the rules of the public arena are respect, temporary interaction, quid pro quo accountability, and action based on one's self-interest. Tension and diversity are present in the public sphere, in which people wear uniforms, titles, and masks as they play out their respective parts.

The dichotomy between public and private is posited for several reasons. It is noted that while everyone's private life is personally important, most people do not have a public life of much significance. This reflects a state of relative powerlessness and oppression. Community organizing attempts to prepare people for a meaningful role in the public arena. The public/private split also helps clarify the process of initiating hundreds of relationships, by defining it in the limited terms of action on common goals and values. In contrast, the notion of constructing a huge array of friends to help each other, out of mutual affection, would seem unwieldy and overwhelming.

Another utility of the public/private concept was demonstrated when Mrs. Jackson, a housewife who had not done much previous public speaking, boldly confronted the mayor. This concept helps people grant themselves permission to adopt new behaviors in acting on their values. Since operating in the public arena is acting out a role protecting one's self-interest, in doing so people can transcend fears that might otherwise restrain them from expressing their desires, especially to authority figures. Mrs. Jackson understood that on the stage at St. James, she was playing a part in a grand drama -- quite unlike her everyday interactions.

The IAF, in developing the public/private concept, drew heavily on the work of Hannah Arendt, in particular *The Human Condition* (1958). She postulated that the classical early Greek notion of "polis" with its explicit separation between private life (the household and its economic necessities) and the public sphere (public policy for the general welfare of the city-state, discussed and debated among citizens) provided the best political life. In the Greek polis, speech and debate were just as essential as action, and the initiator of an action was interdependent with those who collaborated in implementing it. Decision making and action were truly collective enterprises.

Since that time, Arendt asserts, the public/private separation has broken down, muddling the two with lamentable consequences. The emergence of modern mass economics has created a "social" sphere in which private economic concerns are now public. Private life has hence been diminished by losing much of its importance (the sole responsibility for meeting economic necessity), while public life has become preoccupied with questions of individuals' economic needs, in aggregate. Discussion of the common good has been pushed aside. Political activity, instead of growing out of dialogue and interdependent relationship between leaders and citizens, has degenerated into a sterile manufacturing process -- the product of legislators and even worse, bureaucrats.

For community organizing, Arendt's theory offers the benefit of upholding the ideal of empowered citizens who help create public policy for the general good. It encourages political debate, and emphasizes the need for people to interact in the public arena. These are fundamental to the task of restoring democratic process to our society.

Anger and Tension

Anger and tension are important concepts explicitly discussed by some of the institution-based organizing/training centers. The overt treatment legitimizes what are often perceived as negative, even "sinful" feelings. This point underscores the fact that church-based organizing searches for stable moderates, the backbone of the community who can genuinely represent and lead a large circle. Some other forms of organizing, in contrast, seek out marginalized and highly alienated people whose anger is near the surface and therefore need little prompting to get in touch with it.

The root for anger is the Norse word "angr," which describes grief at a sense of loss, held in memory -- a justifiable and healthy emotion. A principal type of loss is being aware that one's values are being blocked from fulfillment. If a person has strong values and knows that she or he is being violated, anger inevitably follows. This is related to clarity of personal vision, which hinges on being in touch with one's values, knowing they aren't being actualized, and having a desire and plan to fulfill them. Anger flowing from frustrated values creates a wellspring of energy to struggle for social justice. Channeling one's anger constructively, though, is not casual; it is proportional to one's self-confidence and degree of clarity of vision.

Tension and face-to-face challenge are elaborated on in a similar fashion. Creative tension is recognized as essential to the social change process, as Alinsky stressed, and so it must be embraced by all who desire change. Tension for social change in the abstract always condenses to personal challenging between people. People should challenge each other around their responsibilities. This applies to holding each other accountable for organization-building commitments as much as it does for keeping officials accountable in the public arena. Each person must examine, and try to overcome, her or his internal reasons for wanting to avoid tension -- in particular, the preoccupation with being liked. Inner rationalizations to stay in the '"comfort zone" must be confronted if one wants to be an effective social change agent.

Leadership

Organizing is frequently portrayed as a creation and altering of relationships, but it is also often described as a process of developing leaders. Various definitions of leadership are employed in direct action organizing, but the institution-based method has some distinctive interpretations, due primarily to the IAF and built upon Alinsky's early ideas. Leaders have a constituency of followers that they are in relation to, or are constructing in their institution. Essential leadership qualities include a strong and self-aware ego, curiosity, imagination, being in touch with one's anger and values, a sense of humor, honesty, a desire to learn from experience (and mistakes), sensitivity about others, flexibility, clarity about one's self-interests, and a vision that one wants to pursue. The fact that nobody possesses all these qualities in ideal measure proves why organizations need multiple leaders who are mutually accountable and operate collectively.

Planning and Executing Actions

The scene at St. James is termed an "action" in organizing jargon, because it is a public event at which the community group's members make a demand of a power figure and obtain a response. In accord with Alinsky's maxim "the action is in the reaction," attention is focused on what the "target" person will do, in reaction to what the group is seeking. If the target opposes the group's request, then that recalcitrance is expected to radicalize the participants.

A few elements prevail in the institution-based training centers' discussion of actions. Actions are depicted as dramas on a stage -- the public arena -- in which participants act out their respective parts. The theatrical reference helps people to visualize their performance, overcome timidity, and stand up to authority figures (reinforced by their "supporting cast"). Actions also help identify and develop leaders. A leader's performance during an action -- including bringing a promised number of people to it -- provides a test of his or her conviction, courage, ability and reliability.[13]

Actions contain three essential phases: preparation, execution, and evaluation. The planning stage considers tactical aspects, including logistical details of the physical setting and how the turnout will be achieved. A detailed agenda with task assignments must be drawn, with contingency plans for whatever scenarios can be anticipated. Role-playing practice is often used. The action itself should be brief and focused, with as clear a resolution as possible. Tension is designed into the event, chiefly in terms of challenging the invited officials around their public responsibilities. If an understanding with the official has been reached prior to the action, however, then the event can take on the air of a ceremony which formalizes the deal.[14] Floor teams are often used to orchestrate mass tactics such as applauding, standing, or singing in unison; these apply pressure to the "target" -- and enable the attendees to be true players rather than mere observers.

Scenario: In our selected scenario, the action at St. James concludes with choir singing, commitments declared by each member church for the amount of money to be generated in a fundraising ad book campaign, and brief evaluation comments from selected leaders. Immediately after the meeting, a core team of 15 leaders plus the staff organizer meet for a 30-minute debriefing.

This initiates the third crucial part of any action -- the evaluation.

Evaluation

A short evaluation must follow right after each action, in order to identify and capture the emotions of the moment -- the gut feelings that might be altered by subsequent rationalizing. A lengthier evaluation is done later with more leaders, to fully analyze what was accomplished and learned, and what this portends for the next steps. The evaluations generate insights, as group digestion of the experience builds a truly collective political wisdom. Staff organizers facilitate and guide the evaluations (although some leaders may help direct it); their experience and judgements inform the crucial learning process. The performance of leaders like Mrs. Jackson and Father Paul is also evaluated after an action, because a continual increase in skills, political awareness, personal courage and confidence are valued outcomes.

Scenario: In the case of ACTION's encounter at St. James, the group's leaders try, in their evaluation session, to ascertain how their relationships with Mr. Green and Mayor Roberts have changed. Mr. Green readily assented to ACTION's request, which indicates that the group had correctly analyzed his self-

interest (getting the bond issue was more important than keeping the chemical station where it was). It also shows that ACTION has developed enough power to pose a credible threat of blocking the bond issue. As for Mayor Roberts, he tried a classic tactic of mixing the private and public arenas -- claiming "we're all friends" -- to evade making a commitment. Mrs. Jackson caught him on it and pressed for accountability, while posing an indirect threat: implying that ACTION could hurt his re-election chances. Her reference to the election brought Mayor Roberts to his senses, demonstrating that ACTION's potential influence with voters was enough to make him worry.

However, there was no direct threat or ultimatum in terms of ACTION's getting involved in the elections. Like most church-based groups, ACTION shies away from participation in electoral politics.[15] This is partly due to fear of reinforcing the general public's proclivity to defer responsibility to, and place false hopes in, politicians, as opposed to holding them accountable through ongoing dialogue and relationship. Promoting the political fortunes of candidates seems to conflict with the priority of developing as much leadership ability as possible from congregation members. The two are not mutually exclusive, but the emphasis on interacting with politicians in formulating policy reflects the institution-based method's ideology of seeking a participatory democratic politics, rather than a republican-style format in which elected representatives make decisions for the masses. The disinterest in elections also reflects an aversion to the consumeristic and deeply powerless routine they often represent.[16]

Underlying Philosophy and Ideology

The organizing/training networks that employ the institution-based method share some underlying beliefs that are usually not articulated in much detail, if at all. It is important to state that to the extent that some philosophies are submerged they are not likely to receive internal critical reflection. In general, these networks refrain from identifying with any explicit ideologies as such, preferring to view and explain their activities in largely pragmatic terms: how to gain the power that average people need but currently lack. Nonetheless, several threads are apparent: the necessity of personal transformation to achieve social change; adherence to Judaeo-Christian values; the expectation that the American democratic system can be made to work as intended; and a vague image of citizen groups eventually combining forces to foster major societal reform.

Personal Transformation

The general phrase "leadership development" refers to an ever-widening circle of people learning to take responsibility for their lives, clarify their self-interests, form collective and accountable relationships, mobilize other people, and engage policy-makers in the public arena. In many instances it entails men and women like Mrs. Jackson, summoning up courage they didn't know they had, or becoming self-aware to an unprecedented degree. For others, it may be a question of utilizing skills they had undervalued, or acquiring new ones. In most cases it includes increased self-esteem coupled with an expanded recognition of their commonality with one another, as well as a growing understanding of how the world actually works.

Institution-based organizing encourages congregations to actualize the values that the members have defined for themselves, by working on issues that emanated from their own conversations. It is evident that the development of individuals should be inextricably linked to the creation of group power. This view expands to a conviction that reform of the world cannot take place without transformation at the personal level. Since a vision of the interdependence of internal and external change fits happily with some elements of religious faith, it is well suited for congregations.

The Judaeo-Christian Tradition

A key component of the values base for institution-based community organizing is the Judaeo-Christian ethic of compassion for others, responsibility to the community, a sense of morality and fair play, and a striving for social justice. Open identification with this tradition is a naturally comfortable association for organizing projects rooted in religious congregations. Quotes from the Old and New Testaments are cited frequently in a variety of organizational settings, and large meetings are typically opened with a prayer. In reciprocal fashion, references to organizational activity, concepts and process can be woven into sermons and liturgy. Yet, the nature of institution-based organizing's relationship to the church is a complex matter. It is sorted out in different ways by the various organizing/training centers, according to their attitudes and experiences. Viewpoints towards liberation theology, for instance, tend to be ambivalent.

The American Democratic Ideal

Institution-based organizing practitioners are faithful to Alinsky's commitment to a democratic ideal, professing optimism that the founding fathers' vision can be made to work. The bedrock faith is in the common sense and fairness of the average person -- the confidence that the majority of citizens will, most of the time, make wise and just decisions for the benefit of society. The image of the New England town meeting, full of participatory debate leading to consensus decisions, is held as an admired ideal, juxtaposed with the recognition that in modern times we have gone far afield of the American system of earlier days.[17]

In recalling the lost art of democracy, community organizers focus on a tradition of dynamic discourse, even agitation. Lively debate, with passionate but nonviolent struggle, results in mutually respected compromise. Competing self-interests are balanced off in quid pro quo dealmaking. Inherent conflicts are tempered by a faith in the consensus synthesized from a diverse pluralism, and a universally accepted conception of the commonweal. This vision of pluralistic politics is appealing, but it presumes the existence of relatively equal actors or balanced forces -- a far cry from current reality. (It is also totally divorced from any Marxian analysis of the subservience of political structure to the economic system.) The long-range aim, then, is to equalize the odds and "level the playing field" to enable the democratic ideal to actually work. In the face of today's intense concentrations of primary power, this can only be described as an enormously daunting, yet inescapably essential, endeavor.

Critique of the Institution-Based Method

Weakness of the Church Focus

Despite the overall logic of basing community organizing in churches, there are some inherent weakness to the approach. People not in a church congregation usually get overlooked, and even willing people who are in a church can get excluded if their pastor is personally against the effort. If the pastor feels merely lukewarm towards the project, then the burden of motivating the congregation falls to the committed lay leaders, who do not have the same credibility as the pastor. Congregations that include prominent decisionmakers often shy away from "controversy"; their leaders may block any organizing effort. Most church-based organizing is sited in large inner cities, and hence churches located in other areas are likely to be passed over. And, this method tends to deal usually with localized issues on a small scale, ignoring larger systemic forces that more deeply impact the same constituency (Miller, 1987).

Furthermore, precisely by strengthening congregations and assisting parish development (helping to develop leaders and energy for the church's internal functions), this method bolsters the same church structure that is often criticized for holding people down in several ways, including legitimizing the prevailing social structure and the church's own hierarchy. This is the essential trade-off in using the churches as an entry point for access to large numbers of people. In a sense, the networks engaged in this model are delving into the long-standing dialectic internal to the Christian church: the impulse to transformative liberation versus the preservation of hierarchical control. The Executive Director of the IAF, Ed Chambers (who was ejected from a Catholic seminary many years ago for challenging authority and then went to work for Dorothy Day), seems to exhibit the central tension that derives from trying to use the church to liberate people while accommodating all of its operational assumptions. He has no expectation of "reforming" the church, but still says that "our job is to gadfly the church to see that it lives up to its own rules and regulations" -- echoing a standard Alinsky attitude towards all institutions of authority (Chambers, 1990).

The Problem with Public/Private

Although the concept of public and private spheres has central importance, there is an artificial and flawed aspect to the theory behind this construct. The original Greek ideal centered on elite male property holders as "citizens." Women and slaves were an essential but unrespected part of the household economy. Their labor had much to do with maintaining the free space that allowed their masters, the "equal citizens," to contemplate and debate public policy. And since the Greek model predated the invention of capitalism, which inextricably linked personal economic self-interest to the realm of public policy, it is hard to imagine how the original notion of Greek notion of the private sphere could ever apply to modern times. A very different kind of free space, allowing wide interaction, needs to be conceived instead.

Private life also includes, in the world as it is, issues of oppression and abuse within many families. The women's movement wants to politicize these "private" concerns, but the institution-based formulation precludes such as approach; these issues would be deemed divisive and unwinnable, and hence against pragmatic strategy. A majority of the people that the institution-based networks have developed into leaders are women, and they have successfully acted in the public arena on issues of great importance to their families. Ironically, other aspects of women's family lives and personal needs that deserve attention may still be ignored by these organizations. This is not surprising, since they are likewise often ignored by the very churches that rely so deeply on their energy and commitment.

Local Versus Larger Arenas

Some institution-based projects have become major players in their local communities. However, key influences on political, social, and economic life are largely directed from a national or multi-national level; and control is increasingly consolidated in fewer and fewer hands. Major economic choices by far-removed megacorporations and financiers, the inescapable effect of mass media and the advertising industry, and the unresponsiveness of national (and even state) government all severely limit what local church-based organizations can accomplish. At best, when several years of toil have produced a handful of large groups within the same state, an impact can begin to occur on state policymakers on selected issues.

The institution-based organizing/training centers do not provide clear answers to the question of how fundamental social change, the ultimate winning of the "values war," might occur. They put forth the hope that, eventually, proliferating numbers of these organizations will result in ever-expanding alliances of groups, inevitably combining at the state and national level to someday successfully confront the dominant corporations and national institutions.

However, the top staff of these networks counsel extreme patience to the local leaders regarding linking up with other groups -- except within their own network. Rivalry between the networks hampers the prospect of joint efforts, and there are no long-range plans to coalesce. Likewise, there is little internal education to examine the uppermost reaches of primary, hegemonic power on the national scale in preparation for the distant day when the battle will be joined. If church-based power grows in the future to the extent that the networks can no longer logically avoid working together, then some difficult negotiations will be needed.

Missing Concepts

The concepts of culture, gender, race, and ethnicity are typically not addressed by the institution-based networks in their trainings. Instead, people are taught by the experience of building their organizations that they must work with other races, religions, and cultural backgrounds because they need them to construct the desired level of power -- not out of appreciation of other people's ways for their own sake. This echoes a principle of Alinsky: getting people to do the right thing for the wrong reason. Respect for the other person's identity and culture should emerge after a working relationship has been forged, in rationalizing one's new situation. Organizers, nonetheless, are expected to be sensitive to the specific culture of the community they are working in, and weave it into the collective vision and story that will unify the organization. Organizers are expected to discern and address the self-interest of all people they work with, and transcend race, gender, and ethnic barriers. (In theory, a good organizer can work successfully with any group; in practice, the results of organizers working with groups outside their own racial or cultural background are very mixed.)

Racial minorities are asked, in effect, to put aside their perception that racism is the problem, and women are asked to minimize concerns about gender and sexual discrimination. They are called on to instead focus on the balance of power relations on specific issues, and strive for a democratic politics. As Ernie Cortes of the IAF remarks, "I don't think you organize around culture . . . I think that what we're trying to do is teach a civic culture, which is important" (Cortes, 1990). The creation of a participatory political process predominates over all else. Ultimately, it should engender a cross-cultural pluralism in which people will be freer to experience, identify and feel secure about their own traditions -- and be more open to accepting the traditions of others.

Growth of Knowledge Within and Among the Networks

The institution-based networks view themselves as testing and refining their empirical knowledge almost entirely from the practical experience of their respective organizations, even though they share parallel activities and a common heritage stemming from the work of the IAF. However, open acknowledgment of these shared roots is virtually nonexistent. The origins of concepts and methods are rarely discussed or put in a broad context. Correlating to the emphasis on pragmatic acquisition of knowledge there is, conversely, scant recognition or integration of other disciplines (professional or academic) that might proffer useful insights.

Ironically, however, the introduction of intellectualized influences has contributed to the development of the church-based model. Ernie Cortes's interest in theology and political philosophy has been credited with assisting the IAF's invention of church-based, values-based organizing. In another example, the PICO network came to embrace the institution-based method through the urging of Jose Carrasco, an academic and activist who is a social work professor, but also worked with Cortes on an IAF project. Perhaps these instances were happy accidents that resulted in some injection of theory into the pragmatics of organizing. But, since these incidents aided the development of the model, some further advance might be possible if there was greater openness to intellectual and academic sources than has been demonstrated to date.[18]

The overall growth of knowledge in this method is impeded by an imposing contradiction: The institution-based networks all avow the centrality of building power by continually expanding organizational relationships, yet at the same time assiduously avoid working with each other. Rivalry and competition for funds are partly to blame. The gap between rhetoric and reality could not be greater. Meanwhile, primary power sources are consolidating on a national and global scale. The obvious antidote to this -- a decision by the networks to work together sooner rather than later -- is precisely not happening. Institution-based organizations could be winning a series of local battles but losing the war.

Numbers Versus Consciousness Raising

The institution-based networks' vision of personal transformation generating social change is challenged by the fact that relatively few people experience notable transformation. The ones who do (the top leaders) generally have received significant attention and agitation by the staff. The "personal development" requirements, from an organizational perspective, are targeted on the people who will articulate the group's vision, mobilize hundreds of others for mass gatherings, drive the one-on-one process, develop issue research and strategy, perform administrative maintenance, raise funds, and interact with officials and the media.

The imperative to build organizational power tends to foster, out of the need for sheer efficiency, the personal development of only the small percentage who will perform the requisite tasks. The mass of followers don't experience much transformation. Everyone needn't become a leader, of course, but one can ask: If institution-based groups are "universities of public life," as the IAF likes to say, then shouldn't we be concerned that only a minor segment of the "class" is truly graduating, while others receive only a partial education? Can systemic social change occur in the long run with this method, since very large numbers of people are not undergoing real transformation?

It seems that political education and consciousness raising of the masses of organizational members gets short shrift. The successful mobilization of large numbers of people which these networks achieve revolves around a leader/follower paradigm, in which a small number of highly competent people become politicized and grow personally -- in a sense creating an alternative elite -- while others merely follow. A valid test of the degree of politicization of "ordinary" organizational members would be to gauge how well oppositional behavior (resistance to cynical authority and unjust structures) carries beyond their involvement in one organization and lasts beyond its existence.

The institution-based networks do not address the issue of whether many more people in their organizations need to become radicalized to any particular degree, and what form of political education is necessary beyond the satisfaction of winning some public policy victories and learning about power. The centering on values has led to a demarcation of positions on many issues, but has not yet advanced to a comprehensive vision of a fundamentally restructured society.

Classroom Exercises and Skill Development Scenarios (Institution-Based)

A. (Role Playing)   You are a social worker who is a chemical dependency counselor at a small facility that is open to trying innovative approaches. You have attended some direct action organizing training sessions, and you want to try to use the one-on-one technique to get a better understanding of your clients' self-interests and motivations. After doing so, you intend to use the technique of agitation to prompt some of your clients to promote continued movement to independence and personal empowerment.

    1.   Think about how you can adapt both of these techniques to this counseling setting. What kinds of prompting questions will you use in the one-on-one to discover what is truly important to the client? How will you create a relationship of mutuality, to foster openness and honesty in the conversation?

    2.   In preparing to agitate the client, what contradiction between the client's behavior and his/her expressed goal or value will you focus on? How will you pose your questions?

B. (Field Practicum)   Imagine that you are employed at the agency in which you are performing your field practicum, and that the administration of the agency is planning a sweeping change which will eliminate the program in which you are working, and your job as well. (For example, a social worker is employed as a guidance counselor in a public elementary school, which the School Board intends to close as part of a consolidation plan.)   Assume that you intend to organize some effective opposition to this change. As a first step, you decide to perform a power analysis.

    Undertake a power analysis of the agency you are placed in, with the goal of answering the following questions:

    1.   Who are the people who participate in making decisions about the operations of the agency, and what are their relationships to each other? What are their respective self-interests in terms of the agency? Who defers to whom, and why?

    2.   Who holds the top positions of decision-making power? What is their authority based on? Are they elected, appointed, hired, or volunteer? Are any of their positions up for renewal soon?
(re-election, probationary hiring period, re-appointment by a newly elected official) Are any of them planning on moving on -- using this position as a career stepping-stone?

    3.   Are there any flows of money to take note of? (election campaign contributions, awarding of contracts to friends and allies, doing banking or financing with certain banks because of connections to the directors)

    4.   What stakeholders are there outside the agency, to whom the agency's decision-makers have to be accountable? (For example, funding sources,

governmental regulators, families of clients, local public officials) What are the key considerations regarding these stakeholders that the agency's decision-makers have to be mindful of? How satisfied or unhappy are various stakeholders with the agency's performance?

5. What does the recent history of the agency tell you about the comparative power of the relevant actors? (Such as internal power struggles, labor union disputes, questions about continuing United Way funding, winning/losing of government grants)

C. (Role Playing) You are an income maintenance social worker in a large county social services department. You and your co-workers have unionized, civil-service jobs, and the union is well respected. The top administrators of the department want to implement job restructuring and work procedure changes which do not violate the union contract. You and your co-workers are against the changes, and want to resist them. Attempts to provide input and response regarding the changes to the administration have, so far, been ignored. You are now part of a team, encouraged by the union, which will plan and execute an action to interact with the administrators. Your intention is to get them to agree to negotiate the proposed changes with the social workers. After the action you will facilitate an evaluation of it. When negotiations are agreed to, you will help prepare the union side for the negotiation.

1. In designing your action, ask yourself: What setting would be appropriate to respectfully but effectively challenge the administrators to react to the social workers' input? When would be the best timing for this action, to maximize its impact? What allies and stakeholders could you bring into the picture to support your position? Who would be the spokespeople to talk to the administrators, and what would they say? What involvement, if any, do you want of the news media?

2. In evaluating the action when it's done, what criteria will you be judging? How do you measure the degree of success of the action? What kind of lessons do you draw from what your co-workers did, and from what the administrators did? What did you learn about the power relations regarding this issue, and the strengths and weaknesses of both your side and the administration's? Did you get any insight as to what a realistic negotiated compromise might look like?

3. Assume that you are now going to negotiate with the administrators, and that you will help prepare your team. What contingencies do you expect might occur in the negotiation? How will you handle each of them? What are you willing to compromise on, and not compromise on? What do you know about the personalities and styles of the administrators' negotiators, so that you can "read" them accurately and anticipate their tactics? What process will you have to discuss and approve any offers made by the administration?

END NOTES

1.   Church-based organizing is reviewed from the perspective of the religious community in Ramsden and Montgomery (1990).

2.   For a discussion of the internal discussions within the IAF on this point, see Rogers (1990), pp.93-98.

3.   The community organizing formulation that was typical of much of the efforts of the 1970s -- just creating a "multi-issue" organization to attract many different self-interests contains at least three problems: (a) there have to be one or more "hot" issues being worked on at any given time, or else people can rapidly lose interest; (b) the shifts between different issue campaigns can exact a heavy toll in turnover of leaders and active members; and (c) there is no automatic mechanism to develop a strong sense of group identity and solidarity.

4.   The IAF formally codified the theory in a 1978 pamphlet entitled "Organizing for Family and Congregation." COPS, which was built from San Antonio's low-income Catholic Mexican American congregations, marked what IAF top staff Chambers, Cortes, and others call the start of the "modern IAF."

5.   Some of the largest church-based organizing turnouts to date have included 8,500 in 1985 at an East Brooklyn Churches gathering, and 4,000 at a South Suburban [of Chicago] Action Conference event in 1991. Multi-group statewide events included one in 1987 with almost 7,000 members of the Southern California IAF Network, and 10,000 in 1990, of the Texas IAF Network.

6.   The description of the organizing drive is based on notes from IAF, Gamaliel, PICO, and DART training sessions; and from the author's interviews with a variety of participants.

7.   The IAF's procedures are widely enough known that nowadays some local religious leaders raise the money before even approaching the network (Ramsden and Montgomery, 1990). Years ago, Alinsky occasionally had required churches to raise money before he would even grant an initial visit, thereby forcing the local leaders who care the most to cross boundaries and forge alliances -- accomplishing some initial organizing before things even started.

8.   The organizer might also gather small groups in house meetings in order to get people to interact and begin to realize that they have common values and concerns, and to whet their appetites for what lies ahead. The "house meeting" also, according to IAF senior organizer Jim Drake, helps the organizer feel a sense of momentum which combats the tediousness of the process.

9.   Material on concepts and skills is from Hanna notes from IAF session; Robinson notes from Gamaliel session; participant notes from PICO and DART sessions; Hanna interviews with Ed Chambers, Ernie Cortes, John Baumann and Jose Carrasco; Robinson interviews with Greg Galluzzo and Joe Mariano; Jim Drake workshop; and from IAF (1978, 1990) and Cortes (1988).

10.   This sort of power analysis has some noticeable resemblance to the strata described by C. Wright Mills in *The Power Elite* (1958), except that it uses an institutional or system analysis instead of Mills's focus on individual elite leaders. In a sense, the community organizing power analysis is a hybrid between Mills's concept and Marx's view of institutionalized decision-making power based on structural economic control.

11.   A lucid explanation of self-interest is contained in Pierce (1984).

12.   For a discussion on the commonplace, and ineffective, forms of church activism, see Pierce (1984).

13.   The IAF, in its training, goes even further by likening actions to three-act plays: an introduction of players and fixing of the plot; a middle containing a build-up of dramatic tension; and a denouement that resolves the tension. Pursuing the metaphor, two audiences are described: the targets and constituencies outside the organization who will be affected by the outcome, and the internal audience of the organization's members. Goals are articulated for the expected changes in attitude, feelings, and relationship of each.

14.   In an IAF action in 1990 in Los Angeles, the act of "cutting a deal" with local businessmen was symbolized by having hundreds of people physically shake hands with the targets on stage.

15.   Pierce refers to partisan electoral politics as an "activist trap" for congregations (Pierce, 1984, pp. 14-16).

16.   Nicholas von Hoffman, an early protege of Saul Alinsky, wrote during his organizing years: "Perhaps the least important duty a citizen has in a democracy is voting. The ballot box is the last resort of a citizenry that has not been looking after its affairs closely enough" (p.43).

17.   That picture is rather romanticized, since of course not everyone was franchised back then. Perhaps more relevant, it is clear that participatory democracy was easier in some ways when the population was a fraction of its

present size and more homogeneous, and the issues of the day were much simpler than now.

18.   Regarding the intellectual influence of Cortes on the IAF, see Rogers (1990) pp. 93-101. The influence of Carrasco on PICO is taken from Hanna interviews with John Baumann, Jose Carrasco, and Scott Reed.

CHAPTER 4

Individual-Based
Direct-Action Organizing

Scenario: On a bright spring day, something special is happening on the steps of the state capitol building. The statewide People's Action group is staging a showcase event in its campaign on hazardous waste reform. Several speakers, including prominent politicians and a movie star who champions environmental causes, are queued up to speak at the microphone. Large banners are fluttering, and on a special platform are displayed a multitude of boxes containing 250,000 cards signed by citizens across the state, urging the legislature to pass the bill sponsored by People's Action. The bill would provide the funding to clean up 25 toxic waste sites, and increase the statutory penalties for violations of hazardous waste disposal. About 150 people are present, plus several TV and radio crews (both state and national), and the major print media.

People's Action's own speakers include their top paid staff person, two labor union leaders, the director of an environmental public interest agency, the president of a senior citizen group, and the chair of a multi-denominational religious legislative coalition. All of their organizations are members of People's Action. Their comments pertain to the legislative session underway, and accuse Republican senators and the Republican governor of being too cozy with major industrial polluters and their Political Action Committee's (PAC) contributions. They repeatedly point out that they are speaking on behalf of the hundreds of thousands of state residents who signed the message cards featured on the platform, and who are angry that big industries get away with hurting the environment and endangering health, just to save some expense and enhance profits. There is an obvious close alliance with the Democratic legislators, sponsors of People's Action's bill, who have a major role in this event.

This scene, in contrast to the gathering of the institution-based ACTION group at St. James church, is an example of a different type of citizen organizing, which can be called the individual-based direct action method. Instead of building a mass organization by reaching people through institutions that are very important to them, and prompting them to act out of commitment to their institutional values, the individual-based method employs a quite different strategy: appealing to people chiefly as individuals, on the strength of specific issues' connection to their self-interest. Although primary reliance is on the attraction of the issues, organizational relations are still utilized, to a lesser extent -- as a vehicle to help define self-interest and channel information about the issue at hand. This method has both strong pluses and minuses when compared to the institution-based strategy.

In practice, the individual-based approach plays out in several significant variations. One of the most prominent, typified by the People's Action state group mentioned above (a composite based on actual examples), derives its organizational muscle from daily canvassing operations that go door-to-door, talking to thousands of people about a particular issue, and garnering support in terms of petition signatures, letter-writing, and dollars for membership and donations. The Citizen Action national network is comprised of about 30 statewide organizations like this, which also have an institutional membership component as well: labor unions; environmental, senior, and farmer groups; and various liberal-progressive interest groups. The organizational members decide on issue positions and conduct activities to advance their campaigns.

The greatest component of these groups' policy-influencing power, however, stems not from their institutional membership but rather from their ability to reach and mobilize, in certain ways, thousands of individuals through the canvass (Kendall, 1990; Max, 1990).[1]

The individual-based direct action variants diverge according to geographic scope (local, statewide, or national); structural format; and on the critical question of commitment to developing grass-roots leaders. In general, the versions of individual-based organizing which are interested in developing leaders operate on a local scale. The ones which do not address leadership development are those which operate on a state or national level and have eschewed the time-consuming, tedious activity of leader recruitment and training in favor of utilizing existing interest-group leaders, and public mobilization, to try to maximize their influence at the highest level of policy-making processes, on issues that impact considerable numbers of people.

Especially given the accelerating concentration of national and multi-national corporate power, and the continuing fusing of economic and political control in fewer hands, many activists feel the urge to combat these forces directly now in the state houses and Washington, rather than waiting for citizen power to slowly percolate up from congregations and neighborhoods.

Issue Identification

How did People's Action choose the issue of toxic dump clean-up funds and penalties for hazardous waste disposal violations? Their process deviated dramatically from that employed by the church-based ACTION group:

Scenario: The monthly meetings of the People's Action steering committee, comprised of representatives from the 12 member organizations (4 unions; 3 environmental groups; a senior citizen and a farmer organization; a legislative coalition of mainline religious denominations; a social progress organization for blacks; and a utility consumers' group) contain regular discussion on a wide array of issues from a liberal-progressive viewpoint. The environmental groups provided initial information on the hazardous waste issue, and the steering committee decided to have People's Action's staff research it further. A key important decision was to test the general public's response to the issue, by means of the door-to-door and telephone canvasses. When the early responses from the canvass contacts proved to be strongly affirmative, confirmed by a robust donation rate, the People's Action steering committee voted to launch a full-scale campaign. The respective organizations committed portions of their own resources to assist in the activities, including generating endorsement letters, conducting legislative contacts, and participating in press conferences.

The dynamics of People's Action's issue selection method reveals the importance of certain concepts and skills at work. An important training center for these concepts and skills is the Midwest Academy (based in Chicago and founded by Heather Booth), which is totally independent of the Citizen Action network, but has nonetheless provided the lion's share of its training (Kendall, 1990; Max, 1990).

Power

As with the institution-based groups, power is a central theme of the individual-based method, although with a slightly different spin. Power is defined in terms of the ability to win meaningful improvements for your constituency, rather than as a means to implement people's shared values in the world. The definition is similar to what is understood in traditional interest-group politics, which usually involves an adversarial stance with other parties, and negotiated compromise as a possible result. There is no overt emphasis on relational power and intentionally making deals with the target based on self-interest. The notion that power is proportional to relationships is directly addressed from a different angle by the individual-based groups, on the subject of seeking allies and building coalitions of organizations around mutual interests. Power is chiefly discussed in tactical terms, as well as strategically in regard to your ability to either hurt or help the target.[2]

Self-Interest

Self-interest is also an explicit concept in individual-based direct action, but in a narrower sense than is found in the institution-based method. Individual self-interest is described primarily in motivations related to economic, class, and constituency-group terms, both short range and long term. There is some, but much less, emphasis on a recognition of individualized, psychological-linked aspects such as the desire for a sense of meaningfulness in life, the well-being of one's heirs, and adherence to moral values. More deep-seated and emotionally rooted drives stemming from childhood and personal experience are not addressed at all, however, and consequently there is no stress on a need for intimate personal relationship building. It is fair to say that the less priority there is on recruiting and developing leaders, the less urgency there is to understand personalized inner motivations.

Underlying Ideology

The focus on economic self-interest connects to a theoretical underpinning of class analysis, common to left political thought with a Marxian bent. It is no coincidence, since many of the founders and top staff of the individual-based organizations and networks matured in the New Left movement of the 1960s, including involvement in SDS (Students for a Democratic Society) and the antiwar movement. SDS thinking viewed low income people, angered by their marginalized status, as the most likely agents of social change. Many of the present-day individual-based groups, however, view the middle class as their primary constituency (necessary to a strategy that hinges on canvassing for financial support), and low income people as an important but secondary one. Steve Max, who trains many Citizen Action staffers (in his capacity as a senior trainer in the Midwest Academy), predicts that the next great historical social movement in this country will be a reaction by the middle class to their eroding standard of living. The belief in a movement theory of social change is consistent with the predominance of individual-based organizers whose activist roots are in the civil rights, antiwar, and feminist movements (Max, 1990).[3]

Citizen Action and other individual-based networks do not openly espouse what might be called "socialist" viewpoints, since that would be self-defeating in the attempts to build a majority coalition that could create deep reforms in our society. Instead, both Citizen Action and the Midwest Academy embrace "progressive populism," a loose term covering a wide range of social change concerns. These are tied together by themes of economic justice, redistribution of wealth, restraint of multinational corporate power, toleration of racial, ethnic, religious, sexual and social diversity, expansion of participatory democratic process, protection of health and environment, and responsible foreign and defense policy. A common thread is the desire for popular control of institutions that have become unaccountable to the public and serve a privileged elite. Much of the agenda is in tune with the liberal-left wing of the Democratic Party, further evidenced by the frequent alliance of Citizen Action organizations with progressive Democratic office holders and candidates. This "new American populism," as defined by Booth, Max and Harry Boyte in 1986, harkens back to the earlier Populists' revolt against concentrated financial power, and back even further to the first American concepts of public interest and commonwealth (Boyte, Booth, & Max, 1986).

Canvassing

People's Action's quarter-million individually signed lobbying cards, and the tremendous public support that they represent, would not have been possible without canvassing. As the main tool of constructing citizen power in the Citizen Action and some of the other individual-based groups, canvassing technology is at the heart of these groups' capacity to affect public decision making. And, since it is often the critical source of funding, the existence of many of these organizations would be doubtful without it.

Within the Citizen Action network, most organizations are dependent on an allied canvassing operation called the CLEC Canvass Network, the largest in the country. CLEC stands for Citizen-Labor Energy Coalition, the national coalition of groups who fought natural gas decontrol in 1977-1982; the CLEC canvass was originally its fundraising arm. CLEC was organized with the help of Heather Booth (who consulted with many Citizen Action groups) and her associates, and so an historic relationship existed between Midwest Academy, Citizen Action, and the CLEC canvass at its inception. CLEC manages canvassing operations that are integral to the various Citizen Action groups, but does so in a standardized way which it has developed. On an annual basis, the number of people contacted runs in the millions (Boyte, Booth, & Max, 1986; Kendall, 1990; Max, 1990).

Canvass contacts are in two categories: door-to-door (or "field"), and on the telephone. Field canvassing is indiscriminate in that all residences in a given area are door-knocked. The contact (if the person is home) does not usually last more than 10 minutes. The organization and the current issue is described, and the person is asked to sign a statement of support as well as give a donation -- hopefully, in a large enough amount to qualify as an organizational member. Some discussion is generated with the person, but not much. Often, a receptive person is asked to write a brief letter, respond to a quick survey, or sign their name to some other indicator of agreement on the issue. The contact is thus largely non-relational, and more akin to a sales technique -- albeit one that connects with the person's self-interest on a progressive policy issue. In a sense, canvassing is a form of mass consumer marketing of political and social change, "harvesting" the latent support in the community. Loyalty to the organization can be fostered to a partial degree by subsequent mailings and phone calls, but there is a high turnover in canvass membership. This is not considered a major problem, however, because the next sweep by the canvass can be reliably expected to generate an adequate number of dollars and letters. Support is measured in total net numbers at a given moment, more so than in continuity of specific individuals.

Telephone canvassing is usually restricted to people who have already donated on the field canvass, to update them on issue developments and maintain, renew, or increase their financial commitment. In one respect, it resembles telemarketing techniques employed to identify and cultivate the people most prone to donate at higher levels, and maximize the efficiency (and hence net revenue-generating ability) of the fundraising process. However, the phone contacts also help procure further activities such as letters and calls to legislators, and on occasion, turnout at a public event.

The canvassers themselves are staffers, paid partly on salary and partly in proportion to the funds they raise. The majority are young -- often college students -- and turnover is relatively high. Although the messages about issues that they convey are quite brief, the canvassers experience significant political education in their ongoing training process, which includes "cross-training" experiences with other Citizen Action groups, and annual conferences featuring issue workshops and speeches by icons of left-progressive politics. Despite their pivotal role in the success of Citizen Action groups, however, the canvassers have very little voice in the organizations' choice of issues or strategy.

Scenario: Back at the state capitol, the People's Action staff and leaders are drawing Republican senate leader Fred Johnson and the governor's top aide out of the building to appear at their makeshift stage, and respond to the organization's arguments for the bill. Their comments, captured by the news media, are not satisfying; the battle lines have been drawn. Senator Michaels, the author of the hazardous waste legislation (whose recent election victory was substantially aided by canvass support from People's Action), gets to have the last word.

One week after the event, at the next People's Action steering committee, the media coverage which was obtained is judged to be very successful, and more pertinent than the relatively small turnout (most of which was generated by the senior citizen group, with a smaller portion brought by the labor unions). Four additional steps are planned for the campaign: a public debate sponsored by Peoples' Action between a nationally recognized environmental expert and the public affairs Vice President of the state's largest industrial polluter; preparation of comprehensive testimony for a state pollution control agency public hearing; a press conference to publicly release a detailed research report on the issue, written by People's Action staff; and last but not least, targeted canvassing in Senator Johnson's home district, aimed at generating letters to pressure him to reconsider his opposition to the bill.

The campaign planning benefits from the strong tradition, in groups like People's Action, of attention to the skill of developing strategy.

Campaign Strategy

Because of the absolute centrality of the success of issue campaigns to make or break individual-based organizations (in contrast to the institution-based method, which views issues as necessary but secondary), this type of organizing devotes primary consideration to perfecting issue strategy. For instance, it is probably the most critical training element in the program of the Midwest Academy, whose centerpiece "product" is the strategy chart -- a device that combines strategy planning, internal and external power analysis, and campaign design into one entity. Arranged spreadsheet-style are five columns: Goals; Organizational Considerations; Constituencies, Allies and Opponents; Targets; and Tactics (Bobo, Kendall, & Max, 1991).

The Goals column is used to state long-term goals as well as specific goals regarding the issue at hand, including its organization-building potential. The second column is used for an internal audit of organizational resources and specific organizational benefits expected from the campaign. The next column analyzes constituencies within and without the organization, and their self-interest regarding the issue; it also looks at opponents' self-interests and their expected involvement.

Targets, the fourth column, is for analyzing the power structure related to the issue, identified in specific people responsible for decision making, and for listing secondary targets -- entities that the target is accountable to, and who could be pressured to lean on the target in turn. Finally, the fifth column is used to list tactics that can be used on each of the specified targets. Contemplating the possible targets and tactics, along with the rest of the chart, provides a comprehensive information base for constructing a specific strategy and set of tactics.

Electoral Politics

One conspicuous element of People's Action's strategy, and of the Citizen Action network, is direct campaigning for and against candidates in elections. It is a preeminent tactic in the basic strategy of building allies -- in the sense of empowering politician allies -- and fits well with these organizations' relationships with labor unions, which have long been involved in election campaigns. It is justified in purely pragmatic terms: since we are trying to influence legislation, it would be self-defeating to not try to shape the composition of the state and national legislatures. Unlike the institution-based groups that shy away from election campaigns, this tactic works well for statewide individual-based organizations, precisely because they are not preoccupied with trying to develop grassroots leaders. Max indicates that electoral strategies came to the fore when Citizen Action groups realized that their canvass operations were beginning to develop a support base large enough to create the possibility of influencing elections (Creamer, 1990; Max, 1990).

Canvassing is ideal for the electoral strategy. The field canvass can reliably identify swing voters, who can then be targeted for repeat phone and mail messages as the election draws near. The mobility of the field crews and the flexibility of the phone crews enable them to be highly effective, on short notice, during election contests as well as during legislative campaigns. In a limited number of instances, Citizen Action groups have gone further and elected their own candidates. This situation sets up a dynamic of trust and common values which helps ensure the accountability over elected officials which is so elusive to citizen groups.[4]

The development of electoral work has resulted in Citizen Action's loose identification with the Democratic Party, in effect committing itself to the task of pushing a progressive platform within the Party. In doing so, Citizen Action overtly endorses American liberal pluralism and interest group politics. The type of social change sought after amounts to the redistribution of economic value in an increasingly just manner, and enlightened social, environmental and foreign policy. Radical restructuring of the economic and social system is not being pursued. Three Citizen Action affiliates originally had in their names the concept "Fair Share," and one still does today.

Staff People as Leaders

In Citizen Action and many other individual-based groups, paid staff people are often seen as visible spokespersons and leaders. This concept is defended by these groups in the context of the coalition model: the organization staff can display neutrality, thereby minimizing rivalry and friction between a coalition's organizational members. It is also explained by the logistical difficulties in providing speakers for the media, when the constituent organizations are spread around the state. Midwest Academy training speaks of a role for coalition staff in developing leadership among the representatives of the member organizations, but this principle is contradicted in some Citizen Action groups where the staff appears to be the primary leader, while the leaders of the constituent organizations are given circumscribed leadership roles within the coalition. This is not a problem where the member organizations' leaders (often paid staff themselves) subscribe to the aim of having a neutral primary spokesperson. Not surprisingly, lead staff in Citizen Action groups are typically titled Executive Director rather than Staff Director (Bobo, et al., 1991; Kendall, 1990).

Local Chapter -- Individual Membership Model

The Citizen Action Format of a coalition of existing interest groups coupled with an individual mass-base, obtained through canvassing, is by no means the only strategy for individual-based organizing. In some ways, the current Citizen Action organizations can tend to resemble the public interest research groups (PIRGS) promoted by Ralph Nader: a small, professionalized staff who perform research, lobbying, press conferences, and litigation on consumer issues, and who are in only superficial or limited contact with a large supporting membership which backs their efforts.

Many other individual-based organizing networks and groups, however, are in much more direct and deep contact with the grassroots than this, although in smaller overall numbers. The most typical formula of the alternate method is individual membership chapter structures, built on a neighborhood, city, or rural county basis. Groups in networks such as Southern Empowerment Project (SEP), Western Organization of Resource Councils (WORC), and Association of Community Organizations for Reform Now (ACORN) use such a system, which aims to recruit and promote grassroots leaders, and identify issues from the local people's perspective. ACORN developed the most regularized model of all the networks for creating chapters, designed to be easily replicated and undertaken relatively quickly. What follows is a description of the organizing drive, based on ACORN's recipe. Other network's variations may be less intense and rapid although the basic sequence of steps remains similar (ACORN, Institute for Social Justice, 1978).[5]

The Organizing Drive

Preparation for the organizing drive in a new locality begins with an analysis of the city, town, or county in question. Items to discover include the demographics, geographical arrangements, power structure, identification of key contacts, role of the local media, and the history of race relations and significant community issues. Next, specific neighborhoods are examined in closer detail, using the parameters above but paying special attention to income levels, obvious issues (like potholes, vacant lots, or abandoned buildings), and local businesses that could potentially agree to membership discounts. The organizer also needs to determine what the natural boundaries of each neighborhood are, in the context of physical divisions, prominent institutions, and most importantly the residents' own perceptions. A crucial step in the set-up process is finding some community leaders or "gatekeepers" such as pastors, social service workers and shop owners who can provide initial credentialing and entree for the organizer, as well as the first lists of names of local residents to start contacting.

With the above information in hand regarding several different neighborhoods, a selection and prioritization is made for the neighborhoods to be targeted, and in which order. The quality of the lists and the initial contacts, and a judgment on how pressing the local issues seem to be, are significant criteria. Of critical importance is the size of the neighborhoods, because it relates to the physical ability of the available staff to knock on every door in the neighborhood within a given time frame. A month to 6 weeks (not counting the preliminary preparations of 4 to 6 weeks) is the standard timeline given for the drive itself. A drive longer than that, it is feared, would lose momentum and a sense of excitement among the neighborhood residents. It would also likely prove demoralizing for the staff organizer, because he or she is expected, during the actual drive, to knock on 30 to 40 doors a day, 6 days a week -- for a total of about 60 to 80 hours weekly. A total of about 1,000 to 1,500 households is thus the maximum that one organizer could cover in the time allotted. If there are two staff, such as an experienced organizer and a trainee, then the number of doors and the size of the neighborhood can be doubled. At the lower end of the scale, a neighborhood of less than 500 households is considered to be too small for the model. A neighborhood larger than the 1,000 to 1,500 size could be tackled by dividing it into smaller sections, and possibly by creating block clubs. These smaller units are feasible only if each has potential issues to work on within the respective areas. A final information-gathering step is to obtain names, addresses and phone numbers for all households in the neighborhood. The information is put on an index card for each household that will be visited. These data are gleaned from city directories, voter registration lists, and other sources.

The drive itself begins with the creation of an organizing committee of residents within the neighborhood. These people are recruited from names given by the initial contact persons, and additional names derived in snowball fashion from interviewing the first round of contacts. The people to bring onto the organizing committee are those who are committed to creating a neighborhood group and are willing to put in some work. There is no great desire to seek out people who are in existing leadership roles, because the ACORN model assumes that people in lower income neighborhoods do not have many leadership experiences, and that ACORN will be developing those roles for them. Other networks, however, are more interested in people who have already been exercising leadership in some manner.[6]

The key purpose of the organizing committee members is to provide authentic grass-roots legitimacy to the drive, create a pool of workers who will help the drive succeed, and become the new group's first leaders. The 12 to 15 organizing committee members elect temporary officers, sign an "organizing committee letter" which will be mailed to all neighborhood residents, volunteer to help door knock, set a date for the chapter's founding meeting, and agree to a standardized, ongoing relationship with ACORN. That contract requires dues payments, organizational affiliation, and distribution of ACORN's literature in return for ACORN's assistance in creating and maintaining the chapter. The organizing committee also discusses potential issues, and decides on a first campaign that will be used to kick off the chapter. That issue is described in the organizing committee letter which is mailed to all residents (excepting any who have been identified as antagonistic to ACORN's goals). The letter also announces the upcoming meeting and gives notice that someone will be knocking at the door.

Systematic door knocking is then done, preferably in two-person teams. The organizer should always be door knocking with an organizing committee member. In the visits, which are brief -- no more than 15 minutes is recommended -- the need for the neighborhood group and the plans to create it are explained, along with a description of ACORN and its dues requirement. The person is asked what issues he or she is concerned about and is asked for a commitment to attend the neighborhood meeting. After the visit, the person's responses are noted on the previously prepared index card. In more rural areas, house meetings are often used as a supplemental method to help build the sense of momentum and consensus.

As the day for the founding meeting draws near, a second mailing is sent out, and telephone calls are made. Posters, press releases and radio announcements are all used to further publicize and reinforce the attendance for the event, which is intended to appear as the largest and most important meeting ever held in the neighborhood. During the drive the organizer has met several times with the organizing committee members, who have been prepared to take leading roles at the founding meeting and launch the first issue campaign. At the meeting itself, the chapter is founded, temporary officers are elected, people pay their individual dues, issues are discussed, and plans are set for the first campaign.

Critique of the Individual-Based Method

Lack of Leadership Development

Whether or not one believes that many personal transformations must precede social change, it is true that the number of a group's leaders and their skillfulness will have a direct bearing on its effectiveness. The individual-based method does not engage in as much leadership recruitment and development as do the institution-based groups, which is partly reflected in less intensive training programs for both staff and leaders, and utilization of fewer concepts. With fewer leaders, organizational operations are more heavily reliant on staff. This has ramifications, aside from the emphasis on staff as spokespeople, in a reduced ability to physically turn out large numbers of people at events, and a harder time with grass-roots fundraising (apart from canvassing). Limits on personal effectiveness in turn tend to restrict how long people make a career of it, which holds down the collective growth of sophisticated expertise and puts experienced mentors in short supply. An important point to note is that in contrast to the Citizen Action Model, the individual-based groups that use a local chapter structure are succeeding in developing some significant grassroots leadership. Yet even with these, there is still usually not the extent and depth of leadership development found in many of the institution-based groups.[7]

Assuming Self-Interest

A strength of the individual-based organizations is that they tackle head-on many substantial economic issues at the state or national arenas, rather than expend a lot of time on minor localized concerns. There seems to be a clear trade-off between forsaking the neighborhood-type issues and their utility in recruiting indigenous leadership, to move instead to an issue-driven, somewhat top-down approach seen as necessary to address the more significant economic forces that are increasingly controlled at the state, national and even international level. In a way, this equates to abandoning the Alinsky dictum of listening for the self-interests that people express on their own, and forming the organizational agenda around that.

What the individual-based groups have instead is a strategic analysis of issues that deeply impact the low and middle income majority, coupled with technology to communicate to the public that these issues are in fact in their self-interest. Citizen Action groups have had good success in doing so, but they run the risk of missing the mark on occasion. There is always the danger of dissonance between what people perceive their self-interest to be versus what the organizers believe that self-interest is. This is the classic mistake that organizers are taught to avoid, but with Citizen Action's determination to advance a progressive agenda, it is a risk worth taking. Canvass operations reduce the risk by giving valuable, immediate feedback on the choice of specific issues, chiefly in the crude measure of the amount of money donated, but also in people's willingness to write letters.

The local chapter-based groups on the other hand, enjoy a more accurate feel for people's concerns at the grassroots, precisely because they are doing more active listening than is possible with canvassing. Yet, they run the risk of becoming preoccupied with small neighborhood campaigns that don't reach higher levels of power. The dilemma is sometimes dealt with by steering the local campaigns in several localities to mesh with the same issue theme that has widespread support. For a group that operates on both a state and chapter level, the ideal situation is for local campaigns (such as going after local corporate property tax delinquents) to evolve logically into a statewide legislative fight (such as property tax reform in the state statutes).

How Much Power?

In contrast to the institution-based networks, which generally engage (so far, at least) in activity primarily at the local level, many of the groups espousing individual-based methods have long been contending for power at state and national arenas. They have been consistently helping to shape many public policy debates and have won some reforms; yet, decisive major victories elude them. They have just not amassed enough power to fully counterbalance the dominant forces on the political scene. In part, this parallels the weakness of many of their coalition members and allies, such as the environmental movement and the labor unions. A desire to strengthen these groups would require a new strategy direction -- to expand and improve leadership.

There is also a question of how much accountability is obtainable with politicians whose election or re-election is well served by the "campaign contribution" of assistance from a citizens group's canvass. Many more politicians, however, feel no need for citizen group aid at all. Given the overwhelming influence of corporate PAC money and mass media in elections, can citizen groups hope to compete in this game other than as a minor player?

Specific Aspects of Individual-Based Variations

National Link-Ups

One category of individual-based direct action organizing involves networking on a national level. The prime example of this, Citizen Action, has already been referred to several times above. Two others are National People's Action (NPA), and Association of Community Organizations for Reform Now (ACORN).

National Peoples Action, which is based in Chicago, operates as a very loose network, comprising a fluid collection of local-based organizations around the country, which are typically individual-membership groups, often constructed on a neighborhood model, and with a predominantly low-income racially mixed constituency. The training arm of NPA is called the National Training and Information Center (NTIC), which gives minimal assistance to about 300 groups each year, and has a more regular, ongoing relationship with about 25 organizations. NTIC, which is headed by Shel Trapp (who was trained in the 1960s by Tom Gaudette, an Alinsky associate), conducts a 3-day training session in the basics, and occasionally places organizer interns with them (Trapp, 1990).

NPA's most noteworthy role is that of issue campaign research center, clearinghouse, and campaign coordinator for the groups in its network. NPA does not wish to decide issue campaigns at the national level and impose them on individual groups; it could not anyway, since the relationship is voluntary and very informal, and the groups have a high degree of independence. Instead, it generates detailed information and encourages activity on a wide menu of issues, supplying vital information to those groups interested in each particular issue. It also coordinates a dramatic event each year in Washington, DC: the NPA Annual Convention, which consists of several hundred people from its affiliated groups who are bussed to the nation's capitol for confrontative actions, or "hits." These actions usually involve disruptive crowding into top bureaucrats' or legislators' offices, demanding some interaction, with the goal of winning agreements to negotiate with NPA members on selected issues such as Community Reinvestment Act (anti-redlining of mortgages), utility rates, and energy assistance. The issue topics for the NPA Convention (which was launched in 1972) are decided collectively, in advance, by leaders from the allied groups. The commitments for future meetings with top officials, secured at the Convention, provide opportunities for follow-up negotiations and actions throughout the year -- with participation in each by those groups involved in the particular issue.

ACORN (Association of Community Organizations for Reform Now) comprises a national network of about 20 groups across the country which have similar constituencies to NPA, but operate under a much more centralized structure. It is greatly reduced from its height in the early 1980s, when (by its own count) it numbered 50,000 members in 27 states; but its earlier peak period is worth noting because of the example it presents (Delgado, 1986; Kest & Streich, 1990; Kest & Rathke, 1975; Rathke, 1977).

ACORN was initiated in Arkansas in 1970 as an experimental project of the National Welfare Rights Organization, in a deliberate attempt to reach beyond the primary base of the lowest income strata by including moderate income people as well. Rapid expansion ensued -- and was initiated in other states -- aided by a rigid, easily duplicated step-by-step model (which relies on large amounts of door-knocking); an in-house training institute; and a large labor pool of low-paid staff organizers, recruited from the ranks of middle-class students. ACORN's direction came from the left-leaning staff, who were much more politicized than the grass roots leaders they recruited. Not surprisingly, the contradiction between highly educated, middle-class staff who deliberately forsook decent wages, and a membership base of low income people who sought a higher standard of living, created some significant tensions between the two.[8]

With a centralized decision-making structure and a mobile staff force, ACORN proceeded with a national strategy which attempted to influence the Democratic National Conventions in 1978 and 1980. There was a partial impact, but it was subsequently subverted by the Democrats' party leaders. ACORN also lost 100 VISTA staff positions which had been key to its expansion capacity, and top ACORN staff became interested in a different venture of labor union organizing, with the Service Employees International Union (SEIU). ACORN thereafter lost most of its momentum, although many local groups still exist. They have converted to the canvass mechanism of fundraising and member recruitment, and work primarily on housing issues.

Regional Link-Ups

In other instances of individual-based organizing, multiple groups are linked not on a national basis but regionally. The two most prominent examples of this are the Southern Empowerment Project and the Western Organization of Resource Councils.

The Southern Empowerment Project (SEP) is a training and support network in the Southeast and Appalachia, focused in Tennessee, Kentucky and North Carolina. Unlike many networks, it was created in the mid- 1980s by five already existing organizations who wanted a collective training and consulting resource to service their groups -- whose number had grown to eight by 1991. It is run as a cooperative by those groups, most of which are statewide and represent low and moderate income people (some white, some African-American). They work on a variety of issues, including the Community Reinvestment Act, solid waste disposal, taxes, mineral land rights, and taxes. Their common format is individual-based memberships, often organized in a chapter sub-structure. They are not involved in a direct electoral strategy, but do frequently hold candidates' forums to press politicians for commitments on their issues.

SEP's training, which features an intensive 6-week program, teaches the concepts of self-interest and power analysis in an Alinsky-derived fashion, and skill areas such as accountability sessions and membership recruitment. An initial influence and resource was Myles Horton of the Highlander Center. SEP also directly treats regional history and socio-political analysis, and the subjects of racism, sexism and classism, and homophobia; there is a clear vision of facilitating cooperation between the races. Less clear, however, is how to engender a broad social vision among their grassroots leaders beyond the focus on specific issues (Rostan, 1991).

Western Organization of Resource Councils (WORC) is a regional network of five state organizations, located in North and South Dakota, Colorado, Montana, and Wyoming. It began with the Montana group, the Northern Plains Resource Council (NPRC), which was formed in 1972 by farmers and ranchers worried about losing land to coal strip-mining. NPRC initiated the other four groups over the next 16 years, combining them into WORC to coordinate activities on some issues and provide a consistent training resource for leaders and staff. A 4-day session provides comprehensive skills training, without treatment of concepts (Sweeney, 1990; WORC, 1991).

WORC's state organizations are comprised of local chapters, usually county-wide. Among the five state groups there are about 40 chapters, with a total individual membership of 5,000. WORC's individual-based, chapter format and recruiting of indigenous leaders is similar to ACORN's method. Land use, oil and gas regulation, taxes and environmental issues are typically addressed, with a variety of tactics that are primarily traditional in nature. Up to 600 people have been turned out for public hearings, and WORC has at times resorted to litigation as a secondary tactic. WORC has had some ongoing interaction with Kentuckians For The Commonwealth, a SEP group. Interestingly, WORC's director, Pat Sweeney, learned much about basic organizing principles from Herb White, a minister who had been involved in an early IAF project in Rochester, NY. White was also instrumental in encouraging John Calkins to start Concerned Seniors for Dade in Miami, and DART, after that.

The Center for Third World Organizing (CTWO) is not a fully linked network like SEP or WORC, but it does have relationships with organizers and groups in many different states. Founded in Oakland, California, around 1980 by Gary Delgado and other former Welfare Rights and ACORN staffers, it is unique in that its mission is to be a resource for minority organizers, and assists groups that are tackling issues from a minority perspective -- such as the racism inherent in placing hazardous waste sites in low income minority areas. Its primary function is to serve as a training center, rather than as a coordinator of various organizations' activity. CTWO's 6-week internship program includes thorough content on cultural diversity and empowerment of women (de Avila & Sampson, 1990).

Other Categories of Individual-Based Groups

Many other examples abound of individual-based direct action groups across the country. Some are multi-issue organizations that are locally based or statewide, but without a connection to a regional or national network. Others are single-issue groups that are focused on a particular constituency and their attendant issues: homeless people, senior citizens, environmental activists, women's organizations, and others. Tactics run the gamut from traditionally accepted participation "through the channels" all the way to civil disobedience such as sit-ins or squatting in vacant buildings. Some of these groups have made use of training programs previously mentioned, and a significant number have received training from the Midwest Academy, which has taught over 20,000 people from 1,000 organizations since 1973 (Bobo et al., 1991).[9]

A final, but important comment is that unlike the Citizen Action format described earlier in this chapter, many individual-based groups do in fact engage in recruitment and development of leaders at the local level, and cultivate issue priorities from a grassroots-up direction. In general, however, the institution-based networks are still more intensive about leadership development, and more patient in the listening process to uncover issues of perceived interest.

Classroom Exercises and Skill Development Scenarios (Individual-Based)

A.   (Class Discussion)   You are a social worker whose job includes helping victims of drug-related violent crimes work with their feelings and develop appropriate strategies to combat helplessness and apathy. Outline a realistic issue campaign which involves the following steps:
    1. Assume there is a definite geographic area where many of these crimes have occurred. Who might have an interest in working to reduce such crime? What are their self-interests and how will you tap into them?
    2. What will be the major steps in your power analysis? What research will you conduct to identify power players who can do something about the crime wave? What resistance might you anticipate?
    3. What initial tactics will you employ to gain legitimacy and get attention of decision makers?

B.   (Class Discussion, Role Playing)   You are a social worker at a nursing home. One of your duties is facilitating and advising the residents' council. There is general concern about Medicaid funding cuts at the legislature, and many residents want to do something to let state legislators know that they are opposed to the cuts, and would be hurt by them in various ways. The question is not whether to do something, but what to do. What tactics would be the best to use? Listed below are some possibilities. What are the advantages and disadvantages of these -- and others that you add to the list?

In thinking about this, make note of logistical considerations that affect the practicality and feasibility of performing the tactic; the willingness of the intended actors to undertake the tactic; the likely reaction to the tactic by the people it is designed to affect; the public perception and opinion that will likely be formed as a result of using this tactic; and how this tactic might fit into a larger plan that could entail a longer-term campaign, and possible escalation of tactics.

1. Invite area legislators to visit the nursing home and meet the residents.

2. Transport a group of residents to the state capitol (30 miles away) and stage a demonstration in the state capitol building.

3. Have family members, school children or others write individual letters on behalf of each resident, and send them to the legislators.

4. Organize a large community meeting at a nearby location to publicize the negative impact of the cuts, and get news media to cover the event.

5. Try to get seniors at the neighborhood senior citizen center to lobby the legislators on the nursing home residents' behalf.

C. (Class Project) You are a social worker who is the activities coordinator at a senior center. Several seniors who gather there daily express interest to you in creating an organization to express their views to politicians on a variety of issues. Help them plan an organizing drive to get the organization off the ground, up to and including its founding meeting. Keep in mind the following:

1. What step-by-step sequence of tasks and procedures will enable you to maximize the participation in the new organization and give it a good chance of success? What is a realistic timetable for the organizing drive, given the people who will be working on it? Are there any other people who could be recruited to help (social work student interns, church personnel, agency personnel)?

2. Whom do one-on-ones need to be done with, who will do them, and how will they be trained and supported in this activity? Which categories of people who use the senior center now will be interviewed? Are there any seniors who do not use the center that you think should be approached? Are there any senior clubs operating in the nearby area in churches, hi-rises or other locations? In each of these groupings of people, how will you select the one-on-ones to target the people with the most promise?

3. If one-on-ones are done with various seniors, but they aren't showing interest in the idea of the organization, what contradictions might they be agitated

on to prompt them to get involved? What sort of needs and self-interests of local seniors do you imagine the new organization might be able to address? If certain seniors seem to show the potential to be leaders of the new group, how would you proposition them to take on that level of responsibility? What specific tasks and activities might you offer them?

4. In preparing for the founding meeting of the organization, what dynamics do you want to take place at the event, and how will you ensure that they occur? What tasks will you and others do to ensure turnout at the meeting? How many people do you seek to have in attendance? What do you need the chairperson to do at the meeting? How many other people need to be prepared to take active parts, and what roles should they perform? Design the agenda for the meeting, and describe what you want to take place. At the conclusion of the meeting, what next steps will the group have likely decided to undertake?

Endnotes

1. A prominent Citizen Action example of the type of scenario presented here, but on the national level, occurred in 1985 when four semi-trailers converged on the US Capitol from across the country. The trucks' contents -- 1.5 million petition signatures and local documentation of toxic waste problems -- were displayed at a major media event, to urge an increase in the Superfund cleanup appropriation. The event was held on the day of a critical Senate vote and succeeded in prompting a major increase in funding (Boyte et al., 1986).

2. Information on concepts and skills is from Bobo et al., (1991), and WORC, (1991); Hanna interviews with Steve Max, Pat Sweeney, Fran Streich and Steve Kest; Robinson interviews with Jackie Kendall, Bob Creamer and Shel Trapp; Amy Self interview with June Rostan; and training materials from SEP, NTIC and ACORN. WORC and SEP utilize some materials developed by the Midwest Academy, including its issue strategy chart.

3. It is noteworthy that SDS had been influenced by the civil rights movement, which encompassed divergent strategies, including the Southern Christian Leadership Conference's high-profile mass mobilizations, dependent on media coverage and charismatic leadership (focused of course on Dr. Martin Luther King, Jr.) on the one hand; and the Student Non-violent Coordinating Committee's low-profile organizing at the local level. In some ways, the Midwest Academy still embodies this dialectic. As for Citizen Action, many of its groups began with a local chapter-based model that included a strong component of low income issues, but have since transitioned to a media-dependent, high-profile format with a less solid grassroots connection and a more middle-income appeal.

4. At least two Citizen Action groups, Illinois Public Action and Connecticut Citizens Action Group, have elected their own to state legislatures. Some national Congressmen, such as Senator Paul Simon, have received critical campaign support from Citizen Action.

5. ACORN's focus on an easily-repeated model stems from its birth in 1970 as a project of the National Welfare Rights Organization (NWRO). NWRO utilized, with great success for a time, a replicable model to demand special needs grants for welfare recipients (known as the "Boston model," for the city where it was developed). The cookbook format provided rapid creation of chapters by staff with little experience.

6. ACORN's disinterest toward most local institutions such as churches and unions is related to a fear that middle class people with leadership experience in existing organizations would take control of ACORN chapters. This is directly opposite to the institution-based method's essential strategy.

7. A disturbing trend among Citizen Action groups, in Jackie Kendall's view, has been the fact that administrative duties and funding shortages usurp the time of directors who have had organizer training, to the extent that they are not transmitting those skills to others; and many organizing director positiions that used to exist have been eliminated. Kendall sees the modest organizer salaries paid in most of the groups she consults with as having created a problem in that many experienced organizers of the 60s and 70s have left the field without passing on their knowledge (Kendall, 1990).
A relevant question is whether Citizen Action's issue campaign focus has rendered many of its own staff too undeveloped in organization-building and leadership development skills. This could be partly responsible for the difficulty in achieving success in grassroots fundraising goals to help provide acceptable salaries.

8. Gary Delgado, a former ACORN staffer who felt that ACORN's direction came from a "staff oligarchy," wrote: "Part of the ideological contradiction is that middle class organizers who have rejected [for themselves] the organization's avowed goals of gaining economic benefits cannot blatantly direct low income members who in fact enter the organization to make the system work in their interest" (Delgado, 1986).

9. One very important example from the women's movement is the 9 to 5 organization, which has grown dramatically since its inception in the mid-1970s, and concentrates on workplace reforms for secretaries and other office workers.

The 9 to 5 leaders received their initial training and encouragement from the Midwest Academy.

CHAPTER 5

Non-Traditional
Labor Movement Organizing

Social Workers and Corporate Campaign

Scenario: Two social workers employed by a 140-bed skilled nursing facility owned by Cleverly Enterprises, Inc. are having lunch. The two, both of whom are only part-time employees, were hired to do eligibility certification, patient intake, and ongoing casework with each patient. Because both are part-time, neither receives health or pension benefits, sick leave, or vacation. In fact the only benefits they do receive are a sub-standard wage and ever-increasing and changing responsibilities. When Cleverly cut back on the number of nursing aide staff, the social workers found themselves having to empty bedpans. When Cleverly eliminated the BSW degree requirement for the social worker positions, our two friends could see the handwriting on the wall and they decided to take action.

The Power Analysis

The social workers knew they were up against the wall with few options. They knew that without a lot more people involved and some leverage, Cleverly

124

would keep on doing what it had been doing across the country for years: resisting unionization and diminishing quality care standards for patients and employees. They decided to conduct a power analysis, combining parts of Brager and Holloway's (1978) Force Field Analysis, and the "TRADES" campaign model, developed by the Special Programs Department, United Brotherhood of Carpenter's and Joiners of America (AFL-CIO). Step one "T" target was the local Cleverly facility. At least initially, the social workers didn't think they had the resources to go after the Corporate headquarters for Cleverly. Second, "R" research, revealed a variety of potentially useful information, which was separated into driving (support change) and restraining (resist change) forces and categorized into three areas: participant forces (within the local nursing home), organizational forces (such as the mission and goals of the nursing home -- purportedly dedicated to care of patients), and environmental forces (including major economic and political elements) (Brager & Holloway, 1978).

After research came "A" analysis, part of the assessment phase involving the weighing and sorting of forces according those most and least likely to be mobilized during the campaign. "D" develop and "E" execute a "S" strategy, the final steps, require the practitioners to decide upon the overall plan of action. Who will act, when, and how? Following the initial definition of corporate campaign, the strategy is to apply continuously escalating pressure, carefully mobilizing the identified forces, using a variety of tactics. The remainder of the scenario narrative describes how our social workers operated to achieve their goals of fair play and quality care.

Driving Forces	***Restraining Forces***
Participants:	
themselves	*facility director*
nursing staff	*facility advisory*
	board
the patients and their families	
the nursing aide staff	
Organizational	
the mission of quality care	*the profit-making motive*
	the ideology of management
	efficiency

<u>Environmental</u>
 <u>Economic</u>
reliance on state funding

the local jobs provided
the expanding network and
corporate economic power
of Cleverly facilities in state
Publicly traded stock

<u>Political</u>
County Department of Social
Services (conduit for patients)
Public Employee Unions

Corporate Political Action Committee
($500,000.00 in contributions per year)
Prestigious Corporate Board
of Directors (golf with Gov.)

Professional Associations for
nurses and social workers
American Association of Retired
Persons (AARP)
Elected County and State officials
Federally mandated Ombudsman
State Attorney General
State Department of Health

three members of County
Board of Supervisors

Assessment Phase

Our social workers immediately saw that other staff must be involved. In fact, it turned out the only unionized staff in the facility were the janitors, who were part of the Service Employees International Union (SEIU), which had had national battles with Cleverly. In addition, the social workers were particularly cordial with one supervising nurse (who was a friend of the parents of one of the social workers. This nurse happened to be Vice President of the local Nurses Association. Another stroke of luck was the fact that the social workers personally knew family members for two patients: among the family members were a lawyer and an accountant. But our social workers were very resourceful. They had made it a point to nurture solid working relationships with the liaison for the County Department of Social Services. The liaison happened to be the shop steward for the county's public employee union, a chapter of the American Federation of state, county and municipal employees (AFSCME).

The social workers figured that they would best do their planning outside of the workplace. The supervising nurse agreed to host a potluck, to which the social workers were certainly invited. The nurse, who had considerably more job security and mobility than the social workers, agreed to invite the family members of the two patients (lawyer and accountant), a janitor and SEIU representative, the liaison and AFSCME representative. Oh yes, the lawyer also invited her friend, the Chairperson of the State AARP. The local NASW representative arrived late with the punch.

It seemed dissatisfaction with Cleverly had been brewing for some time and most of the guests had been looking for just such an opportunity to come together. The social workers, who had studied social change practice in school, simply provided the impetus. After a lengthy discussion, it turned out that the local chapters of the SEIU and AFSCME, along with the Nurses Association, all banked with the same bank, which, as the accountant pointed out (as a shareholder of Cleverly Stock), carried the note on the Cleverly facility, as well as Cleverly stock. The janitor pointed out that Cleverly had cut corners on the purchase of cleaning supplies, downgraded the quality of bedding, and cut back on the room cleaning schedules for some time. The County Social Service Department liaison had not personally heard any of these complaints before, because during each visit the facility clinic director had presented an impressive array of documented improvements and innovations in patient management and participation in governance of the facility. Of course, these visits were scheduled when the social workers were not on the premises.

The group gathered additional research in the next few months which revealed that some of the nursing home's board members were major campaign contributors to three County Board supervisors. Another board member's husband managed a local ambulance company which often transported the nursing home residents to medical visits.

Additional research found that the County Board supervisors in question repeatedly voted against funding for increased inspections, and that the ambulances were used unnecessarily when less expensive wheelchair and oxygen-equipped vans could have been used instead.

Meanwhile, the social workers talked to residents' family members and encouraged the formation of a family council. The group's discussions uncovered complaints of residents having difficulty getting assistance when they needed it from the staff, who frequently seemed overworked. At the family council's request, the federally-mandated nursing home Ombudsman made several 100-mile trips from her office to inspect the nursing home unannounced, and documented numerous quality of care violations. The family council members also complained to their state legislators, who in turn talked to state Health Department officials.

The Health Department issued multiple correction orders, but the Cleverly home dragged its feet on compliance. The family council, SEIU, Nurse Association and AFSCME went public with their charges against the home's board members.

Because of the slow compliance to the correction orders, and bolstered by the public complaints, the Attorney General's office felt compelled to subpoena administrative and financial records. These unearthed two new surprises: The first was that staffing levels had been below the required minimums, with falsified records submitted to the state. The second, a careful review of the books, showed that the administration had systematically siphoned off money from the residents' Medicaid personal needs allowance accounts.

Shortly thereafter, and 9 months after the two social workers began their campaign, the Cleverly facility was forced into receivership by the state, which continued to operate the facility up to standards, hired one of the social workers full-time, and sent the scaliwags who had managed the place to do community service for the local senior center. The state Health Department also set up a special toll-free hotline to receive complaints about the other Cleverly facilities located in the state.

One thing that social change practitioners should note is that campaigns such as the fictitious one above are very fluid and subject to change. Simply making an inventory of forces at a single point in time misses the point that Alinsky made: the action is in the reaction. One must be prepared to flow with the dynamic of change, altering targets and tactics when the timing is right. This is the artistry of organizing which is illusive and unpredictable.

Preface to Corporate Campaign

If social workers are going to increase their involvement with direct action organizing campaigns to achieve social justice, it is imperative to have a basic understanding of the role of organized labor in the development and refinement of these approaches. A wide variety of situations faced by social workers and others working on behalf of oppressed groups require extensive knowledge of the workings of corporate power, even if only to understand the limits of possible change. The long-standing bond between social work and the working class needs to translate into awareness of and support for union activity wherever it is found: in county welfare departments, among service workers, or among traditional trade unions. While organized union membership has declined dramatically during the past decade, the labor movement continues to be an important political force for decent wages and full employment, for family leave and maintenance of health coverage, for gender equity and racial and social justice, all issues central to the profession of social work.

This chapter will provide readers with several narrative descriptions of important components of the corporate campaign approach. Beginning with a definition of corporate campaign, and taking up the relevant historical background, it will illustrate the close connection in history between grassroots and union-initiated social change efforts. A detailed description of recent corporate campaigns and an introduction to some of the leading practitioners will clarify the nature of these campaigns. A description of essential skills and available training for corporate campains will indicate the specialized, yet accessible tools with which change practitioners may equip themselves. Illustrations of coalitions and community outreach between organized labor and grassroots/religious communities provide useful indications of how future grassroots practitioners may effectively tap the resources of organized labor in mutually enhancing social change work.

Traditional organizing strategies employed by organized labor have focused on control over the supply of labor. When disputes over contracts arise, workers for generations have relied upon tactics of withholding labor (as in strike actions), combined with mass demonstrations and pickets of the workplace. Pressure, in these situations is seen to be generated by the cumulative economic losses occurring from enforced production stoppage. Of course, the economic loss to workers and their families, as well as to the unions themselves, frequently meant that bargaining power went to the party with the greatest resources upon which to draw, generally the employing company.

But the accelerated changes of the workplace and the structure of productive enterprise and capital flow has changed these earlier practices beyond recognition. There is in fact a growing sophistication apparent in the use of innovative approaches to increasing the bargaining power of workers and their unions. The names for this genre of approaches are several: Corporate Campaign, Coordinated Corporate Campaign, and Comprehensive Campaign. For our purposes, we will refer to all in the genre as corporate campaign approaches, defined as: *the strategic use of available resources to produce continually escalating tactical pressure which exploits selected political and economic vulnerabilities of a targeted corporation in order to develop the power to achieve a desired outcome.*

There are seven components of this definition which warrant closer attention. (a) *The strategic use* refers to the overall plan of action and a statement of the desired goal. The strategy is not the same thing as the goal, but rather a statement which specifies a general technology to be employed; (b) *of available resources* refers to more than the traditional use of large amounts of money and implies the full deployment of the talents of membership, a non-passive approach; (c) *to produce continually escalating tactical pressure,* meaning a specified plan which describes varieties of tactical options at each juncture of a campaign; (d) *which exploits political vulnerabilities of the targeted corporation,* such as potentially embarassing connections of board members, political operatives and elected officials, etc.; (e) *and economic vulnerabilities of the targeted corporation,* including such things as withdrawal of labor pension funds from important corporate lenders, proxy battles, executive pay disclosure, etc.; (f) *to develop power,* defined as the ability to act, usually in the absence of voluntary consent of an opposing party; (g) *to achieve a desired outcome.*

The remainder of this chapter on corporate campaigns is intended to let students of social change know what is going on today in the arena of direct action and to make connections between local and global struggles for social justice.

Background to the Corporate Campaign

As early as 1936, after workers had won the right to organize with the passage of the National Labor Relations Act, there was a recognition by some that the strike option was one which could play directly into the hands of anti-union employers. But during the sit-down strike at 20 General Motors plans, the CIO general counsel, Lee Pressman, discovered, through an investigation of stockholders, that Judge Black, the issuer of an injunction ordering the CIO to cease and desist from the sit-down strike owned 3,365 shares of General Motors stock, valued at $219,000. This revelation and the fact that Michigan law prohibited a judge from sitting on cases in which there was a personal fiduciary interest, caused the injunction to be thrown out (Alinsky, 1949, p. 116).

John L. Lewis, the president of the CIO, which was seeking recognition for the UAW as the sole bargaining agent for workers, recognized that General Motors' strategy was to limit the bargaining authority to a plant-by-plant basis. This would permit GM to force a strike at one plant, while shifting production and even machinery to other plants where contracts remained in force. Lewis had seen such tactics and resolved that massive sit-down strikes would prevent the moving of equipment and prevent the hiring of replacement workers while the strike was in force.

Matching this shrewdness in blocking GM from continuing production was Lewis's subsequent move, a month later, as GM dealers reported declining sales across the country. The CIO began to call off strikes against certain industries, like aluminum and plate glass, to enable GM's competitors to boost their own production, thus placing even more pressure on GM by cutting into GM's market share (Alinsky, 1949, p. 117).

A Grassroots Organization Uses the "Corporate Campaign"

The year was 1966, the place was Rochester, New York. Alinsky and his Industrial Areas Foundation (IAF) were engaged with organizing the FIGHT campaign against another corporate giant, the Eastman Kodak Company. FIGHT was an "organization of organizations" in the now long tradition established by IAF. But FIGHT sought recognition from Kodak as the sole bargaining agent for the black ghetto in Rochester, in a civil rights campaign which demanded non-discrimination in hiring by the film giant.

The FIGHT campaign had progressed to the point at which a Kodak Vice President had reached an agreement with FIGHT which would have meant 600 jobs for black workers and a substantially reworked hiring process. But Kodak disregarded this agreement and it was now up to FIGHT to react.

It is at this point that Ed Chambers, current Executive Director of the IAF, Alinsky Institute, began to set the record straight. Although Alinsky implies, in *Rules for Radicals* that the "proxy tactic" was his own invention, Ed Chambers described in an interview that it was his idea, as lead organizer, to find out where Kodak was to hold its annual meeting and what FIGHT would have to do to gain entry. The story at this point is worth hearing in Chambers' own words:

> Interviewer (IN): What was your role in "FIGHT?"
> Chambers (CH): I organized it. I was the organizer of the
>   Black\Power organization. Never leaving
>   headquarters.
> IN: Where did the proxy idea come from?
> CH: It came out of the necessity somewhere between minister
>   Florence and I, when they tore up our agreement to hire 600 hard
>   core (unemployed) blacks in Eastman Kodak Company, and then
>   two days later they tore it up as a Christmas present December 22,
>   or 23, 1966. And on about January 6 we took out of the treasury,
>   out of the dues money of the black organization, enough money to
>   buy 10 shares and we went down to the downtown, a delegation of
>   pastors went down and bought 10 shares of Eastman Kodak
>   Company. Of course, that got into the afternoon newspaper.

(Grassroots Corporate Campaign, continued)

I gave Alinsky the idea, and Harmon (Richard Harmon, a former IAF organizer) was there when I gave it to Saul at Buffalo, because he was organizing the Buffalo organization. I met Alinsky in Buffalo and I said "Saul, I think I've figured out the next move." Then I laid the whole thing out for him. He immediately saw it. He did not think it up. He immediately saw it, though, and said "oh, great. Now as I go lecturing around I can bring this up and I can really rub the church's nose in it. `Stuff your sermons, give us your proxies.' Then for three months he went on the circuit and we ended up getting . . . about 750,000 shares of Eastman Kodak, plus, the important ones were the ten that the blacks had bought . . I told Saul to buy a share. IAF had to be a new share. I made IAF buy me a share so I could get in. And so ten blacks, Alinsky and myself trot down center stage at Eastman Kodak. We gave them a big black eye that day. That was, to my knowledge, the beginning of (the proxy tactic) . . . and we voted our 750,000 shares against their 10 million 800,000 shares. So, it was used as a tactic to draw attention to the (injustice) . . . . But, to my knowledge, that was, community-wise, one of the first and largest uses of that.

IN: Spontaneous?

CH: Yeah. My problem was I wanted to have a confrontation with Kodak. I couldn't figure out how to get it locally. Then it dawned on me, where is one place they've got to go public? Once a year by law they've got to have an annual meeting. Ah-h. Let's meet them there. We left the night before with I don't know, maybe 50 busses. About 1,000 blacks down there. And all the churches collapsed. Eight denominations lined up to receive four or five busses so the people could shit and pee, they'd been on a bus all day long, and get coffee. We didn't have money to feed them, particularly. We wanted the church to host them. These are church people from Rochester coming for an annual meeting. Every single denomination collapsed, called a week before, "I'm sorry" . . . . The Catholics collapsed, the Lutherans, the Methodists, bang, bang, bang.

(Grassroots Corporate Campaign, continued)

We were down to one church the night before, Missouri Synod Lutheran Church. That guy called us at 6 o'clock and said "I've got a real problem here. They're going to put it to a vote whether I stay or go if I host your coming tomorrow." And by then he knew that I was expecting him to take all the 900-1,000 people, that he had made special provisions to have men and women on duty, with extra coffee. I've got lot of people. I said, "well, we'll be here, be sure to call us after the meeting, don't you let us down, everyone else has collapsed. We have no place . . . ." 'They closed up downtown Flemington that day. The police, they had 3,000 or 4,000 National Guard on reserve for call-up. They figured there was going to be a riot. They had people posted on top, like the old western with the guy standing up with a gun. There were only two or three-story buildings in downtown Flemington. They had policemen up there with rifles. During the little march through town. This guy called back at 11 o'clock and says "it's OK, come ahead." "What was the vote, pastor?" "Six to five" (Chambers, 1990).

Alinsky subsequently outlined "The Genesis of Tactic Proxy" in his 1971 book *Rules for Radicals* and in some detail discussed the endless possibilities for proxy fights to be used to promote "people power" and social change. His book and the subsequent popularization of proxy solicitation as a tactic used by all manner of organizations and social movements, is a unique part of the history of direct action organizing. The incorporation of the proxy tactic, as well as the tactics of analyzing stock ownership used by the CIO, are important pieces of the development of the modern corporate campaign (Alinsky, 1971).

The Modern Corporate Campaign

Ray Rogers started the Corporate Campaign, Inc. in 1981 after several years of organizing with the federal ACTION program and work with political organizing consultants in Washington, D.C. Prior to these experiences, Rogers worked with the VISTA program in 1967 and was assigned to a rural community in Tennessee. Due to his activism and project work to promote social change in these impoverished areas, Rogers had the bureaucratic "reins" placed on his work. He then entered a period during which he could spend lots of time reading and writing, mostly about organizational subjects, which were a switch from his college studies of astronomy, physics, and sociology. He read Saul Alinsky and Gandhi and Martin Luther King, Jr. He was persuaded by Alinsky's position that one must understand how power works and how to get it and use it. He grew equally committed to nonviolence and combined his views on power and nonviolent tactics with the evolving conflict strategy he came to call the "corporate campaign."

Rogers's tactical skill development received a boost after leaving VISTA and working in Washington, D.C. for a political campaignist, Walter Clinton. Working for candidates he felt he could support, he set about to learn as much as possible of the political campaign technologies, particularly professional canvassing, direct mail, telephone banking and media applications. He also could begin to see how to conduct strategic research on specific targets, and recalls a particular teaching from these experiences: "Ray, there are only four ways you can communicate with anybody . . . and if you can't communicate, you may as well not even be there, right? Mail, telephone, personal visit, or the media." Any good organizer, in Rogers's view, must understand this principle: "If you can communicate with anybody, you can communicate with everybody," meaning that the message has to fit the audience and one needs to approach people with a sensitivity to their interests; not just the people with whom the organizer may share a common view of reality, but fitting a message to the reality which people unlike the organizer may perceive. Rogers recommends political organizing experience for anyone interested in the struggles for justice, if only to develop these skills (Rogers, 1990).

All of these experiences were soon to become invaluable to Rogers as he was hired by the Amalgamated Clothiers and Textile Workers Union (ACTWU) in 1979-80 to work on the boycott campaign against Farrah slacks (as part of the J.P. Stevens boycott) Rogers admits to a certain amount of ignorance at the time as to the legality of secondary boycotts, but he was sent to Birmingham, Alabama, with the mission to get Farrah slacks out of Birmingham stores. Rogers recalls the events:

> *I never put up a picket line, I never held a protest demonstration, I never did what the union did when they would put together labor leaders to meet with the store managers. I used what was called the domino theory. Essentially . . . I began a divide and conquer strategy . . . I did everything very quietly, I did it with no media whatsoever. I found out who the players were, I orchestrated the whole thing . . .in 10 weeks I had broken every retail outlet . . . And Willy Farrah who was quoted at the end of January . . . saying he would never . . . bargain with the union . . . two weeks later (he) contacted the union that someone in Birmingham was knocking the hell out of his business and he was ready to . . . arrive at a settlement. (Rogers, 1990)*

Rogers, in a 1984 interview, describes the specifics of his campaign:

> *First you must develop a strategy that you feel absolutely confident will succeed if you carry it out. In-depth research, a broad understanding of corporate financial-political power analysis and careful targeting are all part of this strategy development phase. (Rogers, 1984)*

This first phase is "conceptual," according to Rogers. The second phase, execution, is an "organizational" problem. Rogers defines his "divide and conquer" strategy in the same interview: "By creating dissension within the corporate ranks, your campaign can cause a multiplicity of internal pressures that disorganize and realign existing power relations" (Rogers, 1984).

These "activities seek to cause each institution and individual heavily tied in with a company's interests to exert its own considerable influence on the primary targeted company to recognize the rights and dignity of the people to bargain fairly" (Rogers, 1984).

The essence of the strategy described by Rogers and used by him and Corporate Campaign, Inc., is to go to the center of the banking, insurance, and investment structure which supports the targeted company and without whose support the company becomes vulnerable to economic collapse. In Rogers's view, the organizer of this type of campaign must be willing, "if necessary . . . to polarize the entire corporate and financial community away from a primary target company" (Rogers, 1990).

In a four-part series in late 1986, Rogers outlined the major rules of the corporate campaign: (a) Research the target, understanding its strengths and weaknesses, its links with other institutions; (b) build a broad community-labor coalition of groups opposed to the target's policies; (c) use all the power that workers have: their creativity and initiative, as well as pension funds, bank accounts, stock proxies, purchasing power, and votes; and (d) divide and conquer corporations by applying real economic and political pressure against the target's allies, such as key banks or insurance companies (Rogers, 1986).

Rogers recommends that the strike be the measure of last resort, and notes that a successful corporate campaign requires pressure to be applied from every angle even before the strike.

The cost of operating a corporate campaign can exceed $40,000 per month. Thus, it is not an inexpensive enterprise, and costs may be other than financial. A few illustrations from corporate campaigns undertaken by Rogers make the point.

In 1982, Rogers contracted with the International Association of Machinists to win a strike involving 1600 unionists against Brown and Sharpe Manufacturing Company of Rhode Island. The "first step was to study Brown and Sharp's proxy and annual report to find links between it and influential individuals and companies" (Rogers, 1986). He pinpointed a local bank and its chief executive who was also a director with Brown and Sharpe, and with U.S. Senator John H. Chafee who had family ties to Brown and Sharpe and another stock-holding bank. Using informational pickets, letter campaigns and the 30 percent unionized worker ratio in Rhode Island to his advantage, Rogers rebuilt the morale of the workers on the picket line. These workers had received little from the parent union except strike benefits and there was no apparent strategy to force the company to bargain in good faith (Rogers, 1986).

But the cost of the Rogers campaign was too much for the International, which refused to extend the contract beyond 3 months, even though the local strongly favored doing so and saw progress being made. The confrontational element of the campaign seemed to diminish the support of international union leaders to support the strike, which ultimately ended in a bitter, concessionary agreement which eliminated many seniority work rules and reduced wages.

The Case of George A. Hormel and Co., Austin, MN

Local P-9, an affiliate of the International United Food and Commercial Workers (UFCW), AFL-CIO, struck the George A. Hormel and Company of Austin, Minnesota in August, 1985, 11 months after unilateral, mid-contract wage cuts from $10.69 to $8.25 per hour were instituted (Hormel, 1987).

Hormel is the trade name on a variety of products, including Spam. The company had built a new pork processing plant in Austin, Minnesota in 1978, but only after workers agreed to substantial concessions, including a 7-year no-strike clause, 20% increase in production, worker loans to the company, and the elimination of 1,500 jobs at the new "hi-tech" plant, from 3,000 jobs to 1,500 jobs.

But Local P-9 of the UFCW had never been a docile union. In fact, the record indicates a fifty-year tradition of militancy and democracy. In 1985, the P-9 President Jim Guyette was certain he had the support of the majority of members and the necessary strength to take on the company which refused to negotiate the newly imposed concessions, stating that the original contract did not prohibit wage givebacks to make the company competitive. Despite the efforts of federal mediators, neither Hormel nor Local P-9 could or would alter their respective positions (Hormel, 1987).

After the wage cuts were imposed and initial efforts failed, Local P-9 hired Ray Rogers to organize a "Corporate Campaign" against Hormel. Rogers did his homework, targeting the First Bank System as major corporate sponsors of Hormel, mobilizing significant support from other unions and developing strategies within the Austin community to ensure preparedness for an effective and if necessary long strike. But unlike traditional strikes, striking Hormel workers would not just walk picket lines. After the strike was called, workers effectively "socialized" the conflict using a broad variety of economic, political and nonviolent pressure tactics including the following: initiating a nationwide boycott of Hormel products; letter writing campaigns by spouses of striking workers, secondary picketing of First Bank System and encouraging roving pickets at other Hormel plants (both roving pickets and actions at First Bank System by union members were later ruled illegal by courts); local picketing and leafleting was picked up by unions throughout Minnesota and grocery chains were covered frequently; outside

138

(Hormel continued)

(non-Minnesota) unions were directly solicited for financial and political assistance and an "adopt a P-9 family" strategy was initiated before the Christmas holidays. During the first 6 months of the strike, the plant remained idled and pickets stopped all traffic into the plant. The initial strategy of building pressure on the system in order to equalize power relationships and increase leverage seemed to be working. But other events closed the circle around P9 more tightly even as the grassroots support seemed to broaden.

- August 16, 1985 -- UFCW International President William Wynn calls P-9 financially "bankrupt" just 24 hours before the planned strike.
- October 4, 1985 -- Wynn attacks P-9 and tells other affiliates to be careful about supporting P-9. In December he asks them to disregard P-9's urgent calls for help.
- January 16, 1986 -- Hormel announces it will reopen with replacement workers and UFCW President Wynn accuses P-9 leadership (and Ray Rogers) of promoting "mass suicide".
- January, 1986 -- Local P-9 workers blockade plant entrance; hold public rally attended by thousands of supporters who travel to Austin, MN; Minnesota Governor Rudy Perpich calls up the National Guard to ensure safe conduct into the plant by scabs. The Guard stays two weeks. Eight hundred P-9 workers cross the picket lines to save their jobs.
- February 20, 1986 -- International UFCW President Wynn accuses P-9 leadership of duping members, comparing them with Nazis.
- March 14, 1986 -- Wynn returns a $10,000 check intended for P-9 Union; International UFCW Executive Board orders P-9 to end its strike and cuts off all strike benefits. Subsequently bills P-9 $1.3 million to pay for strike benefits.
- April 1986 -- UFCW International lawyers get federal judge to force P-9 into trusteeship; subsequently UFCW agents evict P-9 from the union hall, closing soup kitchen and food shelf.
- September 1986 -- UCFW Trustee signs contract with Hormel "providing one cent an hour more in 1990 than workers were making in 1979." Replacement workers and former unionists are covered; 850 striking workers not included in settlement. Striking workers are subsequently thrown out of new P-9 union (Hormel, 1987).

Corporate Campaign, Inc.(CCI) has experienced some setbacks to be sure, but they have had successes and, for better or worse, a spate of imitators. In 1993,

CCI continues to work successfully with a number of unions, including the United Paperworkers International.

Ray Rogers remains convinced of the correctness of the corporate strategy: *Time and again, union leaders enter negotiations armed with statistics on wage and benefit trends, but without any real knowledge or comprehensive analysis of the people, interests, and institutions with whom they are in effect dealing. Therefore, they never consider the fundamental importance of carefully targeting individuals, institutions, and geographical areas for campaign activities aimed at forcefully challenging the true power brokers behind a company's anti-union stand. (Rogers, 1986)*

The United Brotherhood of Carpenters and Joiners of America, (AFL-CIO)

We will look at one union shop, the United Brotherhood of Carpenters and Joiners of America, (AFL-CIO), which does have a well-developed corporate campaign training program, operated out of the Special Programs Department, directed by an attorney, Ed Durkin. Durkin acknowledges that professional organizers who are employed within organized labor tend to be the lowest paid and most dispensible employees. The general approach to labor organizers is to bring in recruits and to work them until they burn out, usually within a few years. There is one encouraging development which promises to improve the situation and opportunities for younger people to take jobs as organizers. This is the new AFL-CIO-sponsored Organizing Institute, which has developed paid internships for prospective organizers in organizing campaigns throughout the United States..

The Special Programs Department was begun in 1982 as a full-service department to respond to the growing needs for comprehensive campaigns in the construction and industrial unions serviced by the Brotherhood of Carpenters and Joiners. Durkin lends a historical perspective to the question of labelling a campaign "corporate, coordinated or comprehensive." The corporate dimension of a campaign, perhaps initially associated with Ray Rogers' work on the J.P. Stevens struggl and particularly, his focus on the banking and insurance linkages, was really only one part of a much broader campaign that included a boycott and much traditional labor tactical work. Durkin finds these different categories interrelated, with choices from one effecting or contradicting choices from others. In Durkin's view:

> . . . *if you try to put a word to describe the tactics, they're not corporate, it's comprehensive. That's what we teach, that's what we preach . . . there's somebody out there in the community giving us a problem, we've got to generate pressure, . . . organizing is about power. So when we have the target, we have to look at how are we going to get that target in the right frame of mind to see that it's better to work with us than against us. . . in order to get them to that point, you can't just file unfair labor practice charges because they have labor lawyers for it, and they can beat that or prevent those charges from every being filed . . . . We have to empower ourselves . . . . In the absence of manpower power (control over the supply of labor, which even in highly organized areas rarely exceeds 15%) . . . we have to look at other ways. Part of that is looking at what the target's vulnerabilities are and then initiating tactics that respond to that. (Durkin, 1990)*

There is a growing recognition in many sectors of organized labor that "corporate" campaigns, (implying the narrower definition of the capital and financing elements of a campaign) may have been oversold "as being somehow magical." This consensus has emerged, and has led to the formation of a Coordinated Campaign Committee (CCC) at the centralized Industrial Union Department (IUD) (the Carpenter's Union is one of the 58 unions affiliated with the IUD). The CCC has as its main purpose to show other unions what can be done with campaigns and particularly to encourage unions (including at the statewide and local levels) to identify and train specific people as resources for such campaigns. A part of this consensus stems from a sentiment that this kind of organizing cannot be done "for" unions from outside the structure of labor. It is necessary to develop the capability of unions from within and to be in a position to conduct "preconditioning activities" before problems develop into crises. It is too often at the crisis point where outside providers are brought in at substantial financial cost and considerable disillusionment. As Durkin states: "I think more unions are coming to a realization that we need to develop the internal capabilities, and we need to extend those capabilities to our field people . . . . We need an army of people because there are so many localized disputes" (Durkin, 1990).

The Special Programs Department has developed an elaborate high quality publication called *New Tools for the Trades*, a handbook of their organizing approach which includes the basic concepts and detailed appendices which make the research and analysis of targets downright systematic.

Target, Research, Analyze, Develop, and Execute a Strategy (TRADES) defines the method and its sequence. The point is made that too often unions think only about the immediate source of a problem, a specific contractor, as the target. As we have seen already with Corporate Campaign, Inc., there are wide arrays of "construction users, banks and other project financiers, general contractors, subcontractors, and construction managers, . . . industry market segments," all of whom have potential as targets. The choice of one or a combination of these will depend upon such factors as the financial and political resources of the union, the degree of union membership participation and overall strength, and the wages/benefits differentials in the geographic area. Above all, a union must be clear about its long-term commitment to organizing (*New Tools for the Trades,* 1987).

At the level of research, three questions will assist the formulation of a data base: "Who are the people, companies, banks, partnerships, etc., that you need to develop information on? What is it that you need to find out about the particular target, and where might you find the information?" (*New Tools for the Trades,* 1987).

Detailed corporate research can be quite tedious and time consuming, thus requiring advance commitment to following through with the process, once begun. The Special Programs Department has identified four levels of corporate research, including corporate structure and personal financial data, corporate interlocks and political/governmental connections. Any given dimension of research is guided by the principle of "strategic" importance. Does the research meet the criterion of clear utility for the overall plan of the campaign?

Analysis of internal information may help to shape this strategy or game plan, guiding one to an understanding of the need to expand or diminish the size of the field, and will serve as a vital feedback loop to make visible the fit of data to strategy, which depends upon the power and resources which can be brought to bear on a selected component of the plan.

The last stage, developing and executing a strategy, requires the consideration of the whole range of tactics for each component of the campaign;

their timing, intensity, duration, resource requirements, and above all, the relationship of each tactic to the overall strategy and goal. The Special Programs Department suggests a variety of strategy options for each of four types of organizing target, which are illustrative of the choices facing any campaign organizer. They list options for a specific construction project (which could as easily be a single store or service provider), such as choosing to pressure each participant; or the owner (director or board member) at job and off-job sites; or conducting a comprehensive campaign from the "top down" (its principal sponsors and supporters) or "bottom-up" (including constituency or client base, if a human service operation) (*New Tools for the Trades*, 1987, pp. 1-12).

Similar strategy options might be developed for other levels of a campaign, including or excluding elements which are within or outside the power/resource capability of the organizing entity.

Coalition Building and Community Outreach

Without the control over the supply of labor to some appreciable degree, unions are having to rethink how they relate to the larger community. They simply cannot rely upon their traditional approaches to prevail in today's disputes.

> *We've got to get out the community. We've got to let the community see that fair construction standards are important. It's important to the tax base, . . . to the quality of life, employing local construction workers as opposed to letting contractors bring workers from out of state. (Durkin, 1990)*

Issues of hiring of local workers can even be raised at the regulatory level; in one Texas community, a construction project has received tax-abatements based on the use of in-state workers. In another state, union members will reach out to the business community, transforming a labor problem of hiring nonunion workers at substandard wages without health benefits, into a community problem of what's going to happen when your customers have less money to spend and your hospitals are paying for the care of uninsured workers? Redefining and coalescing with community interests and participation more broadly in the civic life of the community improves the wages and the influence of unions within specific communities.

Unions like the United Mine Workers (UMW) made very effective use of community outreach during its 1990 strike against the Pittston Coal Company.

Campaign directors for the UMW hired an IAF-trained community organizer from Connecticut, Pat Speer, to mobilize the religious community in nearby Greenwich CT, the corporate headquarters of Pittston. Taking out full-page ads in the Greenwich newspaper, over 100 religious leaders addressed an open letter to Pittston management, excoriating the unfair labor practices (elimination of medical benefits for thousands of retired miners) and calling for good-faith bargaining. Later, 80 miners from the coal fields of Virginia joined 350 people at a rally in Greenwich, carrying 269 crosses with names of miners who died from accidents and black lung disease, in a town unaccustomed to burly, fatigue-clad men picketing on their streets. Such tactics, along with the high pressure, non-violent civil disobedience and corporate tactics, ultimately forced the then-Secretary of Labor Elizabeth Dole, to mediate the dispute, which ultimately ended in a settlement favorable to the union (Coats, 1989).

Labor recognizes today, as never before, that it has much to offer by way of experience, resources and commitment to other community organizations. Proxy solicitation and the whole topic of financial analysis are two areas where unions can make a great contribution to other justice struggles. The pension funds of international unions are huge, some ranging from $12 billion in over 2,000 separate funds across the country, in the case of the Brotherhood of Carpenters and Joiners (AFL-CIO) to over $60 billion for the largest public employees union, California Public Employees Retirement System (CAL-PERS). A working knowledge of these financial relationships and a nurturing of coalitions for social justice may yield labor/community partnerships on housing, environmental, and redevelopment issues all over the country. Pressure may be uniquely applied to financial institutions to gain compliance with an agenda of justice.

More frequent use of the proxy tactic is also possible. One union recently gave enough proxy representation to a citizens' group in Colorado concerned with utility and environment questions, to get them on the agenda for a shareholders' meeting of a company with whom the union just happened to be having labor problems. Another union extended proxy rights to the Greenpeace environmental group, allowing them to gain entrance to an International Paper Company shareholders' meeting and utilize more outlandish tactics to pressure the company than the union might otherwise prefer to use itself.

Such marriages of convenience are but one of the arrangements which have been and of necessity will continue to be discovered and used to address issues of fairness and social change. The corporate/coordinated/comprehensive campaign approach is not a magical wand, but rather a powerful instrument which socializes conflict in a way which broadens its scope and the nature of the participation. Workers now will be recognized for more than simply their productive labor. They will be viewed as public citizens with critical awareness of the nature of community oppression and the viability of options to address the struggles of the future, in solidarity with and in partnership with ever-widening circles of organized resistance.

Issue Coalition Approach

Clearly, with such well-publicized and bitter campaigns as those with Eastern Airlines and its then-president, Frank Lorenzo, the hated "Darth Vader" of the airline industry, labor will receive the sympathy and support of a broad coalition of organizations from churches, political operators, and many affiliated unions. But when the memory of the campaign fades, there is no permanent coalitional structure which might serve to preempt some problems or work collectively in a community to develop strategies for social change. Now, the Industrial Union Department (CIO) does have such organization, called "Jobs with Justice," which is separate from the official structure and which does have the participation of some 20 affiliate unions. It acts as an alliance of forces not just on labor campaigns, but also on campaigns for health care, decent housing, issues of homelessness, and the like.

Labor leaders recognize the deteriorating union membership and increased decertification of existing unions is in some measure linked to the poor credibility and self-serving image which unions project to the public. In addition to wide-scale organizing within labor, there must be a concentrated effort to re-establish union labor throughout the life of every community. Jobs for Justice is a helpful beginning.

Outside Contracting

One of important features of the Industrial Union Department (IUD)(CIO) coordinated campaigns is their consistent use of selected contractors for specialized services which cannot be provided by their own staff. Public relations/media and research are two such areas where contract services are provided. During the lengthy strike against Greyhound Bus Lines, the IUD needed analysis of the company almost overnight. The union's research department usually handles collective bargaining research, which is different from the kind of power analysis required in a corporate type campaign. The Midwest Center for Labor Research in Chicago, directed by Greg Leroy, was able to conduct a very rapid and incisive analysis of the debt carried by Greyhound and they provided IUD a description of the three different debt instruments of the creditors. Another company, Hogan and Denton of Washington, DC, and Santa Fe, New Mexico, then looked in more detail at the loan agreements levels of financial maintenance required under the Department of Transportation regulations. IUD was then able to develop a sophisticated "probability of default" which it could then use strategically with Greyhound's creditors, communicating with the idea that the creditors might then put pressure on Greyhound to settle the labor dispute. Greyhound did subsequently file for bankruptcy (Uehlein, 1990).

Such a specialized research service can be invaluable to the interests of workers; similar research centers have worked with direct action organizing projects, such as the bank redlining campaigns and the family farming campaigns. Social change practitioners will do well to learn about the requirements of such research, clearly one of the useful contributions which professionals may make to grassroots direct action and transformative work.

One final set of tactical considerations will be of use to direct action social change practitioners. These are called workplace tactics, and they reveal the growing dilemma of unions (as well as unorganized employees), which is the possibility of prolonged loss of income from striking or locked out workers.

Operating as part of an overall strategy to maintain income to employees and avoid a strike, many employee groups are getting on the front end of organizing what in many respects resembles the study circle methodology. In this instance, however, the IUD refers to a "workplace organizing committee" which seeks to educate, involve, interest, and empower rank and file members, and to do these things before there is a situation requiring action (*The Inside Game: Winning With Workplace Strategies*). There are many elements of this approach which imply the broadening of leadership and motivation of rank and file (or line staff, in the case of service/professional organizations). But unions have a long way to go to dissolve their fascination with the accoutrements of position and power to which they have fallen prey, an idolatry of management, if you will. But at least there appears to be recognition of a need to trust the rank and file to make decisions often left to the union hierarchy. One IUD publication suggests conducting focus groups and one-on-one interviews to establish rapport with workers and to develop a specific list of problems and priorities, and again, to reinforce the impression that opinions and knowledge of workers are important. A variety of subcommittees may be set up to monitor workplace conditions and to assemble information which may be vital to getting a campaign up and running during contract bargaining or when a strike or lockout is unavoidable. Such advance work might also diminish the increasing number of decertifications of unions that have taken place in recent years (*New Tactics*, 1985).

The pressures against unions from short-term profit-minded managers in many firms has taken many forms. The movement of capital and manufacturing industries to second and third world countries, the technological revolution and increased competition from other countries, have shaped much of the work environment. The kind of tactics employed against the CIO, against the airline and bus unions, and against employees wishing to organize in the country represent a second level of oppression. Many corporations hire consultants to develop strategies for breaking up existing bargaining units. The tactics employed include: claiming financial distress loudly and publicly, well before contract bargaining, then making concessionary demands at the start of bargaining; engaging in superficial bargaining without an intention of resolving differences through compromise, with the idea of declaring an "impasse," which allows companies to legally make a "last, best and final offer," before forcing unions to resort to a strike or to accept concessions; developing elaborate public relations gimmicks and workplace "perks" such as an annual party picnic, to foster the impression of management as "good guy" or company as "family," to cover up the wage differential or fringe benefit deficit from comparably placed unionized firms or to set up workers for decertification campaigns.

The corporate campaign fights power with power and is a highly confrontative strategy which personalizes targets and polarizes communities. Its effectiveness is mixed, but no company leaves a campaign unscathed. It would appear to have its strength in the solidarity it engenders in the workers. Its weakness may be that it demands total commitment and energy from all involved. The costs are high.

The principal disadvantages to the corporate campaign practitioner who chooses to operate outside of the union, as an independent entrepreneur, are readily apparent from the review of Corporate Campaign, Inc.'s work. The instability of the employment relationship between Rogers and the unions which utilize his specialized services are but a surface problem when compared with aftermath of an intraunion battle between a local and its international. The autonomy of the outside operator, however, does have much to say for it. There is a definite status quo bias within the huge institutional labor organizations, which makes creativity and innovation a scarce commodity. When he works on a campaign, Rogers surely trains large numbers of people to carry out their own campaign. There is an empowerment of floor level workers, who gain confidence and skills to take on directly the employers and structures which oppose them. But Rogers and Corporate Campaign, Inc. cannot systematically train employees over a long period of time, preparing in advance for campaigns which may take place. If he were to create a training center, it surely would be quite successful. But in its absence, we may usefully look to some of the unions for examples of ongoing training programs and other models of the corporate type of campaign.

Classroom Exercises and Skill Development Scenario--
Corporate Campaign

How many times have you passed by that abandoned building, trash-strewn vacant lot, or dilapidated housing for low-income or disabled people? You know something should be done but perhaps think there is nothing you can do to the fat cat who owns the place. Well, let's get busy and do a little digging to see what we can uncover about the owner(s). Remember the Carpenter's Union guidelines: Target, Research, Analyze, Develop and Execute a Strategy.

(Small group project) You and several classmates are about to embark on a social
    justice version of a treasure hunt!
        a. Target a property in your town which would be interesting to learn
        about or consult with one of your local unions which may be

interested in doing research on a particular corporate employer. You can make your action research more relevant in this way.

b. Make a sketch of the property, including adjacent properties, street names and numbers, and commercial names listed on signs. Assume you cannot find out from local residents or tenants the name of the person who owns the property. All you have is your sketch and address.

c. Call the county tax assessor's office or the recorder of deeds and find out if they will give you over the telephone the name of the taxpayer for the property in question. If the tax assessor requires the legal description of the property, send a delegation to that office to examine an official property map containing the plot in question, locate the property on the map, and request the name of the taxpayer, who usually is the owner. The tax assessor's office may also make available a list of properties where taxes are delinquent. This information will be useful to publicly humiliate the target if they in arrears on taxes.

d. When you obtain the name, you can then visit the office of the Recorder of Deeds. Look for the grantee/grantor (buyer/seller) index. First look at the current year's grantee index, and go back year by year until you find the property owner's name. The index will also refer to a book and page number which refer to deed books found in the Recorder (Registry) of Deeds office.

e. Proceed to the deed books and examine the deed and other pages which apply to that property of interest. The deed may have on it or attached to it the name of the mortgage lender, which will be useful information to have when you get to the strategy stage (or you may pay to have a copy of the deed made for you).

f. Just for the fun of it, send someone to the county, state, and federal district courts to see if your property owner (or others listed on the deed or associated with the company) has any criminal indictments on record. This can be done by looking at the plaintiff/defendant index (alphabetical). You may learn of financial problems or law suits against the individual or company. Probate and divorce records may also yield information about the assets of the person.

g. For a small fee, or with the help of a friendly realtor, obtain a listing of other properties in the county owned by the same person. Frequently, localities will have Real Estate Information Services (REDI) which offer "abstracting" services. (Check to see if the spouse of the person has a different last name and is "hiding" other assets this way.)

h. Now you can retreat to the quietude of your university library reference room and focus on the personal and family background of this property owner. Begin by checking the telephone directory for name(s), addresses, phone numbers. Look at a "criss-cross" alphabetical address listing (or borrow one from a political campaign office or advertising agency). Examine the various "Who's Who" books for biographical information, check the indexes of your local newspaper for stories about the person of their family; look at the Social Register or Blue Book for your area, which gives information on well-heeled folk. Birth, death, marriage and divorce records can also be helpful, and for 35¢ a piece, you can obtain documents from the Superintendent of Documents, G.P.O., Washington, DC 20402: "Where to Write for Births and Deaths, Marriage and Divorce Records". The Secretary of State for your state also maintains a *corporate filing guide, articles of incorporation, and annual reports* for each corporation operating in your state, including nonprofit social welfare and human service organizations (excluding governmental entities). These are all excellent sources of information about directorates and finances of companies and are just a few of the obtainable materials from these offices.

i. Having done your best to collect this information, sit down as a group and sort through it. Devise a plan which utilizes some of this information to go after the person's vulnerabilities. List some possible tactics which you might exercise to expand the conflict and "bring it to their front door" (or place of business, etc.).

This exercise is of course based upon just a few of the huge number of resources available to the corporate researcher or even to a grassroots organization which regularly engages in community campaigns. Listed below are a few other research handbooks and source materials which any social change practitioner should have ready access to:

Villarejo, Donald. *Research for action: A guidebook to public records investigation for community activists.* California Institute for Rural Studies, Box 530, Davis, CA 95616.

Greever, Barry. *Tactical investigations for peoples' struggles.* Train Institute, 10129 Thornwood Road, Kensington, MD 20895.

Katz, Jim. *Action research.* Institute for Social Justice, New Orleans, LA.

Open the books: How to research a corporation, and *research package: Open up the books,* and *People before property,* all from Midwest Academy, 600 W. Fullerton, Chicago, IL 60614.

Also see previously cited materials from the Industrial Union Department (AFL-CIO), 815 16th Street N.W., Washington, DC 20006; as well as from the United Brotherhood of Carpenters and Joiners of America, AFL-CIO, Special Programs Department, Washington, DC.

Other Reference Sources Available in Libraries:

Directory of Corporate Affiliations
Dunn and Bradstreet's Middle Market Directory
Dunn and Bradstreet's Million Dollar Directory
Moody's Industrial Manual
Standard and Poor's corporation descriptions
Who's Who directories

CHAPTER 6

Transformative Social Change Strategies

*Saul (Alinsky) and I differed because my position was that if I had to
make a choice between achieving an objective and utilizing
the struggle to develop and radicalize people, my
choice would be to let the goal go and
develop the people. (Myles Horton)*

The introduction to this book listed five elements which are common to all of the transformative methods that will be reviewed in this chapter. It is useful to list them again: a small-group orientation; an emphasis on self-directed (non-hierarchical) learning; an emphasis on interpersonal bonds; an analysis linking personal oppression to societal/structural oppression; and a fully collective approach to group decision making and social action. We also said the heart of transformative strategies is adherence to an "adult model" of learning which adheres to democratic principles and maximizes participation by all members.

Social change practitioners will readily see the advantages and disadvantages of each method which will be reviewed. One method emphasizes preselected discussion groups which meet around a content area, another takes up the general topic of women's oppression, and yet another begins as a religiously oriented support group, and so on. Each method is adaptable to a variety of situations and contexts, one to the workplace, another to people's homes.

152

Whatever the setting or situation, no two groups will be the same, even when using the same method. Also, everybody's experience as a participant will be unique, so there is no point in thinking about these methods as you do an ordinary classroom where all aspire to some common objective which a teacher may think can be measured. Take what you will from this chapter and leave the remainder behind.

What is Social Transformation?

The principal failure of traditional social change practice lies in the political philosophy of liberalism which undergirds the system of government, defines the character of its institutions, and narrowly limits participation in the change process. Many types of direct-action social change practice fail, primarily due to the absence of "an encompassing integrative political ideology" and "the decisive theoretical and strategic limits of the new populism" which "contains no critical or transformative approach to power relations, or to domination" (Friedmann, 1987, p. 410). Transformative social change practice, on the other hand, both rejects the central notions of liberalism and embraces an explicitly ideological critique of reality. It is a viable oppositional strategy which finds its essential values in "the reciprocity of awareness . . . among two or more persons" (Wolf, 1968, p. 184). Rather than promoting a society of competing private values, transformative social change promotes "creation of a unified social will" (Tillich, 1977, p. 148) based upon three sets of reciprocal values which are the bases for community, taken from Wolf (1968, pp. 189-192):

1.   "The social values of "Affective Community," referring to "reciprocal consciousness of a shared culture . . . the mutual awareness on the part of each that there are others sharing that culture";

2.   The social values of "Productive Community," referring to the four satisfactions of productive labor described by Marx as coming "from the object itself (felt needs), enjoyment of the laboring itself, the delight of coming to be oneself, and coming to know who one is, . . . and coming to know one another through cooperation in collective productive activity";

3.   The social values of "Rational Community," referring to those achieved through direct participation -- dialogue and common action -- or "a reciprocity of consciousness among morally and politically equal rational

agents who freely come together . . . for the purpose of concerting their wills."

Transformative practice (or praxis) requires this careful consideration of intention and the consciousness of being in relationship, precluding the treatment of other as "object" or "instrument" to the achievement of one's personal satisfaction. Here we can see the implication for the "exchange" or "business" approach, for instance between employees and employers, where there may be, explicit or implicit, the quality of "extracting" work from the "worker" as an object or instrument in the production of surplus value. As Dussel states:

> *Praxis is the experience of constructing the other as person, as end of my action and not as means. We are dealing with a relationship of infinite respect. (Dussell, English Translation, 1988, p.9)*

Transformative social change practice begins with this difficult process of extracting ourselves first, and only then others, from the various forms of systematic oppression, including many destructive aspects of mass culture.

The following pages, describing several approaches to uplifting individual consciousness in the context of face-to-face community, are but a few examples from an abundant tradition of democratic, nonviolent resistance to the forces of oppression. It is useful to keep in mind the following guidelines for the utilization of the transformative method:

1. People and social groups are at different stages in the development of a repertoire of political behavior;
2. Social change practitioners and organizers need to be cognizant of these stages and make an assessment of populations before initiating a particular strategy;
3. There are definite (general) consequences for selecting a direct action over a transformative strategy;
4. Transformative strategy and method tends to require adherence to a long-term process, demanding carefully developed, consistent, small social groupings, which precludes an early entry into social action;
5. For the most marginalized people in U.S. society, the very poor and least educated, among whom are disproportionately people of color, the

transformative approaches appear especially well-suited. Used in concert with traditional methods of political organization, transformative methods may be highly useful in coming years.

Study Circles

- A group of Latino/Latina human service professionals, frustrated about the poor quality and insufficiency of culturally appropriate mental health services in a rural county, meet several times to talk about their problems. The lack of Spanish-speaking mental health professionals severely limits access to services by the large monolingual Spanish-speaking population. The initial impulse of the group was to use their own "influence and prestige" as professionals to initiate bureaucratic responses to services defined by them as professionals. But one group member (who was also an MSW student who had read Friere's *Pedagogy of the Oppressed,* and *Study Circles),* skillfully introduced the study circle methodology. They decided to engage in a study circle approach to uncover the nature of the oppressive structures as well to carefully expand their core group to include other nonprofessionals, for the purpose of developing indigenous leadership in the larger county Latino/Latina population. It would have been more convenient (although not necessarily more effective) for the group to leverage their expertise and reputations to get some modest program revisions. But this "traditional" solution would not contribute to the empowerment of the monolingual population, and the professionals would only reinforce their "separateness" from their own cultural reference group.

- Another graduate student, one of the first Hmong graduates of a social work master's program, used a similar, nondirective, gradual approach when introducing study circle methodology to a group of Hmong businessmen initially interested in some fairly narrow economic development goals. The graduate student, fully aware of the cultural and gender biases within Hmong society, was able to shift the focus of the agenda to include systematic outreach to the larger Hmong community, including the possibility of expanding the core group to include women in business.

• A third graduate student participated in a post-Iraq War forum in a rural foothills community. While careful not to exert undue influence over the group process, in fact reinforcing the democratic process of the group, the student began to use a one-on-one interview process to get at the deeper self-interests of people who seemed unable to translate the post-war events to their everyday situations. After several weeks, all participants agreed to establish a food coop and newsletter as vehicles for solidifying community and continuing to dialogue about issues of importance in their growing community. Two years later the coop thrives.

A Brief History of Study Circles

Even with the long tradition of volunteerism in the United States, it would stretch the imagination to find 60% percent of our working-age population participating in an array of small group study without the usual financial incentives, status rewards, or direct service functions. But this is precisely the lived experience of contemporary Sweden, which in fact, modestly reports 2.9 million Swedes participating (and voluntary is the key word) in 325,000 study circles (Oliver, 1987, p. 24). Indeed, this rather straightforward adult education methodology is considered the foundation stone of modern democracy in Sweden.

Despite their rather recent rediscovery, the use of study circles in the U.S. actually pre-dates their use in Sweden, beginning with the Chautauqua Literary and Scientific Circle of New York, begun during the 1870s. "By 1915, the CLSC claimed seven hundred enrollees and fifteen thousand study circles, using Chautauqua texts and other publications in these colleges for one's home" (Oliver, 1987, p. 2).

Even earlier than this, Benjamin Franklin and Samuel Adams had experimented with civic education, called *juntos* by Franklin, and Committees of Correspondence by Adams. From the Lyceum Movement of the 1820s and 1830s, to the CLSC's of the 1870s, through Jane Addams's citizenship centers, the League of Women Voters, a long list of foundation and university-sponsored issue and readings-based forums, and through documented case studies of the National Issues Forum (NIF) of the Domestic Policy Association (1982) and the International Union (IU) of Bricklayers and Allied Craftsmen (BAC) (1986),

Oliver's book impressively develops the case for the systematic approach to building citizenship and expanding political participation (Oliver, 1987, pp. 90-129).

Principal Guidelines for Study Circles

Numerous assessments of the Swedish Study Circle Movement have been conducted. It is instructive to briefly review their experiences and conclusions.

One can derive a good sense of how to view the model from the Swedish perspective by considering the definition of adult education offered by an influential educator in Sweden who defines adult education: "as a living, activist process that related knowledge to action and social change, to development and creativity, and to social intercourse and collective development" (Oliver, 1987, pp. 22-23).

A short list of the important study circle principles includes:

- Equality and democracy among circle participants;
- Liberation of member's inherent capabilities and innate resource;
- Cooperation and companionship;
- Study and liberty, and member self-determination;
- Continuity and planning;
- Active member participation;
- Use of printed study materials (to supplement circle conversations) (Oliver,1987, p. 23).

Participation in these study circles is completely voluntary and there are no formal teachers. There are study circle leaders, but no special qualifications are needed and the leader is usually chosen or elected from among the group of participants. The leader performs coordinative tasks, pulling together the study plan agreed upon by the group, and facilitating group meetings to ensure fair and complete participation (Oliver, 1987, p. 64).

The Swedish system is very large, with each of 10 national associations providing the integration for the 350,000 study circles. These 10 associations receive a total national subsidy approaching $113 million annually, with nearly one third of this going to the two largest associations, The Workers' Educational Association (ABF) and the Social Democratic Party (SAP). One third of ABF's study circles take place in the workplace, (with 15 % of trade union members participating annually). Trade unions use the services of some 60,000 paid study circle organizers who frequently recruit workers to circles during hours of work. According to Oliver, the principal tasks of study circle organizers are to "recruit circle members, help develop study circle plans, identify and train leaders, obtain materials, and follow-up on logistical matters."

It is important to recognize that Swedish study circle democracy is very highly evolved, largely as a result of significant demographic homogeneity, small size, and political unity within the country. Ninety-five percent of eligible Swedes vote in elections. Trade unions and the Social Democratic Party used study circles methodology earlier in the century, largely due to dissatisfaction with the "formal educational system." Although much of the ABF's circle discussion content revolves around workplace issues, organizers have tried to broaden the appeal to attract participants from the general public. There is still in-depth worker education, termed "crisis education," which is used when economic conditions threaten the future operation of a factory. In fact, 10% of study circles do have a local focus, and united action is not uncommon. Although Sweden's circles have generally moved more broadly into cultural affairs, language, and international discussion and learning, politics and community life are issues taken up by a third of all study circles in Sweden each year.

The rosy picture is not without problems, and the usual demographic characteristics of gender, race, ethnicity, class, and geography still dictate much of the participation patterns even in Sweden. And there remains a tension in Sweden over the question of the degree of government involvement in study circles, with one camp preferring grassroots control, another wishing to stay with government control.

But the success in Sweden seems undeniable, with three central elements of the process being: well-trained study circle leaders, a similarity of interests and objectives for the appointed/elected study circle leader, and the individual circle participants, and a clear relationship of the content ideas and concepts (or skills) with the real circumstances of day-to-day life for participants.

What may be of greatest significance for the application of this study circle methodology to the United States context is the dual role it can play in the process of developing critical consciousness among a broad base of the population, while also moving people to self-initiated direct action for social change. A study of hospital workers engaged in study circles showed that after 4 years of operation, the percentage of participants interested in discussing worker rights, political organizing, and health and safety issues increased from 25% to 50% (Oliver, 1987, pp. 13,67). Four years may seem an interminable amount of time to some direct action practitioners, but it is not that far from the experience of congregation-based projects which may require up to 2 years just to form a sponsoring committee.

Thus, self-directed learning which seeks to bring people to their own power and capability, must utilize a longer range vision and methodologies which have proven successful in engaging masses of people in a course of study which can move people in this direction.

Other Illustrations from the United States

Great diversity and creativity have been applied to the adaptation of the study circle methodology. One of the more successful places of application has been in Minnesota. With the assistance of the Study Circle Resource Center (SCRC), which does have small seed grants available to people wanting to begin a local group and larger grants for undertaking statewide networks, a small number of people active with the National Issues Forum (NIF) expanded their work and started the Minnesota Study Circle Network in 1988. According to the Fall 1991 newsletter of the SCRC, Minnesota now has a growing number and variety of applications, including:

- Sponsoring a statewide forum on study circle democracy, in which Swedish adult educators participated;
- Implemented "A People Informed," which engaged 1000 citizens in study circle fashion to propose resolutions for the Governor to use in discussions with the White House Conference on Library and Information Services; and
- Adult literacy programs and campus-sponsored programs at Macalester College, the University of St. Thomas and the College of St. Benedict. (*Focus on Study Circles*, Fall, 1991)

The same newsletter carries letters documenting growing numbers of study circle applications in the Dayton, Ohio public schools, the Florida Defenders of the

Environment, the Peace Education Center of Pentwater, MI, and the United Methodist Church in Brunswick, ME ("Focus on Study Circles," Fall 1991).

The Study Circle Resource Center, located in Pomfret, Connecticut, publishes a variety of pamphlets which describe in very simple terms the steps usually followed in establishing a study circle. Although the United States is obviously not going to get into this enterprise as has Sweden, one may look to numerous local sources for assistance in the development of reading materials, and the Resource Center is a good place to begin. Pamphlets titled *Guidelines for Developing Study Circle Course Material, Guidelines for Organizing and Leading a Study Circle,* and *An Introduction to Study Circles,* are a sampling of their materials. In addition, The Study Circles Resource Center does prepare detailed study materials on a limited number of subjects, and distributes fliers called *Connections: Youth Programs; Connections: Unions; and Connections: Adult Religious Education,* each of which describes and lists numerous current people and organizations already engaged in study circle development. For convenience, the address of The Study Circle Resource Center is: P.O. Box 203, Pomfret, CT 06258, (203) 928-2616, FAX (203) 928-3713.

Citizenship Schools

What is too big for one person to handle can be figured out by all of us together. We will have a new kind of school -- not a school for teaching reading, writing and arithmetic, but a school for problems. (Myles Horton)

History of the Highlander Folk School

Myles Horton, the modest visionary who founded the Highlander Folk School in Monteagle, Tennessee in 1932, recalls in his autobiography some notes he had recorded during his year of study in Denmark a year prior to the opening of Highlander:

> Students and teachers living together
>
> Peer learning
>
> Group singing
>
> Freedom from state regulation
>
> Non-vocational education
>
> Freedom from examinations

Social interaction in informal setting

A highly-motivating purpose

Clarity in what for and what against. (Horton, 1990, p. 52)

Horton reflected his distrust of bureaucracy in another note to himself:
"The job is to organize a school just well enough to get teachers and students together AND SEE THAT IT GETS NO BETTER ORGANIZED" (original emphasis; Horton, 1990, p. 52).

Horton had been particularly impressed with two schools in Denmark, which he felt reflected the spirit of revolutionary democracy upon which the Folk School idea had been founded a generation earlier. These two schools, The International People's College and the Folk High School for Workers, in Horton's view were quite creative and original, using small group discussion as the central mode of education.

Over the next 50 years Myles Horton lived his life as an educator according to these ideas. He had studied at the University of Chicago with Robert Parks (the widely respected sociologist who also counts Saul D. Alinsky as a former student), and he studied at Union Theological Seminary with other influential thinkers, including Reinhold Neibuhr. Horton (1990) recalled his thinking about the purpose of attending Union Theological in 1929 with the words, "to try to find out how to get social justice and love together" (p.32). Along the journey of his life, Myles Horton was also to learn from and challenge the likes of Jane Addams, Eleanor Roosevelt, and Rev. Martin Luther King, Jr., and to quietly influence the history of the labor movement in the South (organizing and integrating the first textiles union in the South) and help shape the process and thinking of many of the leading organizers of the Civil Rights Movement.

But Myles Horton accomplished these things solely by the force of his commitment to working with the social outcasts of this society: the poor black and white, mostly Southern men and women who came to Highlander to learn about themselves (as people sharing common problems) and to learn from each other what could be done to solve these problems. Highlander reflected Horton's beliefs about social change and about education. "My position was that I believed in changing society by first changing individuals, so that they could then struggle to bring about social change." But Highlander was not a place for armchair philosophers. Like many of the direct actionists we've examined, Horton too believed that action was the best teacher. But at Highlander, protest or organizing of any kind needed to be connected to a larger long range goal of transforming society. Social movements were also viewed by Horton as excellent vehicles for radicalizing people. Horton had learned

> *that educational work during social movement periods provides the best opportunity for multiplying democratic leadership . . . . That is, people learn from the movement to go beyond the movement. It may only affect a minority of the people, but there are so many people involved that thousands of them get radicalized (Horton, 1990, p. 127).*

Instead of the divisiveness and competitiveness found so often among the direct action training centers, Horton felt it was Highlander's job to develop the capacities of ordinary people who might later work as organizers for social change. Getting caught up with limited goals or methods of organizing was not what Highlander modeled. As the title of his autobiography reflects, Horton was committed to "The Long Haul."

Workshop Format

Highlander adhered to two unbending principles in the workshop programs: nondiscrimination and freedom of speech. Everyone was equal in these sessions and all had an equal right to say anything which was germane to the general topic, regardless of ideological position. The format is a discussion among peers, not the traditional teacher-student separation. Six assumptions were formulated to guide workshops: goals for workshops must come from problems articulated by participants; people do have the intelligence to solve these problems; Highlander can enrich the experiences of participants; participants learn from each other and Highlander staff must interact with participants; the "factual information" needs to be in a digestible form to be used by all participants; follow-up must occur with participants once they have returned to their home communities.

In Horton's words, "There is no method to learn from Highlander. What we do involves trusting people and belief in their ability to think for themselves. Our desire is to empower people collectively, not individually," and the informal aspects of workshops at Highlander were as important as the formal, particularly an emphasis on singing and sharing food (Horton, p. 157). These elements support and develop appreciation for how people express themselves and their cultural traditions. Also, although Horton confesses that workshops frequently run into time pressures just as we have seen with the direct action centers, Highlander does have definite leisure time which none can disturb.

By 1953, Myles Horton had crystallized his vision of a "rural citizenship movement . . . to train community rather than organizational leaders." One of the more important early victories of Highlander (which was subsequently taken over by the Southern Christian Leadership Conference (SCLC) during the Civil Rights Movement), involved the lengthy process of building the citizenship of several sea islands off the coast of South Carolina. Gradually, a program of citizen clubs, citizenship classes (to develop reading and literacy, and understanding of laws and procedures for voting, social security, and taxes) and Highlander residential workshops to train people as leaders and teachers, using the adult model of Highlander, effectively altered the political structure of Charleston, South Carolina itself, and led to substantive changes in the patterns of political activity and power relationships among the mostly black residents of John's Island and several other sea islands (Horton, 1990, pp. 141-163).

The essential learning which occurred was that citizenship classes challenged people and communicated with people as active participants in their own learning. Teachers were not there to provide answers, but to assist people with finding solutions to their own problems in daily life. Drawing again on his fondness for our democratic history, Horton used a concept from Jefferson:

> *When you teach a student, you think of his present limitations and you try to help him with these. But you also think of what he can become, and it is in terms of that, rather than the way he is now, that you treat him. This is what I mean by respecting human dignity . . . . You yourselves, as teachers and leaders, incorporate in every small thing you teach your students to do, the values that lead people to look toward the "ought to be" . . . I think that's the genius of our program. (Horton, 1990)*

Within a year of SCLC's taking over the project and with the continued assistance of Highlander, 200 teachers and 200 local citizenship schools had developed. Hundreds of thousands of black people were registered there within two years and the citizenship schools were year-round enterprises.

It is obvious, however, that Highlander Folk School (currently called Highlander Research and Educational Center, Inc.) contains(ed) the tranformational dimensions to which we have referred in discussing study circles, namely: a commitment to self-directed learning, to developing the critical awareness of individuals in the context of the person's environment and the larger society (internationally), and the "challenging of people to act, but not to act alone" (Horton, 1990).

Contrasting Direct-Action and
Transformative Methods

The distance between the direct-action methodologies, the corporate campaign, Citizen Action, or Alinsky type organizations, and the first two transformative approaches is far from subtle. Direct-action methods make no pretense about their priority on goal achievement and organizational power. A definite set of skills and steps to build organizational strength is prescribed by most of the direct action training centers. Discussion and training seminars are quite traditional in their format and a definite "bank" of information is transmitted to participants. Small group exchange or nondirective learning is minimized.

The latter, transformational approaches may in some ways underemphasize skill-based training in favor of the ideological/educational approach. But the study circles and citizenship schools are quite conscious and intentional in the use of their adult learning philosophy.

It may be appropriate at this point to make some additional clarifying remarks about the citizenship school model. There are very obvious parallels and many similar program elements shared by study circles and citizenship schools. Both seem to have many common roots in democratic theory and practice and so one may ask if it is not an artificial distinction to posit both as separate transformative methodologies.

Our answer is yes, but, there are historical and contextual differences which make it worthwhile to describe each separately and let people choose a name which best fits their intentions, resources, and organizational structures. Study circles may be initiated by any unaffiliated individual for practically any purpose of topical inquiry. Its methodology provides some procedures and ground rules which readily prepare people to undertake its use. Its beauty is revealed the deeper one goes into the value premises and ideology of the method's fundamentally egalitarian processes. It is also not a demanding study regime which will deter all but the most hardy and committed from participating. Also, its limited duration requires limited commitments from people who may otherwise may be interested in informal discussions about important or interesting topics and who may not find the setting of the adult schools either stimulating or inviting.

On the other hand we view citizenship schools/clubs as essential, permanent organizations in society. As indicated earlier, such functions have always been served by one or another organization or institution, including the mixed service/direct action experiences of the Community Service Organizations (CSO's), the Migrant Ministry (MM), and Highlander, each of which was a grantee of the Emil Schwartzhaupt Foundation (ESF). While our principal description is of the Highlander experience, it is important to note some distinguishing characteristics among the three.

A basic common characteristic to all three is concern "with helping citizens in a community learn to secure and use rights of which they were being deprived . . . emphasizing the importance of forming citizen organizations and learning how to maintain and use them" (Tjerandsen, 1980, pp. 176-191).

The Industrial Areas Foundation (IAF) was funded in 1947 by the Emil Schwarzhaupt Foundation (ESF) to consolidate much of the work already begun by Fred Ross, Sr., who was organizing Councils for Civic Unity among Mexican-American farm laborers throughout Central and Southern California. The IAF director, Saul Alinsky, hired Fred Ross, Sr. and subsequently Cesar Chavez to develop these Community Service Organizations (CSO).

The activities of a CSO usually included organizing citizenship classes (to prepare for naturalization) and English classes, conducting voter registration and getting out the vote campaigns, bringing pressure to bear against discriminatory practices in dealing with, for example, issuance of motor vehicle licenses, eligibility for welfare benefits, or police misconduct, etc. (Tjerandsen, 1980, p. 178)

Alinsky's guidelines for developing an organization were utilized, but there were two innovations: first, Fred Ross, Sr. insisted that the membership base be individual, not organizational; and second, that among Mexican Americans, the *"house meeting"* approach (a technique of meeting with small groups of people in their own homes) would be used to speed up Alinsky's traditional "one-on-one." Tjerandsen estimates that over a 10-year period as many as "30,000 Mexican Americans had completed CSO-sponsored classes in English and Citizenship . . . and nearly 430,000 were registered to vote" (Tjerandsen, 1980, pp. 85-86).

While CSO's were experiencing growth and success, even in electing Mexican Americans to public office, there were problems which eventually undermined the viability of CSO's as organizations which fought for the right of oppressed Mexican Americans. Success brought with it diminished urgency and interest on the part of people whose issues were resolved. It increased the pressure on volunteer leaders, as they were exposed to much conflict and dissent, which led to the decreased willingness of the individual Mexican-Americans to hold leadership positions while fighting for rights. Thus, gradual bureaucratization took place, bringing middle-class Mexican Americans, even lawyers and county employee managers, into positions of authority, and reducing the CSO's fighting spirit and connection with the mass-base.

The CSO work was in large measure a typical Alinsky "learn through action" approach, and the formal, organized 10-day national training of IAF was not yet developed. In fact, it is of some importance to note that Alinsky seems to have developed an "educational" component to CSO work (and all his subsequent leadership training) under some pressure from the funding agency, the ESF. In 1953, Mr. Tjerandsen, Executive Secretary of ESF, wrote to Alinsky and asked a series of questions, the essence of which were to strongly insist that Alinsky develop an educational component for his organizing program.

> *The great danger in a program such as yours is that the most obvious and the easiest thing to do is to "operate." There are injustices and inequities. It is possible to identify leaders, work with them to build a power organization and apply pressure to correct the injustices. This is good. But is not your basic objective to develop certain capacities among the people with whom you work? In the West, you are working primarily . . . with a particular ethnic group. Are you developing a set of political*

bosses, new style, in the pattern of ethnic political bosses as we have known them in Chicago or Boston? If such a result is to be avoided, must not some understanding of the basic problems be shared fairly widely in the group?. . . This is only a beginning. But it is an educational job. When the drive is to get some results, who is thinking about and doing something about the educational side? (Tjerandsen, 1980, p. 101)

This letter is of particular importance when attempting not just to consider the different emphases of the direct-action methods versus the transformative methods, but to see how easily citizenship organizations can be shifted in one direction (direct action) as opposed to the other (development of critical awareness). It is of course likely that this tension is healthy, with no one clear choice. Nonetheless, its possible ramifications deserve the serious consideration of every social change practitioner.

Feminist Support/Action Groups

Feminist Support Group: Ritual Healing Focus

There are countless examples and varieties of small and large groupings of women (and sometimes men are included) who come together for the purpose of supporting each other's journeys, hearing each other's stories, and participating in processes which expand the consciousness of members. Research also indicates a proliferation of women's groups focusing on victims of abuse, such as incest, rape, and battering. Such groups provide solidarity among the women involved, and extensively utilize ritual healing techniques commonly focusing on female spirituality and symbols and images associated with female strength. The data from one study in particular indicates that such ritual healing groups effect dramatic reductions in fear, anger, emotional pain, and increase the sense of power and well-being experienced by participants (Jacobs, 1989). The groups tend to operate within a format of three acts of participation, moving from (a) acknowledgment of having been a victim, to (b) recapitulation of the experience(s) and catharsis, to (c) a period of guided imagery using a female deity or meditation.

Las Hermanas

Whereas ritual healing groups tend to form among well-educated and acculturated white women, an entirely different type of group was begun by

Chicana/Latina women in 1971, Las Hermanas (The Sisters). Las Hermanas began as an organization of Chicana religious members, but rapidly expanded to non-religious women, and became an integral part of the Chicano/a Movement, supporting the United Farm Workers struggles, protesting the exploitation of Mexican nuns who worked in the United States, and effectively challenging the church patriarchy (Cadena, 1987, pp. 80-82). Las Hermanas is currently a vital national women's transformational organization, and should not be overlooked by social change practitioners who work with Latino/a people.

Women's Reading Circle

Sometimes women's support groups form around a modest focus on moving from reflection to action. In many cases these groups are short-lived. In one particular case, the group is very much alive and evolving at the ripe old age of 18 months. Following is the account of this unnamed group the foothills of the California Sierra Nevada Mountains.

Shortly after developing a food cooperative in late 1991 (see page 155), several women coop members began to consider the idea of forming a women's group. The food coop had been a productive idea, and had served as a bridge from a preceding group/study circle on the Gulf War. The food coop (and its monthly newsletter) were regarded as vehicles for creating a closer community in this largely rural area. There was even some thought that the coop might eventually lead to a more socially activist agenda. But some of the women coop participants, most of whom were married and in their 30s and 40s, as well as a few non-members (including one lesbian couple), simply felt a strong need to combat the sense of rural isolation that accompanied living in the mountains, and a need to coalesce around their particular shared values, which often seemed at odds with the values of the dominant community and rural culture.

So it was that in February of 1992, an informal meeting of several women occurred. Taking some of the democratic leaderless traditions of the Gulf War group, the women began to form some ground rules. One member, who had previously been a member of another women's group, suggested limiting participation to women only. There was agreement. The group decided that they would begin as a social group and reading/study circle. Each month, the group would meet at a different person's home for a potluck supper and discuss a selected book. Meetings would last 2 to 3 hours. The group remained open, with a core of 10-12 women attending regularly, but with an occasional attendance as high as as 20.

Books were ordered wholesale from a Berkeley bookstore, Bookpeople; the feminist perspective was generally apparent from the book titles, such as Amy Tan's *The Joy Luck Club* and *The Kitchen God's Wife*; Gloria Steinem's *Revolution from Within*; Susan Faludi's *Backlash*; Ursula LeGuin's *Buffalo Gals and Other Animal Preserves*; Ann Cameron's *Daughters of the Copper Women*; and Clarissa Pinkola Estes's *Women Who Run with the Wolves*. Meaningful book passages were highlighted, and participants felt free to speak about events in their personal lives, or feelings and thoughts brought into focus by the readings. According to one participant, the feminist perspective was a principal theme, as participants experienced their own sense of oppression as women in a society dominated by men. But it was also clear that the women in this group didn't spend their time "male bashing." Rather, the mutual support and natural experience of women gathering to share stories and ideas was the essential uplifting and unifying theme of these meetings.

The reading/study circle continues to meet monthly, and, while still in a "pre-political" stage of evolution as a group, it continues to evolve. Several of the members have participated in a pro-choice march sponsored by the National Organization for Women (NOW), and the group has expanded its reading to include books written by men, such as that of noted Native American author, Michael Dorris, *Yellow Raft in Blue Water*.

Women's Action Group (WAG)

The Women's Action Group (WAG), in Duluth, Minnesota, is an example of a transformative approach applied to the situation of low-income women. It originated in 1984, from a network of anti-battering activities: a women's shelter, a project working with the police and courts to perform early intervention in domestic abuse cases, and a support group for battered women.

The women who had been meeting as a support group decided spontaneously, out of a sense of indignation, to stage a series of protest demonstrations against a restaurant whose advertisement of "battered mushrooms" on their menu belittled battered women's shelters. Significant media attention was generated, and the restaurant eventually closed (it was also anti-union). Volunteers for the shelter decided to survey 131 women about their concerns on related issues, and called for some discussion meetings. As they continued to meet informally, the group reached a consensus to undertake actions of various sorts over the next few years: neighborhood vigils at locations where several rapes had occurred; "take back the night" marches to emphasize safety for women; protests against AFDC cuts (in alliance with other groups); and vigils in support of a Native American battered woman who had killed her violent husband in self-defense.[1]

The group's members, usually numbering about a dozen, are primarily white, with an occasional minority woman; this reflects the makeup of the local population. Many are single parents, and some are on public assistance. Their predominant common tie is their status as low-income and battered women.

As the Women's Action Group evolved, with continued participation of people from the shelter and the Domestic Abuse Intervention Project, greater clarity emerged around a philosophy of action centering on nonviolence (the value opposite to the target of their greatest concern), based on the work of Gandhi and others. A key text for them was Joan Bondurant's *Conquest of Violence: The Gandhian Philosophy of Conflict*. Another pivotal influence deliberately adopted by the group was the learning process developed by Paulo Freire. His emphasis on political conscientization (development of critical consciousness), collective process to decipher and understand common reality, and equal involvement of all individuals resonated exactly with WAG's style and purposes. Freire's technique of group creation of "codes," or skits that depict a critical problem, has been especially useful for WAG.[2]

True to its support-group roots, WAG has always maintained a high priority on mutual emotional sustenance. WAG members uniformly relate that they have found some of their closest friendships within the group. The significance paid to each other's feelings results in what many of them believe is a stronger commitment to the issues that they decide to act upon than that found in other organizations. The strength of group members' feelings at the moment underlies a decision to undertake an action, not any deference to an issue "campaign" selected and committed to at an earlier date. This often amounts to a reactive protest to a local event which offends them deeply, such as the public appearance of an anti-woman "men's rights" organization (Women's Action Group, 1991).

WAG's disinterest in the structured, multi-step issue timelines typical of direct action community organizations can result in a lack of follow-through which usually hinders the chance of a positive resolution, but that is not the point. The group often engages in what others might disparage as merely symbolic protests, without a focused plan to leverage enough power to win a specific reform. The attitude of WAG members, however, is based on their analysis of the need for fundamental change in the attitudes and behaviors of the police, judges, prosecutors, the welfare system, and men in general. Their actions are aimed at exposing, and bearing witness to, the essential paradigms of their oppression. Many of their protests are, in a sense, Freire-type "codes" aimed at raising public awareness of the underlying contradictions, with the implication that (they hope) many others will pressure the offending parties to change -- or that the oppressors will see the errors of their ways. They are fully aware that the basic societal changes they wish to see cannot possibly occur within a short time frame.

Some WAG members feel that direct action organization reforms of achieving better low-income housing availability, or better health care delivery, are only "fix-it" Band-Aids dealing with the symptoms, not the causes, of their oppression. Having said that, WAG has nonetheless worked on some low-income housing issues in alliance with other groups.[3]   Above everything, WAG's commitment to a non-hierarchical, fully collective, mutually inclusive and supportive process takes precedence. While both are important, issues are clearly secondary to process.

Women who have been part of WAG sometimes go on to involvement in more specialized direct action organizations, and pursue issues in those arenas in a structured, highly goal-oriented fashion characteristic of community organizing. They usually keep ties with their comrades at WAG, as an ongoing support base. WAG therefore functions at times as a transitional experience for women who are on the journey of becoming fully politicized -- "a kind of training ground for community activists," according to Ellen Pence, who helped guide WAG's development. Women come into WAG from isolated, alienated situations, usually battered and with little income or self-esteem. WAG serves, for them, as a safe place to begin to feel a sense of ownership, and sisterhood with others in similar straits. The group nurturing, consciousness raising, and discussions of issues enable them to find their own voice, and figure out what topic or issue they really are interested in. For some, it amounts to a process of self-empowerment and self image-building which results in decisions for personal improvement, such as going to school (Pence, 1990).

WAG constitutes a fairly unusual blend of traditional support group dynamics and purposes, meshed with an embedded desire to act in the public arena, if only symbolically at times. What is deeply significant is that WAG's developers found in transformative methods the only opportunities to combine the two together.

Comments

Obviously, women are engaged in the arenas of traditional and direct-action social change methods as well as these illustrative examples of transformative methods. The numerical dominance of women in many aspects of institution-based organizing and the clear leadership by women in individual-based organizing underscores this point. It is simplistic to convey the impression that women are exclusively involved in one or another strategy of social change work. It is also inaccurate to portray women who do participate in transformative methods as exclusively part of the culture of victim's services. But even such services, when developed or proffered by social work organizations, can be meaningful adjuncts to politically oriented social change work. Particularly when social workers are mindful of the guidelines for transformative work, such as fully -- democratic processes and the perspectives of empowerment and feminism, transformative methods can contribute to the eradication of all forms of gender-based oppression.

Women's Action Group--End Notes:
1. WAG, "A History of the Women's Action Group." (Duluth, MN 1987)
2. WAG's interest in Freire is quite serious, and has involved lengthy trips to talk with his associates. It culminated, in 1990 with hosting a visit by Freire to Minnesota. In true transformative fashion, WAG activists initiated a self-directed study circle for people to learn about Freire's teachings in advance of his visit.

3.   Interestingly, WAG became involved, somewhat hesitantly, in local
       institution-based direct action organizing effort. Perhaps not surprisingly,
       WAG members did not find the experience, with its goal-oriented issue
       approach and formalized structure, very satisfactory.

The Base Ecclesial Community
and Liberation Theology

Community organizing works on issues and doesn't build community . . . or it
may build some kind of community among organizers, but it doesn't build
community out there in the neighborhood. (Fr. Chuck Dahm)

Introduction

The basic ecclesial community or BEC is described by close observers as a
new way of "being church." Also known as base Christian community (BCC) or
base community, this form of church actually seems to approximate the earliest
forms of the Catholic Church in which the faithful were active celebrants of liturgy
and rituals which in modern times have been restricted to ordained priests. BEC's
have been a rapidly growing, organic, grassroots movement throughout Central
and South America for over 20 years. The close association of BEC's with
liberation theology, Marxism, and mass civil disobedience among destitute landless
peasants throughout Latin America has much to do with the resistance to BEC's
found in the United States. Also, the perception that the BEC form of "being
church" is exclusively Catholic and the general antipathy of social work and human
services towards religiously oriented programs contributes to the lack of
understanding of the BEC methodology.

The most immediate context of this revolution of consciousness in Latin
America must be seen as the movement of landless peasants in the grassroots
church communities or base ecclesial communities (BEC's) or base Christian
communities (BCC's). In Brazil alone, one 1989 estimate placed the total number
of active base Christian communities as 100,000, engaging perhaps 5,000,000
people (Hewitt, 1989, p. 123). But it is noted that many other countries have
growing movements of base Christian communities, including: Peru, Argentina,
Bolivia, the Central American countries of Nicaragua, Guatemala, Mexico, and the
Philippines, Sri Lanka, South Africa, and South Korea (Coleman, 1982, p. 65).

The United States, with its significantly different history and institutions, is also beginning to take hold of the BEC methodology, while struggling to evolve a praxis which fits the circumstances and cultural plurality of varied social groupings.

Whereas for the BEC's in Latin America, the motivation to form a community of faith is for liberation from poverty, misery, and death, here and now, in the United States the motivation may be to reduce the isolation and fear experienced among undocumented workers and political and economic refugees from Mexico and Central America, to reach out to alienated youth in East Los Angeles, to develop a strong sense of unity and identity in deteriorating and threatened Latino neighborhoods in Chicago, or to meet the religious affiliation needs of people living in religiously underserved areas, or one of the countless other reasons.

First, however, let us see what the BEC looks like in a North American context.

Catholic Communities of Pilsen (Chicago)

Father Chuck Dahm, a Chicago-bred Franciscan priest with a Ph.D. in political science from the University of Wisconsin-Madison, is pastor for the St. Pius parish, a predominantly Latino (90% Mexican American) area in Southwest Chicago. He spent several years working in Bolivia (although not with base communities) and upon his return to Chicago in 1972, he became increasingly persuaded that traditional community organizing approaches were not doing the job of building community among his parishioners. Having maintained his Latin American contacts and remembering clearly the advantages and disadvantages of the Latin American model of base community, Fr. Dahm began informally to meet with small groups of families, in their homes and in their neighborhoods. Since 1986, a loose confederation of five parishes in the diocese has developed, and 15 base communities, varying in size from 8 to 25 people, have been initiated as of 1990. These BEC's are designed, as previously described, for mutual support of members and the sharing of life with neighbors. The five participating parishes have a written community pastoral plan which states that the base community will be the basis for organizing the community (Dahm, 1990).

Home visits by BEC coordinators, combined with the one-on-one interviewing process and a focus on a limited number of social action issues, provide the basis for a long-range strategy of membership development. The weekly BEC meetings (except for summers and Christmas when meetings are suspended), generally consist of three parts: scriptural readings, songs, and questions intended to promote reflection and raising of the consciousness of members. Fr. Dahm emphasized that there is an effort to place the questions before the readings in order to begin to move people toward an analysis of everyday reality. The BEC coordinators, each receive minimal training in how to run meetings, and how to listen and conduct one-on-one interviews, using prepared questions which may be based upon the current action issues for the 5 parishes. For instance, gangs, drugs, and housing were the three dominant issues recently. Illustrative questions would be: "Have you ever experienced violence in the neighborhood?" "What did you feel like when it occurred?" Or, "what are some of the problems if you own a home?" juxtaposed with "What if you are a renter?" Since most BEC membership is a mix of renters and owners, and since there is commonly much blaming of each respective group by the other group, the questions tend to promote discussion about immediate situational reality and to raise the level of critical awareness in all members. People "hear each other"; this is followed by a discussion of rights and usually tied into what scripture has to teach about the problem (Dahm, 1990).

This scenario covers the first two stages of the BEC approach discussed earlier: to see, and to reflect. It is the third stage of taking the understanding into the arena of action which remains the most difficult for Fr. Dahm and the 15 BEC's in Pilsen. Fr. Dahm is very clear that paid organizers, full or part-time, are needed to nurture the BEC's and to gradually prepare members for social action. In his view, there is really no choice. At the present time, "we have to put all our eggs in housing: buy, fix up and hold tight or we are all going to be moved out," due to urban renewal or gentrification, and he recognizes that "we may run out of time" (Dahm, 1990).

But the alternative to organizing from a BEC approach, that of a more direct action model, is unappealing to Fr. Dahm. In his view, the professional organizing networks take the few really good leaders from the BEC's and turn them into "elites who manipulate . . . to mobilize people, get them on busses"

(Dahm, 1990). It is a short-term approach which formsd neither people nor community and, in Fr. Dahm's experience, the organizing networks tend to work only around issues, espousing a commitment to unity while fighting with each other and the grassroots organizations over power, turf, and resources. "I realize that at some point, in order to get power we will need a citywide movement . . . and I don't know if we are ever going to get it" (Dahm, 1990).

Starting a BEC in the United States

An essentially similar three-phase process (arranged as a 3-day workshop -- a dialectic between reflection and action) is described by Fr. Edgard Beltran, formerly a Pastoral Specialist from the United States Catholic Conference (USCC) Secretariat on Hispanic Affairs and now employed by the Rockford, IL diocese. Edgard Beltran also spent many years working with Latin American BEC's and was involved with the early work and development of the Mexican American Cultural Center (MACC), the training/education center which will be described in association with the BEC methodology.

The first phase is: facing the reality of the world. This is a combination of coming together as people with a variety of needs and sharing openly with others these needs in light of their own experiences; seeking to understand these needs in light of the characteristic of the society around them; but not at this point seeking solutions.

The second phase is: reality of faith. Using a closely aligned method of dialogue developed by Paulo Freire in his 1970 book titled *Pedagogy of the Oppressed*, participants at this level learn to see their concrete experiences and needs in the context of their religious faith (in the case of Catholic workshop participants). "All of the needs and wants expressed earlier are the result of oppression and division" (Beltran, 1990). There is clarification of the fact that social structures are as much the location of "sin" as are individuals, who strive to compete against each other; or, in the words of Edgard Beltran, "The way society is set up, no one can escape stepping on someone in order to survive" (Beltran, 1990). This oppressive situation is then contrasted with the Christian ideal of wholeness, which requires community to overcome separation and incompleteness.

"As God is in community we can then begin to live in communion" (Beltran, 1990).

The workshop develops the theme that living in communion "in Ecclesial" (of the church) is the most natural solution to the dilemma of incompleteness and structural sin which places people (of God and within God) against each other. The BEC is held up as a way of "being church": "The first unit of community in the modern church can be the BCC. Up to this point never had it been suggested that the entire role of the church could be taken up and shared within a BCC. But now, in order to be whole the group gathers up its different talents and finds its threefold mission: to be prophetic (teach, evangelize), liturgical (baptize, celebrate) and socially concerned (live, share)" (Beltran, 1990).

The third phase (and 3rd day of the workshop) is: "What is to be done?" and requires participants (from specific localities) to decide for themselves what action they will take. When groups do decide to initially establish a BEC (or BCC), guidelines (but not specific topics for discussion) are generally discussed, including options for times, duration, sharing responsibilities, and shifting leadership, etc.

Moving to a "Theology of Democracy"

There is some variation between what is going on in Chicago and the activity at the Mexican American Cultural Center (MACC) in Texas. MACC sees itself moving away from the base of liberation theology and toward political organization. The Director of MACC, Rosendo Urrabazo, discussed movement away from liberation theology:

> *Were not there anymore in the sense that that's not a major component of our teaching . . . The thrust I am introducing is what I call "theology of democracy". . . . And basically what it is that I'm finding that liberation theology only goes so far. It is in a certain direction that is ideological . . there is no power base for liberation theologians anywhere I know of. There is no political force. There's no party. There's no organized effort to implement the goals of liberation theology. (Urrabazo, 1990)*

In Urrabazo's view, the base ecclesiastical communities are fine, as an element in the development of critical consciousness, but they do not form *a political organization . . . liberation theology basically inspired movement-type activities . . . and it has inspired us in this country . . . But it really doesn't help us in the day to day . . . In the United States we have the possibility of forming a political organization. In that sense we can go beyond what liberation theology talks about. (Urrabazo, 1990)*

Urrabazo then makes reference to the recently held convention of the Communities Organized for Public Service (COPS), the Industrial Areas Foundation (IAF) initiated project whose lead organizer (and now director of the 10-city project, Texas IAF) was Ernesto Cortes.

What we did Sunday, (referring to a mass public accountability session), that is not liberation theology . . . that's a theology of democracy. That is looking at our democratic process and saying "this is good." We can make it work, for our own theology, inspired in part by liberation theology but also our own social teaching . . . lends itself to saying it's OK to be an American, it's OK to participate in the political process of the United States. We don't get involved in politics . . . And the religious dimension of that is saying . . . it's good to do this (Urrabazo, 1990).

Fr. Urrabazo spoke about a conversation he had with Gustavo Gutierrez recently, in which Gutierrez reportedly said that the theology of liberation is past. We need to go into something brand new today. New statements need to be made now. Urrabazo (1990) states in this regard: "What he (Gutierrez) argued for was not the outcome but the process. And what we're saying is we buy into the process, and we're coming up with something else. We're coming out with statements that make sense to us in this country, in our context" (Urrabazo, 1990).

Classroom Exercises and Skill Development Scenario --
(Transformative Method)

A. (Class Discussion) You are a hospital social worker. Large changes are looming regarding health care reform at both the state and federal levels. In your state, the insurance companies and for-profit medical industries are dominating the reform agenda. You and your co-workers are worried about what might happen in the future, but you feel powerless to have any impact. You decide to initiate a study circle for people to learn more about these issues and the options for reform, and to explore how you might be able to have some influence on the outcomes. How will you go about setting up the study circle? Ask yourself:

1. Who should I invite to participate in the study circle?
2. What should the logistics be of when, where and how often to meet?
3. How should we obtain materials to study and discuss?
4. How will our study group be facilitated?

B. (Individual or small group project) Following up on the study circle methodology, select an existing group with which you are currently involved or with which you could become involved as a regular participant. The group should meet at least monthly, and ideally would meet bi-monthly or weekly. Examples might be a local NASW Chapter, a women's support group, a church-related group, a business forum, or a work-related group. Once you have identified the group, begin to introduce general study circle principles through your own subtle, nonintrusive participation. Consider taking any of the following gradual steps during the course of a semester length project:

1. Observe and keep a journal of the basic group process, including such things as leadership patterns, authority, sub-grouping, supportiveness and commitment of members, extent of participation.
2. Without putting yourself in the designated "leader" or "expert" role, initiate dialogue which either enhances the democratic process, reveals or develops analysis from a socioeconomic or political perspective, or contributes to critical consciousness of the group. These interventions should be very simple things, like asking a probing question, drawing out a reluctant member to greater participation, or discussing a "theme" which you think underlies surface talk. Interventions will vary, depending on whether this is strictly a "task" group or a "process" group.
3. During the interim between meetings, make a conscious effort to initiate a dialogue with, and listen to all members of the group. Use the one-on-one technique to do face-to-face interviews with several people of varied racial, ethnic, and cultural backgrounds. Using the one-on-one approach, try to find out individual self-interests and feelings about the group.
4. Although not to be expected of yourself, opportunities sometimes arise where the group can be moved to engage in some small action step as a part of their transformative group process. Reflecting on action usually deepens the reality of the transformative experience. A caveat here is that unless you are a committed long-term member of this group, do not set the group up for failure and preemptively terminate your participation during a crucial action phase.

5. Discuss your group experience periodically in class, using these opportunities to receive feedback from classmates as "consultants." Be sure that the instructor is committed to a fully democratic classroom and does not fall into the "banking" trap (see Freire for explanation of the concept).

C. (Class Project) Paulo Freire's method uses codes, which are brief skits that dramatize, in a symbolic way, an essential dilemma, problem, contradiction, or aspect of oppression. This helps the participants clarify their analysis of the reality they are dealing with, and it enlightens the observers by heightening their awareness of something they might have been insensitive to.

Have the class divide into small groups of 5 to 10 people each. Each group is to choose and discuss, using a collective process, some aspect of academic life, the social work profession, or some other commonly shared experience which the group's members find oppressive. Then, the group will construct a brief 5 to 10 minute skit which provides a symbolic representation of either the oppressive situation, a solution to it, or a dilemma or contradiction about it. All members of the group must have a role in the skit.

Finally, each of the small groups will present their skit in front of the entire class. The class will discuss each skit, addressing questions such as: What was the group trying to tell us? Does this relate to my reality? What insights do we gain from this symbolic skit?

D. (Class or Individual Project) Conduct a series of one-on-one interviews with local clergy who represent the diverse cultural, racial, and ethnic populations in your area to determine:
   1. their personal and denominational perspectives on social/economic justice.
   2. the specific scriptural (or theological) references or stories which support or undermine a justice commitment.
   3. examples of justice/organizing work conducted by their local congregations; patterns of leadership, strategies, and tactics.

After completing these interviews, take time as a group to discuss the implications of your findings for organizing around contemporary issues among the various populations and neighborhoods, and the likelihood of developing support from this "value" perspective. Ask the question, whether or not a modified base ecclesial community approach would begin to effect a change in the consciousness of these sectors of the community. Who would be in a position to initiate such forums? How could you go about informing them of the process or inviting them to participate?

CHAPTER 7

Decision Rules for Social Change Practitioners

Critical Choices for Social Workers

Where do we go from here? An array of possibilities have been presented in these last six chapters. Traditional, direct-action, and transformative strategies have been explained and case examples and exercises provided to promote familiarity. Some readers may have already had actual organizing experience. Others may have undertaken a class project or tried out the organizer role in the context of field practicum. Almost everyone should be ready to contemplate the first major decision: Do I as a social worker want to have anything at all to do with social change practice? Of course, we hope the answer is yes. But let's take a little more thoughtful tack and examine the major subquestions:

1. In the context of traditional agency-based social work practice, can we transform our perceptions of helping roles, diminish the legacy of paternalism and status differentials between professional and clients, and effectively utilize direct-action and transformative strategies to empower workers and client groups? To do any of these things we must all become liberated educators. We must believe in the capacities of co-workers and clients and take the following steps:

- Develop **circles of resistance** to brace yourself against the seduction or threats by power figures, through cooptation, manipulation, or fear of sanctions. A circle of resistance is any structure, forum, or relationship which provides free associational space within which to discuss or act upon alternative visions of reality. This may include provision for alternative means of income and economic support, selectively "de-linking" from the mainstream economy, forming cooperatives, sweat equity programs, community trust funds, or other grassroots community development options. It may mean unionizing the workplace or finding ways to assert collective will on behalf of threatened co-workers.

- Become risk takers. We may have to challenge employing agencies to get involved in issues of the wider community, as well as be prepared to meet the resistance of the community to intervention and innovation.

- Educate peers and clients. Using knowledge of the steps of building critical consciousness, we may need to engage in a longer term project of political and organizational transformation.

- Build a peer support group. Horton's advice was to act, but never alone. A forum for discussion of issues or problems (what is the social reality you wish to construct?) may be one of the first steps taken by the change-oriented social worker.

- Step outside of your personal comfort zone. Along with peers, begin to move your agency toward an expanded conception of agency-based practice -- one which is more interactive and multi-disciplinary; one which recognizes the importance of politicization of workers and clients and which legitimizes the use of transformative strategies and public action to initiate policy or reform policy.

- Get ready for tough battles and the "long haul." Get accustomed to seeing and using power to make change. Be prepared for a little heat when your political behavior is labeled "professionally inappropriate" by those too timid to make waves. "If you want peace, work for justice."

- Do your part to diminish status differentials. It is perfectly in order to fight for higher wages for yourself. It is vastly more important to support a union of workers who fight for each other. Working with

nonprofessionals, including them in your union and political work, is
also important.

- Embrace strategies of empowerment of clients and oppressed groups
associated with your agency, and form linkages with other agencies
and advocacy groups to move this agenda collectively.

2. Assuming an affirmative response to the question about getting involved, the
next question is, at what level or in what arena of social change do you want to
work?

- Begin by asking yourself about your own self-interests. If your highest
priority is to make a lot of money in private practice and live in a gated
community, you just read the wrong book. But seriously, what are the
personal and financial needs of you and your family? Everyone has
limits on her or his time and energy, and it is important to make a
realistic assessment of where and how you expect to be living for the
next few years. If you plan to leave your current geographic
community within 6 months, it is a safe bet you are not the person to
lead a union, develop a grassroots action campaign, or start a base
ecclesial community. Time-limited commitments -- for instance,
political campaign work, participation in limited public actions, or
loaning out your expertise for a few months to a grassroots group --
may be your best bet. If you are staying put, then you could contribute
to the more patient work of developing the relationships that are
needed to build a permanent local organization. In addition, ask
yourself what you would like to learn within the next few years. What
skills do you want to master? What talents do you have to offer?
- Your choice of social change strategy will to some extent limit your
choice of arena. For instance, none of the transformational methods
can be readily utilized at a national level. These methods are most
appropriately utilized at a local level, a neighborhood, block, or other
geographically proximate setting. While direct-action methods such as
corporate campaign or other mass protest tactics have been
implemented at a national level or statewide, the majority of direct

action organizations and their targets are smaller than statewide in scope. It is the traditional forms of political organization, parties, and interest groups, including public interest advocacy organizations, business, and labor interests, that have dominated the national arena. Access to traditional politics is high, although participation by local entities and individuals is notoriously limited.

- Which brings us to another point about choice of strategy. If your principal interest is in seeing tangible, more immediate results, the direct action arena is probably your best bet. Even though results may be limited in scope, direct action tends to move into "action" more rapidly than either traditional or transformative methods and focuses more on specific, immediate issues. Lots of people can be mobilized through direct action, although it will generally be a smaller core of leaders who get the training and recognition, and whose commitments to ongoing organizing increase as a result of the action.

- If your emphasis is on the identification of new leaders from among oppressed populations or people not normally associated with mainstream organizations, and on effecting longer term, more fundamental changes in society, perhaps the transformative methods (or their adaptations) will be more appealing to you. Within the various direct action methods there are large differences in the attention given to developing an individual's leadership abilities. In general, the institution-based method does the most; the local chapter, individual-based format does a lesser amount; and the Citizen Action model does the least.

- If your emphasis is on broadening the mutual support dimension of a group of people (affective community instead of rational community), then transformative methods will be better suited to your needs.

- If your main desire is to strongly influence policy decisions at a high level (state or national), then your best point of engagement is with the individual-based networks that coordinate issue campaigns at a state, regional, or national level. Much of their activity does not have a strong component of local leadership development, since there is often a tradeoff between the two. It is quite difficult to pursue both goals at once.

3. Do you have a specific constituency in mind to work with? If so, this may dictate the method you utilize.

- Suppose you want to work with senior citizens in a rural setting on issues of importance to them. Sometimes the issues will require coalitions with other groups of seniors to have an effect upon state or federal legislators, while at other times there may be much internal building of the senior organization itself. But the old Alinsky maxim to never to go outside the experience of your own members, probably limits the selection of direct-action tactics.

- In the same way, if you work with low-income people with limited English ability, chances are you will have a lot of pre-political, transformational work to do before the group can move into either traditional or direct-action methods, unless your aim is just to mobilize such people as any ambitious politician might to win an election or exercise limited veto power. Some institution-based networks have succeeded with these constituencies by working through their churches.

- There are also constraints on most social workers when their principal constituency is a disabled group, a victim's support group, or some other traditional client group. There are a host of ethical considerations which social workers must weigh when organizing among clients, including such things as manipulation, safety, and confidentiality. These sometimes conflict with the goals of justice and empowerment, although ethical prescriptions (and the vaunted "professionalism") have too often been made excuses for not doing anything. Generally, direct-action methods are those of last resort in these instances. Traditional methods (read weak!) often substitute for true empowerment and democratic self-governance by client groups.

- The motivation of most people involved in social change includes not just anger at injustice, but also a complementary inner guidance from faith-based ethical or spiritual values. While some utilize this as just a personal drive, others seek to openly challenge their own religious community to collectively live by the group's stated social justice values. Two very different ways to pursue this are the institution-based direct-action method to put faith into action, and the transformative method of creating base communites.

4. Have you made a decision about organizing in the workplace or outside the workplace?

- Organizing in the workplace is a mixed bag. Some social workers find it too intimidating to consider organizing in their place of business, where their livelihood depends upon conforming to narrowly defined behaviors -- generally a kind of mildly coerced passivity which is a veil for a not-so-benign form of corporate control. If no labor organization or collective bargaining agreement is available to protect your rights and serve your interests, this enforced passivity is usually a stage on the way to an environment of covert resistance on the part of workers. Too many social workers have had to spend large parts of their careers in such environments. This is intolerable, and changing this environment takes courage and skill with social change methods. Brager and Holloway's 1978 book, *Changing Human Service Organizations*, is a fundamental resource for low- and middle-level workers, even where collective bargaining is present. But without collective bargaining, social workers could consider transformational methods, particularly study circles and feminist or worker support groups. Modest improvements in work environment can be effected with the first sign of worker unity. Longer term organizing really should include traditional labor organizing to keep the managerial mentality firmly in check.

- Outside the workplace, some social workers still feel the watchful eye of corporate "big brother." Whether one chooses to serve on a board of directors for a slightly radical advocacy organization or to pursue left politics, even large towns can feel awfully small. But protection (and legitimacy) only comes when challenges to status quo power politics are forcefully made by organized groups of citizens. Plenty of wage earners are involved in broad-based (church-based) direct action organizing, just as they are involved in more traditional interest group and party politics. Social workers are very well-suited to these strategies and are uniquely qualified to undertake transformative work at a local level, given their extensive training in group work. Commitments to organize outside of the workplace are probably the most common affiliations, just below the more "service-oriented" volunteer activity so prevalent all over the United States.

- In the experience of the authors, people active in organizing in the workplace are also the same people active in volunteer organizing outside the workplace. And there are those who are motivated to initiate social change work no matter where they work or live. Ideally, there would be a ripple effect as social workers begin to focus more on sharing their knowledge of organizing with other social workers who are new to the idea. In other words, sacrifice some attention to the material goals of organizing to develop the next generation of organizers. This shift is really away from traditional and direct action toward the methods, goals, and ideology of transformative organizing.

5. How does the preference to work on specific issues affect the choice of strategy or method?

- The biggest advantage of deciding to organize around a specific issue, whether homelessness, drugs, crime, or the mentally ill, is that participants are going to self-select. This usually means that participants will have a higher level of personal motivation and probably greater specialized knowledge of the issue, the players, the power dynamics, etc. Organizationally, this tends to focus resources and facilitate their mobilization around particular goals. Less time needs to be spent sorting out conflicting interests and arranging quid pro quo's over whose issue receives initial attention. Also, with single issues, a stable leadership emerges, internal and external relationships get fixed, and constituencies supporting the aims of leader-defined goals can be brought on board more quickly. Dissent is minimized and higher levels of organizational efficiency are achieved. In short, traditional political systems generally come into existence, with all the pluses and minuses this form of organization brings with it.

- Multi-issue organizations are much better than those with a single issue at developing and sustaining for the long term; a diverse grassroots power base which can respond to the interests and tap the talents and needs for involvement of large numbers of people. Leadership can be broader and shifting (or revolving), and the loss of a single key leader, which can effectively kill a single-issue organization, usually will not be fatal to multi-issue organizations.

6. Have you a sense of what it means to you personally or professionally to be a part of an oppositional community?

- Oppositional community is about taking a stand for justice. It isn't particularly important how small the step or how huge the battle; the essential point is to make the initial commitment and to find opportunities to express that commitment in action. Not necessarily direct action of the confrontational type, but action in the sense of consciously affirming your choices and your belief that human beings, working together, make their own history in the smallest of day-to-day actions. And it is important to realize that the essence of commitment is accountability. Perhaps you like to operate alone and think that silent witnessing of your own inner feelings and beliefs (ideology) is sufficient. When is the last time you heard of an Alcoholics Anonymous meeting with one person attending? When we are hurting and most of the mainstream societal messages say, "drink, escape, forget," staying conscious, awake, and dry is a heavy burden. Even at the level of "witness," a collective or community approach is preferable to operating alone. What is the sound of one hand clapping? In the face of massive propaganda, media seduction, and conformity to the ideology of mass consumer culture, people need human community to effectively hold on to oppositional ideas.

- It has been stated in other places in this book that much of what passes for politics in this day and age is the manipulation and manufacture of consent. The dominance of big money and the marginalization of democratic processes within traditional electoral and party politics means that many well-meaning people (social workers and populists alike) simply end up accommodating and getting deeply coopted in the process. Transforming the structures of oppression and domination isn't like a campaign to elect someone to office. It is more like a slow-burning ground fire or guerrilla warfare. The simplest collective enterprises -- the food-cooperative, the study circles, the neighborhood "sweat-equity" projects -- are far more central to the liberation of society than are the slick television advertisements to push commercial products into new and expanding markets.

- In a project of social transformation, it's our time that is the valued commodity. If we can't allocate some of our time to voluntary community organizing work because we are overcommitted to our careers and making money, perhaps it is time to reassess priorities. Oppositional community comes at a price -- not in money, but in time!

Overview of Organizing/Training Centers and Networks

The following section is aimed at giving the reader a basic sense of the various community organizing/training centers and networks, and includes some information about their unique features, training programs, and constituencies. It is grouped according to the categories of organizing strategies described in this book. The comments on each training center or network close with ideas on "How To Get Your Feet Wet," for those who are interested in exploring the possibility of additional training or organizing.[1]

Direct-Action, Institution-Based Method

1. Industrial Areas Foundation (IAF)
36 New Hyde Park Rd., Franklin Square, NY 11010 (516) 354-1076

Having been around the longest of all the networks, it is natural that the IAF has the most highly developed training program and concepts. While the ongoing challenging, teaching, and coaching by on-site organizers is the heart of the development of leaders, the centerpiece of the IAF's training process is the national 10-day session, held three times a year at rotating locations around the country, near IAF projects, with about 100 attending each session. Observation of a major action is usually incorporated, and the most senior staff (who are predominantly white males) conduct the training.

In addition to the institution-based method's concepts and skills described in Chapter 3, the concept of accountability is stressed more by the IAF than any other network. Besides adhering to commitments for turnout and other tasks, accountability also involves large doses of constructive criticism for leaders, even using letter grades. Leaders are taught that internal accountability takes precedence over, and is almost mutually exclusive with, affective bonds with each other. Hesitation to break relationships to enforce accountability -- because of personal friendship -- is utterly frowned upon. The high degree of internal discipline pays off in impressive turnouts and tightly run actions, but at the price of occasional bitterness.

Two skills that are stressed besides the ones mentioned in Chapter 3 are strategic planning, borrowing from business management techniques of Peter Drucker, and individual reflection (combined with personal organization). In general, an alternating praxis of action and reflection is seen as the best way to learn and grow -- both for individuals and collectively in organizations.

The IAF generally operates in declining inner-city sections of large cities. It is concentrated in the Southwest and Mid-Atlantic states, the strongest area being Texas, where the COPS success has inspired nine other organizations (as of 1991) that have combined their power at the level of state policy, even assembling 10,000 people for a statewide action. Southern California and the New York City metropolitan region are areas of focus, but there are also projects in Arizona, Maryland, Tennessee, Kentucky, and Philadelphia. As of 1991, the IAF's 28 projects involved over 600 congregations and 1.5 million families. The number of IAF projects had reportedly risen to 40 by 1993.

Some of the IAF's largest victories include winning public works improvements for low-income neighborhoods, the building of homes for low-income families, agreements from businesses to hire high school graduates, and raising the California state minimum wage. An issue of increasing attention is public school reform, and gun control has also been addressed. The IAF has begun talking about a national strategy, but it is premature to tell where that will lead.

An explicit philosophical thread in the IAF is an insistence on being absolutely nonideological, with a focus on political pragmatism, fluidity, and compromise. Pragmatism is essential for effective action, but the IAF's extreme position on this (including dismissing principles as irrelevant to politics) seems to also serve as an easy excuse to sidestep all discussions of political viewpoint. The long-range vision of the world as it should be -- what people are spending enormous energy to ultimately achieve -- remains, in Alinksy's memorable words, "a bit blurred."

The IAF cleaves to an unstated, implicit value that might be called the "ideology of the family." While the IAF claims to be a champion of the family, they evidently have in mind the ideal of a two-parent family with one wage-earner, traditionally the husband. This approaches a romantic attachment to a bourgeois ideal of the family which is not on the verge of coming back, although some may see it as a goal for "the world as it should be." The IAF, it seems, is not fully coming to terms with realities of single-parent families, the large extent of dsyfunction, and the fact that two-income households seem to be here to stay.

This dilemma connects with the IAF's concept of public/private, seasoned with a dose of sexism: the desired public/private separation works best with a single-income family where one person (usually the woman) stays home to tend to children and household, while the spouse (usually the husband) thrives in the public arena. The IAF's own reality contradicts this, since the majority of its leaders are women. Ironically, they can claim their public roles partly because volunteer community service is often unfortunately stereotyped as "women's work."[2]

How to Get Your Feet Wet

The IAF does not just take in anyone who is interested, and is perhaps the most highly selective of all the networks. In some instances, people seeking employment have been told to get experience elsewhere and then come back. It is usually not very possible to gain entry, as an outsider, to one of the national 10-day training sessions. Approaching an existing local IAF project might enable an interested person to get involved and eventually gain access to training workshops, many of which are on-site. Staff positions are occasionally filled by a local person who has been involved in a project on a volunteer basis. As a rule, involvement occurs through an institution that is a member of the local project. If this is not feasible, then there should be at least some opportunity to learn through observation of organizational activities.

2. Gamaliel Foundation

220 South State St., Suite 2026, Chicago, IL 60604 (312) 427-4616

The Gamaliel Foundation is the second most extensive network in this category, and operates in the midwest, which was the area of the IAF's earlier projects. It is an enormous irony that Gamaliel is employing, in the IAF's original territory, the workable methods that the IAF finally succeeded in developing outside the midwest -- after many years of experimentation there that left little in the way of permanent organizations.

Gamaliel's national training sessions are held three times a year in its home area of Chicago (where the IAF was originally located), but they are only 1 week in length. Gamaliel uses a mixture of senior and some junior organizers to conduct the sessions. Like Chambers, Gamaliel's director, Greg Galluzzo, had been a Catholic seminarian.

Gamaliel's menu and treatment of concepts and skills follows the IAF's fairly closely, including attention to strategic and individual planning, but is not a duplicate. One critical organizing skill that Gamaliel has recently worked into its training program is an explicit workshop on agitation, which consists of pointing out contradictions between people's values and their actions, in order to challenge them to change -- to alter their behavior to be more in line with their stated beliefs. This requires an individual's relationship with and knowledge of the other person. Gamaliel's week-long session also is somewhat unique in spending some attention on fundraising skills and strategies to deal with the news media.

Another recent development is a women's leadership development project, initiated in response to pressure from women in the network who have reacted negatively to the predominance of males among the trainers and some "macho" characteristics of training style.

A subtle contrast to the IAF is that Gamaliel talks more strongly of a goal of reforming churches -- trying to get them to consciously and truly live out their credos -- to "make the word flesh" and fashion a new theology from the experience of organizing. Additionally, liberation theology, which the IAF has no use for, is referred to briefly.[3]

The network has grown relatively rapidly since its establishment as an organizing/training center in 1985. It now (in 1993) operates in eight midwestern states with 28 organizations. The average strength of each project (in terms of number of congregations and turnout at actions) is smaller than the IAF's. Many of the groups are in the greater Chicago region, but there are also a few each in Iowa, Minnesota, Wisconsin, and Michigan. Groups in the same state are now being encouraged to start talking with each other, pointing the way towards probable joint action at some point in the future. The constituencies are similar to the IAF's, encompassing racial, ethnic, and religious diversity, primarily but not exclusively in inner city areas. Examples of issues that have been and are being tackled include school reform (parent involvement in decision making), mortgage funds and construction of low-income housing, shutting down crack houses, and encouraging job creation.

How to Get Your Feet Wet

The Gamaliel Foundation's week-long training in Chicago, held in March, July, and November, is usually open to a small number of people not in existing affiliated projects, although the vast majority of participants are in that category. The network's main office might be able to suggest possible opportunities for interested people to investigate with local projects. The best route would probably be to approach a local project directly and express interest in helping out, and in attending on-site training sessions.

3. **Pacific Institute for Community Organization (PICO)**
171 Santa Rosa Ave., Oakland, CA 94610 (510) 655-2801

PICO became involved in the institution-based form of community organizing only after undergoing a remarkable transformation in the 1980s, departing sharply from the style of its earlier years (1972-1983). John Baumann, the Jesuit priest who founded PICO in Oakland and still heads it, had begun with a neighborhood block-club model which he learned in Chicago from Tom Gaudette (an associate of Saul Alinksy).

Baumann and his staff learned the IAF-style values-based model from Jose Carrasco, who had worked with Ernesto Cortes to create an IAF organization in Los Angeles, modeled on COPS. Carrasco explained the theory and practical advantages of the method, which PICO staff and leaders incorporated first in Oakland and then, by 1990, throughout their network. The results were convincing: turnouts at actions went from a previous 300 - 800 to 1,000 - 2,000. PICO staff now disparage their earlier style as mere "activism," feeling it failed to connect deeply enough with people and therefore was limited in how much organized power could be constructed with it.

In its training program, PICO puts special emphasis on discussing values and the role of the church. However, there is scant reference to religious terminology, other than the general connection between acting on faith and empowerment. In the week-long training session for leaders there is a detailed description of the roles and tasks in actions.

PICO operates primarily in California, but has several projects in other areas (including New Orleans, Denver, and Mobile, Alabama). As of 1993, PICO reports 18 organizations located in eight states. Its constituencies are inner-city populations that are predominantly African American, but also include white, Hispanic, and Asian. PICO has worked especially hard on drug issues, with some concerted efforts by its various groups in California. However, a strong statewide effort is not likely in the near future, because the IAF also has strong organizations in the state. There have been direct clashes between the two networks, with no imminent resolution.

How to Get Your Feet Wet

PICO's training sessions, like those of the other institution-based networks, are geared to the projects in the network, but a limited number of unaffiliated people are allowed in the sessions. An interested person could try approaching a local project to help out and learn, or to get suggestions from PICO's headquarters about opportunities with local projects.

4. Direct Action and Research Training Center (DART)
137 N.E. 19th St., Miami FL 33132 (305) 576-8020

DART is based in Miami, and nurtures those organizations in its network, which is focused in southern Florida. Recently, DART has begun consulting with a few groups in the midwest as well. Its constituencies are primarily low-to-moderate income black, but also include Hispanic, white, and Haitian. While following the basic church-based model, its projects often include a few community groups as well. DART has been especially successful in working with a variety of black churches of different denominations.

The first organization which led to the formation of the DART network was not church-based, but rather a senior citizen group -- Concerned Seniors of Dade (County), or CSD, started in 1976. The organizer of CSD, John Calkins, next began an organization in the area's black churches in 1982 -- partly at the urging of the black seniors in CSD. In the next 2 years he initiated, along with the lead staff of CSD, the DART center as a training resource for these two groups. The training center was also intended as a launching pad for other projects, and with a specific intention to train minority and women organizers.

DART's formalized training session is a 3-day event held twice a year (March and October), which serves as a basic introduction to concepts and skills. The session treats the concepts of power, public/private arenas, self-interest, leadership, and issue identification ("cutting" of issues), and also spends time on organizational structure, funding, and the role of paid organizers. The skill of planning and conducting actions is given significant attention. The comparative shortness of DART's session necessarily means that concepts are not examined as deeply as in the other networks, and DART's training style at these sessions tends to be less agitational and participatory than that of some of its counterparts. As with all the networks, of course, most of leadership training takes place on site, in the individual organizations.

How to Get Your Feet Wet

DART's training sessions exist to serve only its network projects. It sponsors some intern positions for organizer trainees in its projects, and interested people should contact DART's main office.

5. Organize Training Center (OTC)

1095 Market St., #419, San Francisco, CA 94103 (415) 552-8990

OTC was founded in 1972 by Mike Miller, an organizer highly experienced with a variety of constituencies and groups, including labor unions. OTC played a major role in the development of the Citizens Action League (CAL), a statewide multi-issue organization in California that did extensive work on low-to-moderate income people's concerns on utility rates and taxes, and was affiliated for a time with ACORN (but is no longer around). OTC is not rigidly wedded to the institution-based model, but the majority of its consulting and training activities (primarily in California, but also in Nebraska and Colorado) currently utilize the congregation-based method.

Rather than concentrating on constructing an integrated network, OTC operates in a more flexible multi-purpose mode, performing a variety of training and consulting functions, short term and long term, for various groups. It puts on a 4-day basic organizing training session, usually two or three times a year, which addresses values and philosophy of organizing as well as important skills. OTC also has an ongoing training relationship with the Office of Social Justice and Peacemaking of the Presbyterian Church (USA), and with the United Church Board for Homeland Ministries. OTC distributes a quarterly compilation of assorted articles related to organizing concerns, entitled *The Organizer Mailing*.

How to Get Your Feet Wet

OTC's 4-day introductory training session is open to any interested person, and also serves as an opportunity to learn about the groups OTC relates to. OTC lines up some field work placements, either full-time for 6 months, or half-time for a year. For people who want to seriously pursue organizing work, individual internships of various durations can be arranged.

6. **Organizing & Leadership Training Center (OLTC)**
   25 West St., Boston, MA 02111 (617) 728-9100

OLTC, begun around 1985 by Lew Finfer, grew out of a perceived need of local community organizations in Massachusetts, especially groups involved in housing issues, for a local training resource -- especially since some previously operating ones had phased out of operation in the early 1980s. In recent years, the center has become more interested in institution-based organizing with churches, and is actively creating projects using this model in Massachusetts and the New England area; but it also continues to put effort into a statewide housing coalition. OLTC divides its energy between assisting church-based organizing on the one hand and individual-based multi-issue and housing organizing on the other.

The center has conducted a 2-day introductory training session twice a year, geared to basic skills for people new to organizing. Concepts are not given much attention, but the historical context of organizing is discussed. Other, more specialized 1-day workshops are set up throughout the year for the benefit of more experienced persons and for the needs of the projects that are in a consulting relationship with OLTC. The center is in the process of more fully developing its training program for institution-based organizing.

How to Get Your Feet Wet
   Contact the center directly to find out what introductory training sessions are currently being offered, and to learn of local projects affiliated with OLTC that an interested person could approach to help with or observe.

7. **Regional Council of Neighborhood Organizations (RCNO)**
   5600 City Ave., Philadelphia, PA 19131 (215) 878-4253

RCNO is involved exclusively with church-based organizing, and is building a network in southeastern Pennsylvania. Its executive director is Joseph Kakalec, a Jesuit priest. RCNO, which was founded in 1983, goes to extensive lengths to develop scriptural, biblical references to organizing, in order to ground organizing concepts and philosophy directly in the words of the Old and New Testaments. For this reason, clergy can more easily relate to RCNO's training. RCNO also publishes a quarterly magazine, entitled *Organizing*.

How to Get Your Feet Wet

RCNO conducts a week-long training session twice a year, geared to serve the projects in its network. Interested people can contact RCNO's headquarters to learn about possible attendance at sessions or involvement with local projects.

Direct-Action, Individual-Based Method

1. Midwest Academy (MWA)

225 W. Ohio St., Suite 250, Chicago, IL 60610 (312) 645-6010

MWA was founded in 1973 by Heather Booth, who had worked in the civil rights movement in Mississippi and also organized women's groups in Chicago. She recruited as a co-trainer Steve Max, who had been a leader in Students for a Democratic Society as well as being experienced in civil rights and electoral and community organizing. The thinking behind MWA blended Booth's and Max's civil rights and New Left student antiwar backgrounds together with the emerging women's movement and multi-issue community organizing as practiced by the IAF in its last project in Chicago, the Citizen Action Program. Booth was determined to create a training program which, in contrast to the IAF style (at the time), would not disparage women organizers, reject all ideology, or intimidate trainees with a confrontational technique. Many activists in the women's movement were attracted to MWA for these reasons.

MWA receives a broad spectrum of trainees from across the nation, but has two prime constituencies. One of these, as mentioned in Chapter 4, is the Citizen Action network of (mostly) statewide organizations. The second, more recently developed, is the United States Student Association (USSA), with which MWA has created a joint training program entitled Grassroots Organizing Weekends, or GROW. GROW is a condensed and specialized version of MWA's regular training session, and is presented on campuses around the country. MWA's other constituencies include a wide range of community, labor, environmentalist, women's movement, senior citizen, church-based, peace movement, minority and other groups. It invites attendance from people working for "progressive" causes, and will design customized training to suit an organization's needs. MWA has provided training to over 20,000 people from over 1,000 groups in its 20-year history. Its current Executive Director since 1982 is Jackie Kendall, who was mentored by Booth.

As various organizational forms evolved in the 1970s and 1980s, MWA took on a broad view, "not bound by the limitations of any one form of organizing," in Kendall's words. The Citizen Action groups, which had to a large degree been fostered and trained by Booth and MWA, evolved into the coalition format with a canvass base, described earlier. A conscious decision was made at the time to not have MWA be the official training arm of Citizen Action, in order to preserve its ability to relate equally to all models. MWA, as distinct from Citizen Action, views its role as contributing to the development of progressive social movements for various constituencies, beyond the scope of specific organizations. The underlying strategy is predicated on the notion that movements arise from the development of historical conditions, and that community leaders can be trained to take advantage of these opportunities to help liberate people from societal and corporate oppression. Steve Max explains: "The idea was to build organizations and position yourself so that you would be there when the next [wave of social movement] came; and if that happened, you could greatly accelerate the progress and the social change" (Max, 1990).

One of MWA's strategies for fostering progressive movements is to facilitate a loose but expanding national network of activists engaged in various causes. The chief vehicle to this end is the annual MWA retreat initiated in 1974, now titled the Midwest Academy/Citizen Action Annual Conference. It brings together each summer over 1,000 people for a weekend of workshops, speeches (including progressive Democrat politicians), plenary sessions, celebration and renewing of contacts.

Each year, MWA conducts 5 to 8 sessions, each 4 1/2 days in length, limited to 25 participants, and usually held in Chicago but sometimes in other locations. Citizen Action leaders and staff are in the minority at these sessions, since they are more usually served by special MWA on-site trainings set up for them. MWA sees its week-long session as being of best use for people who have some experience under their belt (1 to 1 1/2 years, according to Max), but some people go to the sessions as an introduction to organizing. Part of MWA's strong reputation is probably due to its deliberate emphasis on creating a supportive, nurturing, positive-feedback atmosphere in its sessions.

How to Get Your Feet Wet

Contact MWA to learn of training sessions that are scheduled in Chicago and elsewhere, including GROW workshops on-campus. MWA also serves as a kind of clearinghouse for job openings, since many groups who have benefited from MWA training, as well as those with current consulting relationships, let MWA know of available staff positions. Someone who is interested in working with a particular constituency can probably get information from MWA regarding groups around the country that fit the interest. MWA also published in 1991 a comprehensive manual which gives the reader a sense of much of the material addressed in MWA training sessions.

2. National Training and Information Center (NTIC)
810 N. Milwaukee Ave., Chicago, IL 60622 (312) 243-3035

NTIC, as mentioned in Chapter 4, is the center officially linked with National People's Action (NPA). It is directed by Shel Trapp, who was trained as a United Methodist minister, but does not articulate a connection between religious values and organizing unless it is useful with a particular audience. Because NPA is a relatively loose network, NTIC is very open to working with groups in varying degrees of relationship. NTIC's training style focuses on specific issue campaigns and actions facing the people in question at the moment, and utilizes role playing to a large extent -- together with reflecting on lessons drawn from the action, during evaluations scheduled with key leaders immediately following each action. NTIC favors quick motion into action and hard-hitting tactics, and has on occasion terminated consulting relations with groups who just wanted to talk but not act. Since the low-income constituencies that NTIC works with are generally angry at specific injustices and ready to take action, there is no perceived need to delve into deep conceptual understandings of concepts other than a basic pragmatic understanding of power, self-interest, and strategy.

NTIC's 3-day core training, which is primarily skills-based, is offered three times a year in Chicago, to a limit of 20 participants. Over 15 other sessions, however -- including the 3-day core -- are presented around the country at the request of various groups. The Chicago sessions include a mixture of people who have done a little organizing as well as some who are brand new to the game. NTIC also places about 10 organizing interns a year in projects around the country.

How to Get Your Feet Wet

NTIC's 3-day session in Chicago is open to people who want to learn about the basics of organizing, especially with an aim to work with low-income constituencies. Attending the session could serve as a lead-in to getting an internship position. If a person shows promise and interest in working as an organizer, Trapp will promote the person to groups in the NPA network and help locate possible staff openings.

If someone simply wants to get in touch with community groups with a particular constituency or a particular issue agenda, NTIC can provide information about groups in the NPA network in various locations around the country.

3. Southern Empowerment Project (SEP)

323 Ellis Ave., Maryville, TN 37801 (615) 984-6500

SEP, which is described in brief in Chapter 4, embodies the philosophies and styles of the groups who jointly founded it in 1986: a multi-issue, individual-based format that operates in urban and rural settings. SEP also incorporates a particular mix of influences from existing training resources. These influences included Myles Horton of the Highlander Center, Si Kahn of the Grassroots Leadership project (who was directly involved in SEP's creation), the Center for Third World Organizing, academics from the Appalachian region, and the general Alinsky tradition of direct-action organizing around self-interest (but not the IAF's institution-based method).

SEP's member groups intend for the center to produce organizers who will work with them. The training program therefore concentrates on an intensive 6-week internship program each summer that involves about 15 trainees directly with the eight member groups in Tennessee, Kentucky, and North Carolina. Training on research skills, for example, involves actually performing tactical research for one of the member groups. The specific history and sociopolitical aspects of the region are described in detail (usually with the help of local academics), and there is discussion of the area's labor movement. While most of the training is skill based, certain sessions address the questions of racism, sexism, homophobia, and classism as they affect organizing, and exhort people to deal with these issues within their organizations. The program rotates to several locations, and includes 2 weeks of classroom format as well as 1- and 2-week placements with a local group. It is highly participatory, with extensive group exercises and discussions, and includes trips to locations such as strip mining sites, homes of long-time activists, and inner city neighborhoods.

A few other important aspects to the SEP operation are the job placement files maintained by the SEP staff and the follow-up/outreach services provided to training graduates. Bibliographies and limited educational resources such as films can also be obtained by SEP training graduates.

How to Get Your Feet Wet

In each summer internship program, the majority of participants are from SEP member groups, but there are openings for people not involved with these organizations. Admission to the internship program is somewhat selective, however, in that SEP staff make some judgments about a person's suitability and commitment to organizing. June Rostan and Walter Davis staff the SEP office, and you can speak with either one of them.

4. Western Organization of Resource Councils (WORC)
412 Stapleton Building, Billings, MT 59101 (406) 252-9672

WORC's structure and orientation is outlined in Chapter 4. The current director, Pat Sweeney, is also the founding director. WORC's format of chapter structures and individual members (with no institutional memberships) was decided upon by the leaders who created the organization, without any direct outside prompting. Shortly after the founding of the first WORC group in 1972, Wade Rathke of ACORN began consulting with them, and confirmed the validity of the model they had already implemented. (Unlike ACORN, however, WORC is less staff-intensive, and has clearer ownership and direction on the part of the grassroots leaders rather than staff.) Herb White, who began consulting with WORC in 1975 and still does, provided deeper levels of understanding of organizing concepts and philosophy, which complemented the ACORN emphasis on "nuts and bolts" skills.

Because of the rural setting, and the inclusion of many farmers and ranchers in WORC's membership, Sweeney points out that the key motivations in the organization include not only the usual self-interest and anger, but also a sense of stewardship and emotional attachment to the land. Thus, a benchmark battle for WORC was to win the ability for land owners to veto coal companies' claims to mineral rights for the same land -- a victory which was codified in the passage of the Federal Strip Mining Act of 1977. WORC has some relationships with Native American reservations in the area, and a small number of WORC's own staff organizers have been Native Americans.

WORC's 4-day training session, held in February and July, is an introduction to organizing mechanics, including the WORC chapter-building model. It is primarily for the benefit of newer staff and leaders. About half of the session trainees are WORC leaders, but there are also prospective leaders, leaders from organizational allies, and others interested in organizing from around the country. The sessions rely heavily on small group discussions and role plays. Various internal training events are also held for organizers, and once a year there is a training for senior staff conducted jointly with some groups from the SEP network. A large number of 2-hour "mini session" trainings are held on site for organizational leaders on specific topics.

How to Get Your Feet Wet

WORC's 4-day sessions are open to interested persons, but WORC people get first priority. WORC does not conduct internships, primarily because it does not have a large need to recruit staff. Its staff is relatively stable with little turnover, and some organizational leaders make a transition to part-time or full-time staff. Interested persons can contact WORC about getting involved on a volunteer basis with, or observing, one of the state-based groups.

5. Center for Third World Organizing (CTWO)

3861 Martin Luther King Jr. Way, Oakland, CA 94609 (510) 654-9601

CTWO evolved more gradually and organically than most training centers. It emerged out of a series of discussions with organizers around the country on the question of how to generate new organizers, especially people of color. Gary Delgado, its founder, had worked in ACORN and seen its rise and fall in terms of attracting, and later losing, large numbers of staff people. CTWO started in 1980 by distributing articles on various issues. Next, it held issue seminars, and tried a local, short-lived, organizing project, and then began conducting training sessions for various organizations. In 1982-83, CTWO set up a week-long training session, twice a year. A key aspect of it is to explain the various organizing models and methods employed by the different networks, to arm trainees with a repertoire of styles to choose from. CTWO has worked extensively with groups that are not in an established network; it is attractive to such organizations precisely because it is not promoting one model over another, nor trying to create its own formal network. With its interest in people of color, CTWO is keenly aware that for many minority communities the questions of cultural/ethnic identity and survival are often paramount issues.

In 1985, CTWO began what has become its feature offering: An 8-week program in the summer, called the Minority Activists Apprenticeship Program (MAAP). It consists of a week-long session on basic organizing skills, followed by a 6-week internship placement with a community organization, to help with a current issue campaign. The final week is spent back in Oakland, debriefing and evaluating. Three to four interns (out of a total of about 30 per summer) are sent to a placement site together, and CTWO staff also travel to the placements to provide on-site training and guidance. CTWO's focus is on young people of color, and many interns come straight out of college.

CTWO initiated a serious local organizing project effort in Oakland in 1989, Campaign for Accessible Health Care, which is aimed at creating a multi-racial, multicultural organization. With it, CTWO hopes to test its own organizing ideas, and provide a more secure, long-term training opportunity -- perhaps a year-long mentoring apprenticeship. CTWO also has an organizing project operating in Denver, Colorado, where former intern Sonja Pena is the staff organizer.

How to Get Your Feet Wet

The MAAP program is geared toward people just getting out of college. It has a strong reputation, and CTWO reports that people who go through its internship program are much in demand for community organizing jobs. The 8 weeks are intense and exciting, and require long hours. Not everyone succeeds in completing the program. CTWO "graduates" recruit incoming interns from many sources, including prestigious universities, and many of the graduates continue their ties with the center. Persons who do not intend to go through the 8-week program, but are interested in organizing from a minority perspective, will find CTWO a valuable resource.

In addition to the MAAP program, CTWO also sponsors numerous training workshops in the Oakland area for individuals interested in expanding their organizing abilities and learning more about culturally sensitive organizing. You don't need to be young or a person of color to participate in these periodic workshops and they are well received by participants.

6. Association of Community Organizations for Reform Now (ACORN)
523 W. 15th St., Little Rock, AR 72202 (501) 376-7151

ACORN, although diminished from its height of about 10 years ago, is still active in about 20 states. As of 1989, however, only 7 of these had ACORN offices in more than one city: Arkansas (ACORN's birthplace), Florida, Louisiana, New York, Missouri, Pennsylvania, and Texas. ACORN still has a centralized national network, but the grand plans to pressure the Democratic Party are a thing of the past.

The original basic strategy since ACORN's founding is intact: "organizing the unorganized" (in total contrast to Alinsky's and the institution-based method's credo of organizing the organized), meaning building a potential majority constituency of low-income people plus those from working-class and moderate-income sectors. Mainstream institutions like unions and churches are to be viewed as conservative and thus to be mistrusted, coopted, and neutralized. The strategy of generating social change from economically marginalized people stems from the SDS background and philosophy of Wade Rathke (ACORN's founding staff director) and other staff from the early years.

ACORN's current mode of operation at the local level has changed little from what was developed 20 years ago, utilizing a standardized step-by-step approach to organize neighborhood chapters, as well as a "maintenance model" to keep existing chapters going. Extensive amounts of door knocking are still the key to recruiting and renewing members, and finding people who will become active and eventually serve as leaders.

Training methods are different than they were before. ACORN's Institute, a week-long session provided several times a year in different locations around the country, is no more. What does exist is 10-week-long internships at three locations: New York City, Chicago, and Washington, DC. Until recently, ACORN also conducted a week-long training for leaders as an extension of the annual national convention, but the training has been suspended due to shortages of experienced trainers. ACORN does have a wealth of written guides and articles developed by its Institute that it still uses today.

In addition to their tried and tested organizing model, ACORN has undertaken ambitious low-income housing development projects and most recently has been at the forefront of the national movement to expose discriminatory bank mortgage lending practices in the United States.

How to Get Your Feet Wet

The 10-week internships are for people who want to learn the ACORN model, with an aim to work for the organization. An experienced staff person guides the trainee through a long daily routine (10 am to 7 pm) of in-office teachings on skills, readings, and role-playing, followed by about 4 hours of door knocking in the mid-afternoon to early evening. After week 1, the door knocking is solo. The intern learns the organizing drive model by doing it; basic training and screening consists of seeing whether the person can create a new neighborhood chapter (or tenant's group or parent's group). ACORN's staff wages, as they have always been, are among the lowest in the organizing field.

7. **AFL-CIO Organizing Institute**

1444 I Street, NW Suite 701 Washington, DC 20005

(202) 408-0700 or (800)-848-3021(for applications)

The Organizing Institute is a relatively new player in the area of formalized training centers. The central task of the institute is to find people committed to the goals of organized labor, to train them briefly, and put them into union organizing campaigns around the country. The institute recruits organizers from within and outside labor unions and has recently begun to recruit college students. The institute has developed an apprenticeship program which proceeds through a four-step process: a 3-day training workshop to ascertain organizer potential, a 3-week field internship (which pays a $210/week stipend plus housing and transportation), an apprenticeship of 12 weeks, which pays $400/week plus housing, transportation, and health insurance; and finally, job placement as a union organizer in local or national unions, paying $18,000 to $30,000 per year.

The professional staff and executive director of the Organizing Institute are long-time grassroots organizers and the institute has a large amount of big labor resources behind them. Reports from people who are accepted into the program are that the experiences are powerful and exhilarating, while requiring some long hours and a willingness to relocate. The program is a great step forward for organized labor, which has been faulted for not putting enough resources into grassroots organizing of the unorganized.

8. Highlander Research and Education Center

Route 3, Box 370, New Market, TN 37820 (615) 933-3443

The origin, history, philosophy and format of Highlander is discussed in Chapter 6. For information on current training sessions, contact the center directly.

9. Mexican American Cultural Center (MACC)

3019 W. French Place, P.O. Box 28185, San Antonio, TX 78228
· (512) 732-2156

The MACC has been described in earlier chapters as one important place where liberation theology has made its transition from Latin America to the United States. Although many of the programs are designed specifically for Catholic clergy, other denominational clergy and non-clergy are increasingly drawn to MACC's Spanish-language programs. These are offered for varying durations during summers and also throughout the calendar year. Because of San Antonio's historical and geographical significance for Hispanic culture, the language training is a great opportunity for "immersion" in all aspects of cultural transmission.

The atmosphere on the MACC campus is very conducive to study and there is much informal time spent with a very prestigious and knowledgeable MACC staff and time in surrounding communities, with visits to the Communities Organized for Public Service (COPS) organizing project in San Antonio and towns in Mexico. Costs are very reasonable and dormitory housing is available. MACC also has a very interesting and well-stocked bookstore for anyone interested in cultural and religious themes.

Final Comments

This book has provided readers with detailed descriptions and analyses of current and widely used organizing methods and strategies available in the United States. We don't claim to have covered all the territory with equal attention to every detail. Partly, this is due to our stated preferences and because community organizing research still doesn't get the attention or support it deserves. Partly it is because in the 4 years it has taken to research and write the book, new methods and practices are coming to the fore, or old practices get renamed and recirculated, and it is impossible to learn about, let alone observe and evaluate their utility for social work and social change practitioners. So take what you will from this book and seek out personal experiences to shape and give reality to your practice repertoire.

We are encouraged with developments in the profession which have raised the visibility of and strengthened the emphasis on a commitment to social justice. We refer here specifically to conceptual efforts by social work and community psychology to define and operationalize an "empowerment" perspective, or practice which focuses upon liberation or transformation, particularly at the level of large systems. Although social work has traditionally been aligned with values which reinforce a social justice theme, we seem to have been marching to the drum of individualistically oriented practice for a very long time. It would be a large step forward for social work to once again align itself with and participate in the social justice/community organizing efforts described in this book. It has never been enough to "talk the talk"; we must also "walk the walk," if we are interested in social change.

We also want to encourage readers to experiment with these methods in the context of their agency-based practice. Synthesis will only come from praxis tested in day-to-day situations. There really is no formula which will serve up the perfect community power analysis or the flawless community campaign. There is no sense laboring over the latest spin on politically correct ideology or some "perspective" presumed superior to your own common sense and professional ethics and values. But it is essential, in our view, to find creative (and oppositional) ways to engage the community around you in a dialogue about social change. If we can get our somewhat inward-looking social welfare organizations to sanction broader and deeper relationships with organized and unorganized communities, social change doesn't have to wait for the next charismatic leader, the vapid political promises of city hall or Capitol Hill, or the next visitation of the populist movement. We each can contribute in our own way, according to our own preference and situation, to the realization of justice in our lifetime.

When all is said and done, we recognize that traditional political organizing for candidate election, public referenda, and policy advocacy, presents the most accessible form of participation in organizing for social workers. This work is important and should be encouraged for its own sake as well as for its service as initiation to many practical organizing skills which inform direct-action and transformative strategies. But practical limitations on time and energy available for community service and public citizenship force each of us to make choices about where this time and energy is invested. Professional value commitments to address interests of low-income and oppressed people, coupled with an empowerment perspective consisting of capacity-building and equity demands, persuasively call out for a greater emphasis on direct-action and transformative social change practice. We hope this book brings readers one small step closer to this goal.

Endnotes

1.   Brief but succint descriptions of the training centers mentioned in this section, plus some additional ones, can be found in Wolter (1992). An overview of different networks' approaches is discussed in Miller (1987).
   Information for the institution-based centers in this section is from Hanna notes from IAF session; Robinson notes from Gamaliel session; participant notes from PICO and DART sessions; Hanna interviews with Ed Chambers, Ernie Cortes, John Baumann and Jose Carrasco; Robinson interviews with Greg Galluzzo, Joe Mariano and Lew Finfer; Hanna conversations with Mike Miller and Ed Chambers (1990).
   Information for the individual-based centers is from Hanna interviews with Steve Max, Pat Sweeney, Steve Kest, Fran Streich, Alfredo deAvila and Tim Sampson; Robinson interviews with Jackie Kendall, Bob Creamer, Shel Trapp and Tom Gaudette; Amy Self interview with June Rostan; Robinson conversations with Lee Staples; participant notes from SEP (recorded by Amy Self) and CTWO sessions (recorded by Maria Espinoza-Helm); Bobo et al. (1991); WORC (1991); Delgado (1986); and Boyte et al., (1986).

2.   Regarding staff, there are some interesting observations to make. While the IAF has come a long way from its earlier reputation of being unable to even imagine the existence of a female organizer, there is still a fair distance to go. Females approach almost half of the IAF's current staff roster, but almost none are rearing children, and most of these are women religious -- typically in Catholic

orders. Cortes mentions that the IAF has had only one successful woman organizer who had family-raising responsibilities. Many of their top male organizers, however, have wives and children (Cortes, 1991) The inference is that a male organizer who fully shared child-rearing and household duties with his wife would not likely turn out to be a successful IAF organizer, either. One can at least see that the IAF wants to be faithful to its ideology; Chambers believes in paying a qualified organizer (who is expected to work 55 hours a week) an income that a middle-class family can live on (Chambers, 1990).

3.   The IAF disparages liberation theology precisely because of its goal of reforming the church, which the IAF feels is an unwinnable fight.

Bibliography

ACORN. (1978). *ACORN community organizing model.* New Orleans, LA: Institute for Social Justice.

Alinsky, S. D. (1971). *Rules for radicals.* New York: Random House.

Alinsky, S. D. (1949). *John L. Lewis: An unauthorized biography.* New York: G. P. Putnam's Sons.

Anguiano, L. (1990, May 22). Personal interview with Mark Hanna.

Arendt, H. (1958). *The human condition.* Chicago, IL: The University of Chicago Press.

Bachrach, P. & Baratz, M. S. (1970). *Power and poverty: Theory and practice.* New York: Oxford University Press.

Baumann, J. (1990). Personal interview with Mark Hanna.

Beltran, E. (1990, September 19). Personal interview with Buddy Robinson.

Berger, P. L., & Luckmann, T. (1966). *The social construction of reality.* Garden City, NY: Doubleday.

Betten, N., & Austin, M. J. (Eds.). (1990). *The roots of community organizing, 1917-1939.* Philadelphia, PA: Temple University Press.

Biegel, D. E. (1984, Winter/Spring)). Help seeking and receiving in urban ethnic neighborhoods: Strategies for empowerment. *Prevention in the Human Services, 3,* 119-143.

Billings, D. B. (1990, July). Religion as opposition: A Gramscian analysis. *American Journal of Sociology, 96.*

Bobo, K., Kendall, J., & Max, S. (1991). *Organizing for social change: A manual for activists in the 1990's.* Washington, DC.: Seven Locks Press.

Boff, L. (1988). *Faith on the edge: Religion and marginalized existence.* New York: Harper and Row.

Boff, C. (1987). *Theology and praxis.* (Trans R. Barr). Maryknoll, NY: Orbis Books.

Boff, L. (1986). *Ecclesiogenesis.* (Trans. R Barr). Maryknoll, NY: Orbis Books.

Boggs, C. (1984). *The two revolutions: Antonio Gramsci and the dilemmas of Western Marxism.* Boston, MA: South End Press, Boston, Massachusetts.

Boyte, H. (1984). *Community is possible.* New York: Harper and Row.

Boyte, H. (1989). *Commonwealth.* New York: Free Press.

Boyte, H., Booth, H., & Max, S. (1986). *Citizen action and the new American populism.* Philadelphia: Temple University Press.

Brager, G. & Holloway, S. (1978). *Changing human service organizations.* NY: Free Press.

Brager, G., Specht, H., & Torczyner, J.L. (1987). *Community organizing.* New York: Columbia University Press.

Burghardt, S. (1982). *Organizing for community action.* Beverly Hills, CA: Sage Publications.

Cadena, G. R. (1987). *Chicanos and the Catholic Church: Liberation theology as a form of empowerment.* Unpublished Doctoral Dissertation, University of California-Riverside.

Candelaria, M. R., (1990). *Popular religion and liberation.* Albany, NY: State University of New York Press.

Carrasco, J. (1990). Personal interview with Mark Hanna.

Chambers, E. (1990, June 13). Personal interview with Mark Hanna.

Coats, S. (1989, Sept. 25). Churches respond to the Pittston strike. *Christianity & Crisis.*

Coleman, J. A. (1982). *An American strategic theology.* NY: Paulist Press.

Cone, J. H. (1975). *God of the oppressed.* New York: The Seabury Press, New York.

Cone, J. H. (1986). *Speaking the truth.* Grand Rapids: Wm. B. Eerdmans.

Cortes, E. Jr. (1988, July 11). Organizing the community. *Texas Observer.*

Cortes, E. (1991). Personal interview with Mark Hanna.

Cox, F. M., Erlich, J. L., Rothman, J., & Tropman, J. E. (1987). *Strategies of community organization* (4th ed.). Itasca, IL: F.E. Peacock Publishers, Inc.

Creamer, R. (1990, September 19). Personal interview with Buddy Robinson.

Current, Population Reports. Population Projections of the United States, by Age, Sex, Race, & Hispanic Origin: 1992-2050. By Jennifer Cheeseman Day, U. S. Department of Commerce, Economics & Statistics Administration, Bureau of Census, November, 1992.

Dahl, R. A. (1989). *Democracy and its critics.* New Haven CT: Yale University Press

Dahl, R. A. (1961). *Who governs.* New Haven, CT: Yale University Press.

Dahm, C. (1990, September 18). Personal interview with Buddy Robinson.

de Avila, A., & Sampson, T. (1990, March 2). Personal interview with Mark Hanna.

Deck, A. F. (1986, May 17). Hispanic ministry comes of age. *America.*

Delgado, G. (1986). *Organizing the movement.* Philadelphia, PA: Temple University Press

Domhoff, G. W., & Ballard, H. B., (1968). *C. Wright Mills and the power elite.* Boston, MA: Beacon Press.

Drake, J. (1988). Transcript of a workshop given in Duluth, MN, College of St. Scholastica.

Durkin, E. Personal interview with Mark Hanna, June 6, 1990.

Dussel, E. (1988). *Ethics and community.* (Trans. R. Barr). Maryknoll, NY: Orbis Books.

Dussel, E. (1978). *Ethics and the theology of liberation.* (Trans. G. F. McWilliams). Maryknoll, NY: Orbis Books.

Ecklein, Joan, (1984). *Community Organizers* (2nd ed.). New York: John Wiley & Sons.

Ehrenreich, B. (1989). *Fear of falling.* New York: Pantheon Books.

Ellis, M. H., & Maduro, O. (Eds.). (1989). *The future of liberation theology.* Maryknoll, NY: Orbis Books.

Erdman, D. (1983, Winter). Liberation and identity: Indo-Hispano youth. *Religious Education, 78*(1).

Espinoza-Helm, M. (1991, August). Notes from CWTO training.

Evans, S.M., & Boyte, H. C. (1986). *Free spaces. New York:* Harper and Row.

Finks, D. P. (1984). *The radical vision of Saul Alinsky.* Ramsey, NJ: Paulist Press.

Fisher, R., & Romanofsky, P. (1981). *Community organization for urban social change.* Westport, CT: Greenwood Press..

Fisher, R. (1984). *Let the people decide: Neighborhood organizing in America.* Boston MA: Twayne Publishers.

Fisher, R., & Kling, J. M. (1987). Two approaches to the role of ideology in community organizing. *Radical America, 21 (1), 31-46.*

Focus on Study Circles. (1991, Fall). Study Circle Resource Center, CT.

Freire, P. (1970). *Pedagogy of the oppressed. New York:* Herder and Herder.

Friedmann, J. (1987). *Planning in the public domain: From knowledge to action.* Princeton, NJ: Princeton University Press.

Galluzzo, G. (1990, March 26). Personal interview with Buddy Robinson.

Garcia, J. A. (1982). Ethnicity and Chicanos: Measurement of ethnic identification, identity, and consciousness. *Hispanic Journal of Behavioral Sciences, 4*(3), 295-314.

Gittell, M. (1980). *Limits to citizen participation.* Beverly Hills: Sage Publications, Inc.

Gutierrez, L., GlenMaye, L. & DeLois, K. (1993, March 1). *Organizational issues for empowerment practice.* Paper presented at the Symposium on Community Organization and Social Administration. Annual Program Meeting of the Council on Social Work Education, New York City.

Hanna, M. & Robinson, B. (1992, April). *Report to participating training centers and survey respondents: Overview of selected data from 1990-91 Organizer Training Participant Survey.* Unpublished Research Report.

Hasenfeld, Y. (1983). *Human service organizations.* NJ: Prentice-Hall, Inc.

Hayden, T. (1970). *Trial.* New York: Holt, Rinehart, & Winston.

Hayden, T. (1980). *The American future: New visions beyond old frontiers.* Boston: South End Press.

Hewitt, W. E. (1986). Strategies for social change employed by comunidades eclesiais de base (CEBs) in the archdiocese of Sao Paulo. *Journal for the Scientific Study of Religion, 25* (1), 16-30.

Hormel, *Rank and File Fightback* (1987, Feb.) . P.O. Box 903, Austin, MN, February, 1987). 'The United Food and Commercial Workers vs the members: Whose union is it anyway?'.

Horton, M. (1990). *The long haul.* NY: Anchor Books.

Industrial Areas Foundation. (1978). *Organizing for family and congregation.* Franklin Square, NY.

Industrial Areas Foundation. (1990). *The first fifty years.* Franklin Square, NY.

Industrial Union Department (IUD), AFL-CIO. (1985). Developing new tactics: Winning with coordinated corporate campaigns.

Isasi-Diaz, A.M., & Tarango, Y. (1988). *Hispanic women: Prophetic voice in the church.* San Francisco: Harper & Row, Publishers.

Jacobs, J. L. (1989). The effects of ritual healing on female victims of abuse: A study of empowerment and transformation. *Sociological Analysis, 50* (3), 265-279.

Jesudasan, I. (1984). *A Gandhian theology of liberation.* Maryknoll, NY: Orbis Books.

Johnson, R. M. (1988). *The first charity.* Cabin John, MD: Seven Locks Press.

Kahn, S. (1982). *Organizing: A guide for grassroots leaders.* New York:McGraw-Hill

Kendall, J. (1990, March 30). Personal interview with Buddy Robinson.

Kest, S. (1990, June 12). Personal interview with Mark Hanna.

216

Kest, S. & Rathke, W. (1975). *ACORN: An overview of its history, structure, methodology, campaigns, and philosophy.* Dallas, TX: Institute for Social Justice.

Kramer, R.M. & Specht, H., (Eds.). (1969). *Readings in community organization practice.* Englewood Cliffs, NJ: Prentice-Hall, Inc.

Labriola, A. (1903). *Essays on the materialistic conception of history.* Chicago, IL: Charles H. Kerr & Company.

Lee, B. J., & Cowan, M. A. (1986). *Dangerous memories.* Kansas City, MO: Sheed and Ward.

Liebert, R. J., & Imershein, A. W. (Eds.). (1977). *Power paradigms and community research.* Beverly Hills, CA: Sage Publications.

Lukes, S. (1978). *Power: A radical view.* Hong Kong: The Macmillan Press LTD.

Mac Anghusa, P., & O Reagain, L. (Eds.) (1967). *The best of Connolly.* Cork, Ireland: Mercier Press.

Macquarrie, J. (1972). *The faith of the people of God: A lay theology.* NY: Charles Scribner's.

Mariano, J. (1990, March 28). Personal interview with Buddy Robinson.

Max, S. (1990, June 15). Personal interview with Mark Hanna.

Menchaca, M. (1989, Aug.). Chicano-Mexican cultural assimilation and Anglo-Saxon cultural dominance. *Hispanic Journal of Behavioral Sciences, 11*(3), 203-231.

Miller, M. (1987, Feb. 2). Organizing: A map for explorers. *Christianity and Crisis, 47.*

Mills, C. W. (1971). *The power elite.* New York: Oxford University Press.

Milofsky, C. (1988). *Community organizations: Studies in resource mobilization and exchange.* New York: Oxford University Press.

Neilson, M. (1988). *Reaching beyond charity: The preferential option for the poor.* Liguori, MO: Liguori Publications.

O'Brien, D. (1975). *Neighborhood organization and interest-group processes.* Princeton, NJ: Princeton University Press.

Oliver, L. P. (1987). *Study circles.* Cabin John, MD: Seven Locks Press.

Pearce, J. L. (1980). Apathy or self interest: The volunteer's avoidance of leadership roles. *Journal of Voluntary Action Research, 9,* 85-94.

Pence, E. (1990, November 6). Personal interview with Buddy Robinson.

Pierce, G. F. A. (1984). *Activism that makes sense.* Chicago, IL: ACTA Publications.

Poole, T. G. (1988). The role of the church in black education. *The Western Journal of Black Studies 12* (3).

Ramsden, W. & Montgomery, J. (1990). *Biblical integrity and people power: A new look at church-based community organizing in the 1990's.* Institute on the Church in Urban-Industrial Society.

Rathke, W. (1977). *ACORN Update: More of a movement, more of a people's machine.* Dallas, TX: Institute for Social Justice.

Reed, D. (1981). *Education for building a people's movement.* Boston, MA: South End Press.

Reed, S. (1990). Personal interview with Mark Hanna.

Reitzes, D. C., & Reitzes, D. C. (1987). *The Alinsky legacy: Alive and kicking.* Greenwich, CT: JAI Press Inc..

Rivera, F. G., & Erlich, J. L. (Eds.). (1992). *Community organizing in a diverse society.* Boston, MA: Allyn and Bacon.

Rogers, M. B. (1990). *In cold anger.* Denton, TX: University of North Texas Press.

Rogers, R. (1984, Dec.) *The Unionist.*

Rogers, R. (1986, Oct./Nov.) How labor can fight back. (four-part series). *Racine Labor.*

Rogers, R. (1986, Aug. 23) *Business Week.*

Rogers, R. (1990, June 14). Personal interview with Mark Hanna.

Ross, C. E., Mirowsky, J., & Cockerham, W. C. (1983). Social class, Mexican culture, and fatalism: Their effects on psychological distress. *American Journal of Community Psychology, 11*(4), 326-399.

Rostan, J. (1991, February 12). Telephone interview with Amy Self.

Rubin, H. J., & Rubin, I. S. (1992). *Community organizing and development* (2nd ed.). NY: Macmillan.

Ruether, R. (1985, Mar. 5). Feminist theology in the academy. *Christianity and Crisis.*

Schattschneider, E. E. (1975). *The semisovereign people.* Hinsdale, IL: The Dryden Press.

Self, A. (1992). *Southern Empowerment Project: Pedagogy and Practice.* Unpublished Master's Project: California State University, Fresno.

Solle, D. (1984). The Christian-Marxist dialogue. *Monthly Review, 36* (3).

Taylor, S. H., & Roberts, R. W. (1985). *Theory and practice of community social work.* New York: Columbia University Press.

Tillich, P. (1977). *The socialist decision.* New York: Harper and Row.

Trapp, S. (1990, March 29). Personal interview with Buddy Robinson.

Turner, R. H. (Ed.) (1986). *Annual Review of Sociology, 12.*

Uehlein, J. (1990, June 7). Personal interview with Mark Hanna.

United Brotherhood of Carpenters and Joiners of America, AFL-CIO, Special Programs Department. (1987). *New tools for the trades.*

Urrabazo, R. (1990, May 22). Personal interview with Mark Hanna.

von Hoffman, N. (1962, April). Reorganization in the Casbah. *Social Progress.*

Walzer, M. (1985). *Exodus and revolution.* New York: Basic Books.

Washington, G., & Beasley, W. (1988). Black religion and the affirmation of complementary polarity. *The Western Journal of Black Studies 12* (3).

Waste, R. J. (Ed.). (1986). *Community power.* Beverly Hills, CA: Sage Publications.

Watts, J. G. (1986-87). Black power or powerful Blacks: An analysis of Jesse Jackson's 1984 presidential electoral effort. *Humboldt Journal of Social Relations, 14* (1 & 2), 236-268.

Williams, R. (1976). *Keywords: A vocabulary of the culture and society.* NY: Oxford University Press.

Wolter, P. (1992, Fall/Winter). Consumers' guide to organizer training. *Organizing,* Fall/Winter.

WORC. (1991). *Principles of community organizing.* Billings, MT: Western Organization of Resource Councils.

Zimmerman, M. A. (1990). Taking aim on empowerment research: On the distinction between individual and psychological conceptions. *American Journal of Community Psychology, 18* (1), 169-177.

INDEX